POPULISM AND THE
FUTURE OF THE FED

Edited by
James A. Dorn

INSTITUTE
Washington, D.C.

Copyright © 2022 by the Cato Institute
All rights reserved
Cato Institute is a registered trademark.

ISBN: 978-1-952223-54-9
eBook ISBN: 978-1-952223-55-6

Library of Congress Cataloging-in-Publication Data available.

Printed in the United States of America
Cover design: Jon Meyers and Mai Makled

Cato Institute
1000 Massachusetts Ave., N.W.
Washington, D.C. 20001

www.cato.org

CONTENTS

EDITOR'S PREFACE

The 2008 financial crisis and 2020 pandemic greatly expanded the Fed's scope and power. *Populism and the Future of the Fed* features highly readable essays that avoid technical jargon and provide a broad perspective on core issues—including the populist challenge to Fed independence, fiscal dominance and the return of inflation, the limits of Fed power versus the expansion of its dual mandate, and the strange world of helicopter money and fiscal QE (i.e., using the Fed's balance sheet to support off-budget spending).

One could argue that those who want the Fed to allocate credit, help fund a Green New Deal, engage in helicopter drops, and so on, are well intentioned. However, the real issue is whether such actions are consistent with long-run price stability and the rule of law.

Thus, several questions come to mind: (1) What are the limits to what the Fed *can do* and what it *should do* in a free society? (2) Where do we draw the line between fiscal and monetary policy? (3) Do we want an activist central bank with wide discretion or a limited central bank guided by a monetary rule? (4) What are the risks populism poses for the conduct of monetary policy, Fed independence, and central bank credibility? (5) Can the Fed control inflation if populism and fiscal QE become pervasive?

The distinguished contributors to this volume address those questions in a clear and compelling manner that will help improve both policymakers' and the public's understanding of the complex relationship between politics, policy, and the rule of law. Moreover, the authors provide different perspectives—legal, philosophical, historical, theoretical, and ethical—in reflecting on the role of the central bank in a democracy. We are reminded that the Fed is an agent of Congress bound by the rule of law with limited powers that are ultimately shaped by public opinion. This book will help shape that opinion.

All the essays in this volume (except for those by Charles Plosser and myself) were first presented at Cato's 39th Annual Monetary Conference, held virtually on November 18, 2021. I thank the authors for their diligence in preparing their papers for publication. I also would like to thank the George Edward Durell Foundation and the Harold J. Bowen, Jr. and DuVal Bowen Family Foundation for supporting the conference and this book. Finally, my colleagues in Cato's Center for Monetary and Financial Alternatives were instrumental in helping me organize the conference, especially George Selgin and Nick Anthony; Eleanor O'Connor, as always, oversaw the publication process with grace and wisdom; and Connie Moy ("eagle eyes") did an outstanding job proofreading the final text.

—J. A. Dorn

Part 1

The Populist Challenge to Fed Independence

1

CENTRAL BANKING, POLITICAL PRESSURE, AND ITS UNINTENDED CONSEQUENCES

Raghuram Rajan

The proper role of central banks, the frameworks they use, and the range of tools they believe they can legitimately employ, have changed considerably over the last two decades. Interestingly, this has come after perhaps their greatest triumph, taming inflation. What led to this rethinking? And what are its consequences, some possibly unintended. What have been the effects on financial stability? These are the questions this chapter examines.

To preview my answers, central bankers escaped lightly from the Global Financial Crisis (GFC), getting little of the blame, but acquiring an aura of possessing extraordinary powers as they helped resolve the crisis. One consequence, however, may have been more pressure on central banks to deliver for Main Street. As they subsequently and continuously undershot their inflation target, the pressure on them to aid economic activity increased. Perhaps tinged somewhat with hubris, central banks did not reject these pressures and make the case that there are limits to what central banks can properly do. Instead, they embraced the challenge and embarked on a much broader set of interventions, including direct interventions in asset and credit markets that they eschewed in the past. Arguably, these interventions have not helped central banks measurably in achieving their inflation targets. Instead, they have left them poorly positioned for an environment

Raghuram Rajan is the Katherine Dusak Miller Distinguished Service Professor of Finance at the University of Chicago, Booth School of Business. He is the former Governor of the Reserve Bank of India. This chapter is based on his keynote address at the Cato Institute's 39th Annual Monetary Conference, November 18, 2021.

where fiscal spending has ramped up and inflation, not disinflation, is the key problem. Furthermore, central banks have continued under-emphasizing financial stability throughout this time, which also leaves the world poorly positioned for future shocks, including from the changing climate. In trying to do too much, central banks have not just compromised on their fundamental responsibility—monetary stability—they have added to financial instability. In sum, this chapter is a call for central banks to go back to the knitting and reassess both their goals as well as their use of tools.

A Short History of the Recent Evolution of Central Banking Thought

The actions of the Federal Reserve, no doubt influenced by developments in academia and by the actions of other central banks, have broadly framed the consensus in central bank thinking. After all, it was Paul Volcker's determination to push short-term nominal interest rates really high, and hold them there until inflation came down, that broke the back of U.S. inflation, raised the Fed's credibility as an inflation fighter, and contributed to decades of falling nominal interest rates. Kydland and Prescott's (1977) theory of time inconsistency of policy and the need for commitment, and Rogoff's (1985) arguments on how to achieve that commitment through an independent, inflation-minded central bank made the case for central bank independence. The Bank of New Zealand, in turn, became the first central bank to formally adopt inflation targeting in 1990, and this spread across the world. Meanwhile, John Taylor (1993) described central bank behavior with a simple model that then became the standard for evaluating whether a central bank was ahead or behind the curve in its fight against inflation. Indeed, so remarkable was the worldwide fall in inflation that Rogoff (2004) suggested that it could not just be attributed to central bank independence and policy, and conjectured that global competition must also have helped.

Be that as it may, with inflation quiescent over long periods, central banks no longer had to raise interest rates periodically. As Borio (2012) notes, this allowed the financial cycle—the unholy correlated increases in asset prices and leverage—to play out over longer periods and with greater amplitude. In this chapter, I argue there are many channels through which more accommodative monetary policy can initiate and propagate such a cycle. For instance, as interest rates fall, long-term expectations of growth account for a larger and larger share in asset valuations. Given there is little to anchor such expectations, a wide distribution of valuations is possible. The more optimistic among poten-tial buyers buy more long-dated assets financed with borrowing (see Geanakoplos 2010 for a related model). Their wealth is further enhanced by falling rates, allowing them to exercise more of an influ-ence in setting asset prices. Sustained periods of low and falling infla-tion could thus be accompanied by optimistic asset prices, leverage, and risks to financial stability when prices and leverage correct.

In late 1996, Fed Chairman Alan Greenspan came as close as a central banker can to saying he thought stock prices were overvalued, and that the Fed would potentially take that into account in setting monetary policy (Greenspan 1996). Yet, his speech warning of "irrational exuberance" at the American Enterprise Institute on December 5 was shrugged off by markets—and markets were right. The Fed did not act, perhaps warned off by the vociferous political reaction to his speech. The Fed watched while stock prices contin-ued rising during the internet boom, and even cut rates following the Russian debt default in 1998 and the collapse of hedge fund Long-Term Capital Management.

When the stock market eventually crashed in 2000, the Fed responded by cutting rates, ensuring the recession was mild even if subsequent job growth was tepid. In a 2002 speech at the Kansas City Fed's Jackson Hole Conference, Greenspan argued that, while the Fed could not recognize or prevent asset price booms, it could "mitigate the fallout when it occurs and, hopefully, ease the transition to the next expansion" (Greenspan 2002). His speech seemed to be a post-facto rationalization of why he had not acted more forcefully on his prescient 1996 intuition. He was now saying the Fed should not intervene when it thought asset prices were too high, but that the Fed could recognize a bust when it happened and would pick up the pieces. Given that inflation was quiescent, the resulting monetary policy was asymmetrical. The recipe was to take little action, other than a normalization of interest rates, when the economy was booming; but to take increasingly aggressive actions to support the economy when activity (and, not coincidentally) asset prices were down. Effectively, the Fed offered traders and bankers a "put option," whereby if they collectively gambled on similar things, the Fed would not limit the upside; but if their bets turned sour, the Fed would limit the downside.

Clearly, no central bank wants such asymmetric incentives, yet with one interest rate tool, central banks believed they could not simultaneously achieve both monetary and financial stability. Therefore, it was left to an often poorly defined set of macroprudential policies to curb risk taking. It was convenient for the powerful monetary policy-setting arms of central banks to delegate this messy task to someone else. It was also dangerous for the system. First, as Kohn and Kerr (2015) pointed out, even today the Fed has no central body with macroprudential responsibility. This is particularly problematic since macroprudential regulation has the politically difficult task of constraining risk taking just when the risktakers have tasted success and are more influential. When responsibility is diffused, it is all too easy to leave action to someone else. Second, as Stein (2013) points out, vast areas of the financial system are regulated lightly, if at all. Macroprudential regulation has little bite there. The value of monetary action is that "it gets in all of the cracks."

Be that as it may, the Global Financial Crisis of 2007–2009 was evidence that the system of fractured responsibilities did not work. No doubt, bank regulation has increased considerably since then, and banks are much better supervised, capitalized, and incentivized than before the GFC. Yet the nonbank periphery of the financial system, also termed the "shadow financial system" continues to have considerably less oversight or regulation, and risks tend to migrate there, periodically coming back to ensnare the banking system—as evidenced by recent blowups such as Archegos or Greensill. With the rise of cryptocurrencies, stablecoins, and decentralized finance, the size and complexity of the unregulated shadow system has only grown.

Further offsetting the post-GFC increased bank regulation is the fact that, post-GFC, central banks have not been achieving their inflation targets, and therefore have come under greater pressure to be aggressively accommodative on monetary policy. For instance, in the United States, personal consumption expenditure (PCE) inflation, the Fed's preferred measure, averaged about 1.4 percent from 2012 to 2020, below the 2 percent target. That policy interest rates were at the zero lower bound seemed to be no defense. From the political side, pressure on the central bank mounted in a time of low growth. If the central bank is not meeting its target, there must be some stimulus it is not delivering, or so the thinking went. Pressure on central banks also came from a potentially appreciating exchange rate, as the European Central Bank (ECB) realized over 2010–2013, as other central banks found new, innovative, ways of easing financing conditions. But central bankers did not also reject their own responsibility for excessively low inflation, perhaps because they were worried about losing credibility if they claimed they had done all they could. They always seemed to suggest they had more tools to push inflation up, even after repeated failures. Indeed one can discern a hint of smugness in their lament that fiscal policy and reforms were not working, and monetary policy was the "only game in town." But while Volcker had taught central banks how to bring down inflation, there was no obvious playbook for reflating an economy, especially when nominal rates were already at zero and fiscal policy limited.

How Did Monetary Policy Change after the GFC?

Following the Global Financial Crisis, with interest rates at zero, further unconventional monetary interventions took three broad forms: repairing markets, altering asset prices, and directing credit. At the core of all these was a greater willingness of the central bank to intervene in markets.

Repairing Markets

A number of financial markets had broken down during the GFC. Some of this was due to lack of confidence, some to lack of liquidity, and some because key players were undercapitalized. Of course, there was also a possibility that some of the financial claims being traded were worthless because the issuers were insolvent. Nevertheless, central banks attempted to alter perceptions and engender a virtuous circle by intervening. The hope was that the restoration of public confidence through the central bank's support of financial markets, coupled with the liquidity injected through purchases, would recapitalize market players, increase their participation, and restore values and volume to asset markets. In its first round of quantitative easing (QE1), the Fed invested in the disrupted mortgage-backed securities (MBS) market while the ECB, through its misleadingly named "ordinary monetary transactions" (OMT) policy, backed sovereign bonds of periphery governments.[1] Whether the

---

[1] As Mario Draghi (2012), the then-ECB president put it, "Within our mandate, the ECB is ready to do whatever it takes to preserve the euro. And believe me, it will be enough." Indeed, just this statement seemed to be enough, and no OMT actions were actually undertaken.

central bank changed perceptions of market fundamentals or whether it merely made explicit put options that it had written for these markets is hard to tell. Regardless, the interventions seem to have restored transaction volumes and prices to more normal levels, ensuring their place in future toolkits.

Altering Asset Prices

Monetary policy works, in part, by signaling the path of short-term interest rates, and therefore affecting long-term interest rates. With policy rates at zero, and with little room to cut them further, central banks looked for other ways to affect long-term rates more directly. One way was to expand central bank balance sheets through an announced program of buying long-term government bonds, with the intent of depressing long-term interest rates. Whether this worked by taking long-term assets out of private hands and forcing private portfolios to rebalance by buying more long-term assets (Tobin 1969), or by committing that policy rates would not be raised so long as the central bank is buying long-term assets (see Krishnamurthy and Vissing-Jorgensen 2011), is unclear. Indeed, whether it had much sustained effect on long rates (Cochrane 2018; Greenlaw et al. 2018) is also a matter of debate. Other central banks such as the Bank of Japan practiced "yield curve control" where they sought to keep the yield of a specific bond such as the 10-year bond at a targeted level through direct central bank purchases or sales of the bond. While the effects of such interventions on long-term rates were much clearer, there was little compelling evidence that those efforts helped enhance real investment or economic activity.

Of course, there were parallels between various forms of QE and the discredited past direct financing of governments by their captive central banks. Monetary economists frowned on this practice because the central bank essentially gave the government a "soft budget constraint," which proved to be inflationary. Central bank independence required them to stop financing governments directly. What distinguished the new central bank asset purchase programs from the discredited programs of the past was a fig leaf and circumstances. The fig leaf was that the central bank typically purchased in the secondary market, not directly from the government, though once the program was announced, markets anticipated such purchases, and this was a distinction without a difference. However, after the GFC, the circumstances were different from the typical situation where central bank financing of government debt is problematic. Interest rates were at the zero lower bound and developed country governments were typically not strapped for cash, so central bank financing was not critical for their budgets.

I say "typically" because European periphery countries were indeed strapped. With the onset of the pandemic, this has become the case with more governments, and central banks have become key players in bridging government financing gaps.

Directed Credit Programs

Another element in the new toolkit was central bank participation in providing cheap refinancing for any bank credit that met specific conditions—loans to small and medium firms, households, or sometimes even any loan expansion at all. Once again, this cheap refinancing for bank credit revived old practices abandoned by central banks, who had argued that directed credit distorted the working of the capital markets and could lead to political rather than market allocation of resources. Worries about distortions and politicization seemed minor when set against the enormity of the post-GFC economic downturn. Once again, directed credit programs were revived and expanded following the onset of Covid-19, in March 2020.

Did These Policies Work?

At a narrow level, some of these unconventional policies seemed to work in that some of the stated intent was met. For instance, the MBS market recovered. Di Maggio, Kermani, and Palmer (2016) show that Fed MBS purchases in QE1 led to an increase in refinancing, a reduction in mortgage payments, and an associated increase in consumption. Once again, whether the MBS market recovered because the central bank restored confidence (good), or because it offered the market a long-term put option (less good), is less clear.

Central bank actions did not always work as intended. Acharya et al. (2019) show that banks that held more European periphery sovereign bonds when Draghi boosted their value by announcing OMT lent more. The effective recapitalization they obtained seemed to release constraints on lending. However, Acharya et al. argue that a number of the additional loans went to economically unviable "zombie" firms, whose continued financing and survival may have held back the recovery of industry. Central bank activism also "worked" at second or third remove, even when support was targeted. For instance, Grosse-Rueschkamp, Steffen, and Streitz (2019) show that ECB purchases of corporate bonds reduced yields for eligible firms, allowing them to repay bank debt with bond issuances—enabling banks to lend to riskier firms.

Of course, there is also evidence that central bank actions worked as intended. Foley-Fisher, Ramcharan, and Yu (2016), for example, offer evidence that the Fed's maturity extension program (also known as "Operation Twist") allowed firms dependent on long-term debt to issue more of it, expanding employment and investment.

Despite such positive microevidence, the broader macroimpacts, including on real activity, of these new central bank tools are harder to discern. Fabo et al. (2021) examine 54 studies on the effects of QE on output and inflation in the United States, United Kingdom, and the euro area. While the papers by central bankers typically report a statistically significant QE effect on output, only half the academic papers do. Interestingly, studies by the Bundesbank, a rare central bank opposed to QE, finds even less effects of QE on output than the academic papers. While it is inappropriate to conclude that central bank research is necessarily biased, the fact that specific assumptions can drive conclusions suggests that the evidence is fairly noisy—that is, the new tools do not offer overwhelming evidence of effectiveness.

Why then did central banks embrace them? The nature of the tools suggests that post-GFC central banks had much less faith in the effective working of markets. Perhaps "irrational exuberance" was followed by irrational pessimism, with asset values significantly below true fundamentals. If so, central banks could put their balance sheets to work to correct misperceptions. Of course, there was always a danger that valuations would be altered not because the market recognized true fundamentals, but because the central bank intervention altered fundamentals. If true fundamentals eventually converged to central bank-altered-fundamentals, the central bank might indeed be providing a valuable service. But if they did not converge, we would realize this only too late—when central banks have little room to expand their balance sheets to deliver on their contingent guarantees. Put differently, a key question today is have central banks induced market dependence with their new tools, and consequently tied their own actions to market performance?

Altering Frameworks

The Fed did more in the post-GFC low inflation environment than just adopt unconventional tools. It also set about changing its framework so as to alter public expectations. Essentially, by committing to be more tolerant of inflation in the medium term, the Fed would have greater credibility in signaling that interest rates would stay "lower for longer" even in the face of higher inflation. It would thus allow inflationary expectations to move higher. Put differently, the Fed had to erode some of its hard-won credibility for fighting high inflation in order to combat "low" inflation.

A key element of the Fed's new framework (see Levy and Plosser 2020; Plosser 2021) is that it will no longer be preemptive in heading off inflation. Instead, it will be measured and reactive. The old Fed mantra, that if you are staring inflation in the eyeballs it is already too late, has been put to bed. Instead, the Fed will watch inflation rise until it has made up any shortfalls in past inflation, so that *average* inflation is around the target. Of course, since the period over which the average is taken is undefined, the Fed can allow higher inflation for a while and not be criticized for falling behind the curve. Monetary policy can be more discretionary and can be used to meet a broader employment mandate, where unemployment should not only be low but employment broad based and inclusive. Since minorities unfortunately are last to be hired, this means the Fed will potentially tolerate a tighter labor market than in the past. Finally, the Fed's employment mandate has become more asymmetric: rather than minimize deviations from maximum employment, it worries only about shortfalls now, leaving it to the now-more-accommodative inflation mandate to react to an overly tight labor market.

Isn't discretion good, especially for a professional apolitical organization? Possibly, but perhaps not when the environment changes in a way that was not envisaged by the framework and becomes vastly more politically charged.

What Changed?

Central banks were only partly responsible for the low inflation environment over the last few decades. Part of the responsibility also lay with deeper structural forces affecting demand and supply, such as globalization, population aging, and rising income inequality within developed countries. But these also were changing.

11

One important prepandemic development was growing impediments placed on global trade and investment. Earlier, the rise of emerging markets, which were moving more workers from low-productivity agriculture into industry and service jobs, created a truly global goods and labor market. Greater competition reduced goods prices and wages, but a longer-lasting effect (which is what matters for inflation over the medium term) was, as Rogoff (2004) argues, that greater competition reduced central bank incentives to raise inflation to boost growth. However, with growing protectionism, trade disruption, and investment disputes between the two biggest economies in the world, borders are no longer as seamless as they once were. So even before the pandemic, the conditions holding down inflation were turning.

The pandemic further altered those conditions. Apart from the tragic and widespread loss of lives and livelihoods, the pandemic has disrupted the market for goods, services, and labor. The short-run disruptions will fade, and whether they will have lasting effects on the public's inflationary expectations is hard to tell. However, there are a number of channels through which the pandemic may have longer-lasting influences. The pandemic certainly seems to have led to a change in personal and public attitudes toward low-paying, low-benefit, precarious jobs. Such jobs have typically been on the pandemic front line, involving high contact with people, long hours, and little job flexibility. Not only are workers reluctant to return to such jobs, the public is also more supportive of higher pay and benefits for such work. More generally, wage demands are more likely to be accommodated in the postpandemic environment.

The pandemic has also increased the public's perception of the likelihood of tail events, increasing the political will behind combating climate change. This will imply higher costs of new investments, fully pricing emissions, and compliance with stricter regulations. Of course, these measures are needed. But if firms pass through the higher costs, which will likely come as a steady stream rather than as a one-off, they will also contribute to inflationary impulses.

Perhaps the biggest change in the pandemic response, relative to the response to the GFC, has been on the fiscal side. There are many possible explanations for the dramatic opening of fiscal taps across the world. These include: the imperative for policymakers to act quickly; the need to obtain consensus in a sharply divided polity by spreading the benefits around; and the political pressure to exploit the change in attitudes toward fiscal deficits—driven perhaps by respectable economists whose convenient message (to politicians) seemed to be that developed countries could afford significantly more debt at current interest rates. Be that as it may, the consequence was a massive resource transfer to the private sector (i.e., to households, firms, and banks). In the United States, disposable personal income went up while bankruptcies fell, both firsts for what was ostensibly an economic downturn. Cash savings and pent-up demand have risen to extraordinary levels. With spending focused initially on goods, supply chains have become snarled. Of course, none of this need imply sustained inflation if the central bank acts according to its mandate. There are, however, reasons why central banks will not simply bring out the old Volckerian anti-inflation playbook.

Impediments to Policy Normalization

In the past, current levels of inflation would have prompted central bankers to square their shoulders, look determinedly into the TV cameras, and say, "We hate inflation, and we will kill it"—or words to that effect. But now they are more likely to make excuses for inflation, assuring the public that it will simply go away. Clearly, the prolonged period of low inflation after the 2008 Global Financial Crisis has had a lasting impression on central bankers' psyches. The obvious danger now is that they could be fighting the last war. Moreover, even if they do not fall into that trap, structural changes within central banks and in the broader policymaking environment will leave central bankers more reluctant to raise interest rates than they were in the past. Consider why, focusing on the Fed.

Framework Dominance

As argued earlier, the Fed changed its framework to allow itself to keep policies more accommodative for longer, believing it was in an era of structurally low demand and weak inflation. Ironically, the Fed may have given itself more flexibility just as the economic regime itself was changing.

But shouldn't greater flexibility give decisionmakers more options? Not necessarily. In the current scenario, Congress has just spent trillions of dollars generating the best economic recovery that money can buy. Imagine the congressional wrath that would follow if the Fed now tanked the economy by hiking interest rates without using the full flexibility of its new framework. Put differently, one of the benefits of a clear inflation-targeting framework is that the central bank has political cover to react quickly to rising inflation. With the changed framework, that is no longer true. As a result, there will almost surely be more inflation for longer. Indeed, the new framework was adopted—during what now seems like a very different era—with precisely that outcome in mind.

Market Dominance

But it is not just the new framework that limits the effectiveness of the Fed's actions. Anticipating loose monetary policy and financial conditions for the indefinite future, asset markets have been on a tear, supported by heavy borrowing. Market participants, rightly or wrongly, believe that the Fed has their back and will retreat from a path of rate increases if asset prices fall.

This means that when the Fed moves, it may have to raise rates higher in order to normalize financial conditions, implying a higher risk of an adverse market reaction when market participants finally realize that the Fed means business. Once again, the downside risks, both to the economy and to the Fed's reputation, of a path of rate hikes are considerable.

Fiscal Dominance

The original intent in making central banks independent of the government was to ensure that they could reliably combat inflation and not be pressured into either financing the government's fiscal deficit directly or into keeping government borrowing costs low by slowing the pace of rate hikes. Yet the Fed now holds $5.6 trillion of government debt, financed by an equal amount of overnight borrowing from commercial banks.

When rates move up, the Fed itself will have to start paying higher rates, reducing the dividend it pays the government and increasing the size of the fiscal deficit. Moreover, U.S. government debt is at around 125 percent of GDP, and a significant portion of it has a short-term maturity, which means that increases in interest rates will quickly start showing up in higher refinancing costs. An issue that the

Fed did not have to pay much attention to in the past—the effects of rate hikes on the costs of financing government debt—will now be front and center.

Therefore, even as inflationary pressures rise, central banks are predisposed to waiting longer than in the past to see if they will simply go away. If the post-2008 scenario repeats, if new Covid variants undermine growth, or if China and other emerging markets send disinflationary impulses across the global economy, waiting will have been the right decision. Otherwise, the present impediments to central bank action will mean more, and sustained, inflation, and a more prolonged fight to control it. The problem is that a long period of monetary accommodation, and diminished attention to financial stability while the problem of low inflation was being addressed, have accentuated the financial cycle and exacerbated the risks to financial stability from tighter money.

Risks from a Prolonged Period of Accommodation

The economic system has gotten used to a period of very easy money. What are the risks when central banks do overcome the impediments that we just discussed and embark on policy normalization?

Untested Financial Innovation

There has been substantial financial innovation since the Global Financial Crisis—indeed, the dominant cryptocurrency, bitcoin, was conceived as a substitute to fiat currencies after the failure of Lehman Brothers, since central bankers could not be trusted to avoid the temptation of inflating away currency value. Innovative products already have significant valuations and market shares but are untested through a serious downturn or through a normalization of monetary policy.

We will eventually learn answers to a number of questions. For instance, will credit be more available in a downturn because data substitutes for collateral, or will it become more skewed because everyone coordinates on the same data and similar algorithms to avoid difficult credits? Will stablecoins experience traditional bank runs in a period of higher anxiety about valuations? How will loan losses shape up and how easy will recoveries be on lending platforms and buy-now-pay-later schemes in a serious downturn? How will high frequency trading affect prices then and who will provide market-making services? It is unlikely that all the answers will be comforting.

Financial innovations can also enhance the speed of capital flows and thus traditional sources of fragility. For instance, countries with weak macroeconomic indicators and banking systems may see significantly more capital outflows in a period of rising interest rates than in the past, with cryptocurrencies offering new, effective channels for bypassing capital controls.

The point is that the shadow financial system has only grown since the GFC, and regulators, still using spreadsheets and pdf files, have to make significant strides to both understand financial innovations as well as how to regulate them, including through the use of technology (see Coeure 2021). The change in monetary environment may come before they are ready.

The High Level of Asset Prices

Periods of low rates inspire a search for yield from market participants with fixed nominal liabilities such as pension funds (Rajan 2006). Rising asset prices, especially for innovative "alternative" asset classes, can also induce a fear of missing out among asset managers. Narratives about future use value, especially those with little falsifiability today, can imbue certain long-dated assets with high values when discounted at low long-term rates. How, for instance, will the value of cryptocurrencies, essentially long-dated, zero coupon bonds priced on the hope they will dominate payments or be the new gold, adjust when interest rates move up? Given their value is cumulatively over $2.5 trillion on a good day, this is not an insignificant concern. What of a tech company, scheduled to make losses for the foreseeable future, but priced at astronomical levels because, after all, Amazon made losses for a long time?

As argued earlier, the high level of asset prices can make the central bank's task in removing accommodation more difficult. If markets believe that the central bank will pause or reverse itself if prices fall, they may simply ignore the threat of higher policy rates. However, the price reaction, once markets understand the central bank is determined to remove accommodation, can be larger.

The key to whether asset price volatility leads to magnified real-sector volatility has to do with financial leverage. And high levels of asset prices both cause, and are supported by, high degrees of leveraging.

Leverage

All manner of leverage—private, public, and market, explicit and implicit—has gone up since the GFC. As one example of disguised and implicit leverage, Archegos, a family office run by a convicted trader, was able to borrow about five times its size from multiple banks, all the while betting on a few equities such as Viacom.[2] Not only were the targeted companies themselves leveraged, Archegos held total return swaps on the equities that were themselves funded by margin loans. Archegos blew up when Viacom decided to take advantage of its unrealistic equity price by issuing more shares, thereby tanking the equity price and prompting margin calls that Archegos could not meet, leading to further equity fire sales as banks sought to protect their positions. High asset prices and high leverage were clearly an unstable combination.

Debt that is supported by the cash flows generated by the borrowing entity is inherently safer, especially if the borrowing is long term. Debt that is supported by asset prices is inherently more fragile, yet quite widespread. In an economy with falling long-term interest rates stemming from accommodative policies, the rise in asset prices gives leveraged players more equity to support yet more borrowing. Moreover, the prospect that other healthy players will be around to buy assets if a current borrower is unable to repay gives the borrower greater debt capacity. Debt capacity stems not from the cash flow the borrower generates, but from the lender's greater ability to sell the underlying assets to other players in the industry if the borrower defaults (Diamond, Hu, and Rajan 2020). The cycle is virtuous: greater debt capacity leads to higher bids for assets, which leads to greater equity among prospective buyers in the industry.

---

[2] See www.thetradenews.com/kbc-am-fixed-income-dealer-departs-for-tradeweb -product-development-role.

Of course, when rates rise, asset prices could fall, and the cycle could become a vicious one—prospective buyer equity falls, making potential buyers less able to buy at high prices, reducing the debt capacity of assets. The problem is compounded by the fact that, in times when borrowing based on prospective asset sale values is easy, both borrowers and lenders may neglect the underlying cash flows that will ultimately be needed to service debt when asset prices fall. The mortgage loans made prior to the GFC to borrowers with no income, no job, and no assets ("Ninja loans") came back to haunt lenders when house prices plummeted, and it was no longer possible to sell repossessed houses easily to recover amounts loaned. It is not difficult to see parallel forces at work in the red hot market for private equity transactions today, raising concerns for the period when accommodation ends.

Liquidity Dependence

Central banks have been accommodative not just by keeping rates low but by expanding their balance sheets. The counterpart is an expansion in the central bank reserves held by commercial banks. Ordinarily, one would think that an expansion in the very liquid reserves should increase liquidity in the system. Yet the financial system has experienced severe liquidity shortages, both in September 2019 and March 2020, at times when reserves were four times what they were before the GFC.

The reality is that the supply of liquidity through reserves creates new demands for liquidity, sometimes exceeding the initial supply (Acharya and Rajan 2021). Specifically, commercial banks finance reserve holdings with wholesale deposits, which can turn into claims on liquidity in periods of stress. They also explicitly sell claims on liquidity such as committed credit lines. Regulators themselves want banks to set aside liquid assets to meet various regulatory ratios. Finally, if all these demands come due at the same time (and systemic stress tends to precipitate such correlated demands), some banks prefer to hoard liquidity, further exacerbating liquidity shortages. Of course, all this puts pressure on central banks to accommodate the stress by supplying yet more liquidity. To wean the system of such liquidity dependence is not easy, yet the alternative of an ever-expanding central bank balance sheet is also not feasible, in part because of the consequences for fiscal health.

Balance Sheet Expansion and Fiscal Fragility

When the central bank buys long-term government debt and issues reserves (for instance, when engaging in QE), it effectively shortens the duration of the debt held by the public on the consolidated central bank/government balance sheets. Here is why: the central bank finances those purchases by borrowing overnight reserves from commercial banks on which it pays interest (also termed "interest on excess reserves"). From the perspective of the consolidated balance sheet of the government and the central bank (which, remember, is a wholly owned subsidiary of the government), the government has essentially swapped long-term debt for overnight debt with the public. QE thus drives a continuous shortening of effective government debt maturity and a corresponding increase in (consolidated) government and central-bank exposure to rising interest rates.

Does this matter? Consider the 15-year average maturity of U.K. government debt. The median maturity is shorter, at 11 years, and falls to just 4 years when one accounts for the QE-driven shortening because of the government debt held by the Bank of England. A 1 percentage point increase in interest rates would therefore boost the U.K. government's debt interest payments by about 0.8 percent of GDP—which, the U.K. Office of Budget Responsibility notes, is about two-thirds of the medium-term fiscal tightening proposed over the same period. And, of course, rates could increase much more than 1 percentage point. In the case of the United States, not only is the outstanding government debt much shorter in maturity than that of the United Kingdom, the Fed also owns one-quarter of it.

The broader point is that along with the expansion in public borrowing discussed earlier, the shortening of the duration of that borrowing exposes economies to the risk of fiscal fragility as rates move up.

Cross-Border Spillovers

Easy monetary policy in the core reserve countries leads to cross-border capital flows to periphery recipient countries. When the core countries tighten, capital flows back. The sensitivity of credit flows to U.S. monetary policy is much greater in emerging markets and developing countries and is disproportionately focused on riskier emerging markets and riskier firms within (Brauning and Ivashina 2018).

To the extent that recipient countries are unprepared, given the phase of their business cycle or given the extent of borrowing, to accommodate outflows, stress spreads across borders. Since much has been written about both the monetary policy spillovers and the spillbacks (of reduced activity in recipient countries to core countries), I will confine myself to noting they could be sizable and that we need to consider whether these should be incorporated into monetary policy settings (see Mishra and Rajan 2020).

The Way Forward

So where do central banks go from here, given the impediments to acting and the costs of acting aggressively in a system that has become dependent on continued accommodation? Clearly the temptation is to stay accommodative, hoping that inflationary pressures will die of their own accord. Yet inaction in the face of mounting evidence of the need for action will eventually be disruptive, perhaps even more so. Central banks have to recognize that the pandemic has changed the world in many ways, so they have to be data driven. At the same time, they do not have the luxury of waiting for certainty. They have to act firmly given their best interpretation of incomplete evidence, recognizing there are dangers of being aggressive as well as passive. The fragilities that have built up over the years of accommodative policy will not disappear and will have to be navigated. But as the world moves on, central banks should ask how we got here.

Populism and the Central Bank

Populism implies distrust in elite institutions, their objectives, and their operational decisions. According to the populist demagogue, tough policy choices are an elite conspiracy, intended by the elite to feather their nest while imposing pain on the masses. Central banks are the most elite of institutions, staffed by pointy-headed economists from elite institutions, speaking in an argot that only a chosen few understand. Central banks are easily captured by the demagogue.

There are then at least two ways of looking at central bank actions in recent years. First, their actions could be seen as a laudable response to a stubbornly disinflationary environment. The untried unconventional policies are brave attempts to deliver on their mandates. The neglect of financial stability is partly a consequence of a limited set of central bank tools and the greater importance of reviving growth. This is the interpretation that most central bankers buy into.

Second, there is a different diagnosis, perhaps dating from Chairman Greenspan's failed attempt to talk down the market. It is that central banks have shied away whenever tough policies are required to deliver on their responsibility for monetary and financial stability as they attempt to retain public approval in an increasingly fractured polity. While central banks are ostensibly independent, the resemblance of some of their policies to long-abandoned interventionist policies of the past is not coincidental. In this rendering, central banks have become more political, in line with the change in their societies. The truth probably lies in between.

Clearly, central bankers have made the economy even more dependent on their actions. However, only time will establish whether these new tools have aided macrostability or created new sources of volatility. It certainly has made good central banking policy far more difficult, even as it has become far more critical for economic well-being. Perhaps that is the way central bankers want it!

What changes would I advocate? Almost surely, central banks have to pay more attention to financial stability. Clearly, they have to enhance their understanding here, as well as their supervisory and regulatory capabilities. If they were dozing when the risks to subprime lending built up, they have been in deep slumber as the cryptocurrency market has exploded. In the United States, macroprudential responsibility needs to be firmly allocated to one regulator, which should develop the capabilities to monitor and act or press relevant regulators to act.

The more difficult question is how should monetary policy change? My belief is that it can do more by being more realistic in public communication about the limits of monetary policy and the dangers to financial stability of monetary policy overextension. However, since it is an evolving area of debate, perhaps it is best to end this chapter with questions.

Questions That Need Answers

- What should the inflation mandate of central banks be? Should the mandate recognize that some aspects will be difficult to reach under certain conditions (e.g., higher inflation under disinflationary conditions)?

- What responsibility should the central bank have for financial stability? How should it choose between price stability and financial stability when the objectives conflict and macro-prudential tools are likely to be ineffectual?
- Should central banks take on more responsibilities than just price and financial stability?
- Should central banks explain the limitations of their traditional tool box to the public, even at the risk of undermining faith in, and credibility of, central banks?
- What new tools are permissible? How much should central banks interfere in the functioning of markets beyond setting policy rates and auctioning liquidity? How much should their ability to intervene be constrained after every unprecedented intervention so that the market does not become dependent?
- How much should central banks nod to public opinion? How do they retain their ability to take actions that may be necessary for long-run growth and stability but might result in unpopular pain in the short run?

References

Acharya, V.; Eisert, T.; Eufinger, C.; and Hirsch, C. (2019) "Whatever It Takes: The Real Effects of Unconventional Monetary Policy." New York University Working Paper.

Acharya, V. and R. Rajan (2021) "Liquidity, Liquidity Everywhere, Not a Drop to Use: Why Flooding Banks with Central Bank Reserves May Not Expand Liquidity." University of Chicago Working Paper.

Borio, C. (2012) "The Financial Cycle and Macroeconomics: What Have We Learnt?" BIS Working Paper No 395.

Brauning, F., and Ivashina, V. (2018) "U.S. Monetary Policy and Emerging Market Credit Cycles." NBER Working Paper No. 25185.

Cochrane, J. (2018) "Slok on QE, and a Great Paper." Available at https://johnhcochrane.blogspot.com/2018/02/slok-on-qe-and-great-paper.html#more.

Coeure, B. (2021) "Finance Disrupted." Speech at the 23rd Geneva Conference on the World Economy (October 7).

Di Maggio, M.; Kermani, A.; and Palmer, C. (2016) "How Quantitative Easing Works: Evidence on the Refinancing Channel." NBER Working Paper No. 22638.

Diamond, D.; Hu, Y.; and Rajan, R. (2020) "Pledgeability, Industry Liquidity, and Financing Cycles." *Journal of Finance* 75: 419–61.

Draghi, M. (2012) "Speech by Mario Draghi, President of the European Central Bank at the Global Investment Conference," London (July 26). Available at www.ecb.europa.eu/press/key/date /2012/html/sp120726.en.html.

Fabo, B.; Jancokova, M; Kempf, E.; and Pastor, L. (2021) "Fifty Shades of QE: Comparing Findings of Central Bankers and Academics." SSRN Working Paper.

Foley-Fisher, N,; Ramcharan, R.; and Yu, E. (2016) "The Impact of Unconventional Monetary Policy on Firm Financing Constraints: Evidence from the Maturity Extension Program." *Journal of Financial Economics* 122: 409–29.

Geanakoplos, J. (2010) "The Leverage Cycle." *NBER Macroeconomic Annual 2009* 24 (1): 1–65.

Greenlaw, D.; Hamilton, J. D.; Harris, E. S.; and West, K. D. (2018) "A Skeptical View of the Impact of the Fed's Balance Sheet." Chicago Booth Working Paper. Available at https://research .chicagobooth.edu/-/media/research/igm/docs/2018-usmpf -report.pdf.

Greenspan, A. (1996) "The Challenges of Central Banking in a Democratic Society." Speech at the American Enterprise Institute (December 5). Available at www.federalreserve.gov/boarddocs /speeches/1996/19961205.htm.

_____ (2002) "Opening Remarks." Federal Reserve Bank of Kansas City, Jackson Hole Conference (August 30).

Grosse-Rueschkamp, B.; Steffen, S.; and Streitz, D. (2019) "A Capital Structure Channel of Monetary Policy." *Journal of Financial Economics* 133: 357–78.

Kohn, D., and Kerr, R. (2015) "Implementing Macroprudential and Monetary Policies: The Case for Two Committees." Brookings Institution Working Paper.

Krishnamurthy, A., and Vissing-Jorgensen, A. (2011) "The Effects of Quantitative Easing on Interest Rates: Channels and Implications for Policy." *Brookings Papers on Economic Activity* No. 2 (Fall): 215–65.

Kydland, F., and Prescott, E. (1977) "Rules Rather than Discretion: The Inconsistency of Optimal Plans." *Journal of Political Economy* 85 (3): 473–92.

Levy, M., and Plosser, C. (2020) "The Murky Future of Monetary Policy." Hoover Institution Working Paper.

Mishra, P., and Rajan, R. (2020) "International Rules of the Monetary Game." In J. H. Cochrane, K. Palermo, and J. B. Taylor (eds.), *Currencies, Capital, and Central Bank Balances*. Stanford, Calif.: Hoover Institution.

Plosser, C. (2021) "The Fed's Risky Experiment." Hoover Institution Working Paper.

Rajan, R. (2006) "Has Financial Development Made the World Riskier?" *European Financial Management* 12 (4): 499–533.

Rogoff, K. (1985) "The Optimal Degree of Commitment to an Intermediary Monetary Target." *Quarterly Journal of Economics* 100: 1169–89.

_____ (2004) "Globalization and Global Disinflation." In Jackson Hole Symposium Proceedings, *Monetary Policy and Uncertainty: Adapting to a Changing Economy*, 77–112. Federal Reserve Bank of Kansas City. Available at https://scholar.harvard.edu/files/rogoff/files/rogoff2003.pdf.

Stein, J. C. (2013) "Overheating in Credit Markets: Origins, Measurement, and Policy Responses." Speech given at a symposium sponsored by the Federal Reserve Bank of St. Louis (February 7).

Taylor, J. B. (1993) "Discretion versus Policy Rules in Practice." *Carnegie-Rochester Conference Series on Public Policy* 39 (December): 195–214.

Tobin, J. (1969) "A General Equilibrium Approach to Monetary Theory." *Journal of Money, Credit and Banking* 1 (1): 15–29.

2

POPULISM AND CENTRAL BANKS

Barry Eichengreen

Let me start by thanking Cato for their kind invitation. My quali-fications to speak on the connections between populism and central banking are two. First, I published a book entitled *The Populist Temptation* on the history of populism in 2018, which now seems like eons ago. Second, I have a project with Nergiz Dincer constructing measures of central bank independence and transparency historically and currently.[1] The irony is that the two projects are nonintersecting. I didn't write about monetary policy and central banking in *The Populist Temptation*; the term doesn't appear in the index.[2] Nergiz and I analyze the legal relationship between central banks and gov-ernments, but we don't look at the political coloration of the execu-tive, the rhetoric government officials use when speaking of the central bank, or other indicators of populist tendencies and pres-sures. So I'm grateful for the opportunity to take a first step in bring-ing the strands together.

Defining Populism

To avoid emulating Justice Potter Stewart (as I say in my book), let me start with an explicit definition of populism. I take this to be a

---

Barry Eichengreen is the George C. Pardee and Helen N. Pardee Professor of Economics and Political Science at the University of California, Berkeley. This chap-ter is based on his keynote address at the Cato Institute's 39th Annual Monetary Conference: "Populism and the Future of the Fed," November 18, 2021.

[1]See, for example, Dincer and Eichengreen (2014) and Dincer, Eichengreen, and Geraats (2022).

[2]To be sure, there are a couple of incidental mentions of the Federal Reserve.

movement with anti-elite, anti-institutional, or nativist and national-ist tendencies. Anti-elite refers to lack of deference and respect for experts, specialists, and other successful and powerful individuals. One can well imagine that the term "elites" might apply to the PhDs, bankers, and business people who sit on central bank boards.[3] This unwillingness to defer to expert opinion is often associated with dis-regard of technical concepts such as budget constraints, which gives populist policies their characteristic volatility and inflationary bias (Dornbusch and Edwards 1990).

By anti-institutional I mean lack of deference to the political norms and constitutional institutions of government, such as the sep-aration of powers. One can readily see how this could apply to the statutory independence of a central bank, as institutionalized for example in the Federal Reserve Act. Indeed, we not infrequently see populist leaders criticizing the central bank, seeking to overturn its decisions, threatening to fire the central bank governor, and attempt-ing to replace him or her with a more compliant successor.

By nativist or nationalist tendencies, I mean hostility toward for-eigners, peoples of other national origin, and especially immigrants. This one is more of a stretch when it comes to central banking. I am however reminded of congressional criticism of the Fed for having extended dollar swaps to foreign central banks during the global financial crisis. One can also detect nationalist rhetoric and sentiment in complaints of finance ministers and other officials about so-called currency wars.

Because it is highlighted by the title of this conference, "Populism and the Future of the Fed," I should note the considerable debt the Federal Reserve owes to the populists. None other than William Jennings Bryan strongly supported the creation of the Fed: he described it in a 1913 letter to Carter Glass as "a triumph for the people" (the people, as opposed to the elites, being a classic populist trope). The Fed freed the country from depending on elites such as J.P. Morgan for dealing with financial crises like that of 1907.[4] By

---

[3]Rajan (2017) put it well, that central bankers "with their PhDs, exclusive jargon, and secretive meetings" are the "rootless global elite the populist nationalists love to hate."

[4]Bruner and Carr (2007) tell the story of the crisis. Creating the Fed didn't free the people, however, from dependence on Morgan's right-hand man, Benjamin Strong.

providing the "elastic currency" the people demanded, it promised to protect them from the deflation that haunted Bryan. The decentralized structure of the Federal Reserve System, with its 12 regional reserve banks, chimed in with populist antipathy to concentrated financial power. The one thing Bryan and his fellow populists failed to achieve was preventing bankers from serving on the boards of Reserve Banks. This was something for which another notorious populist, the radio preacher Father Charles Coughlin, famously campaigned in the 1930s after the Fed's signal failure to meet its mandate of preventing deflation and financial crisis.[5]

Populism: A Problem for Central Bankers

Clearly, populism is a problem for central banking, and for central bank independence in particular, whatever your preferred theory of the latter. If you think that central banking is a complex task requiring careful deliberation by thoughtful, experienced individuals, then there is a danger that a populist leader will appoint individuals lacking appropriate temperament and background. If you view an independent central bank led by a conservative, inflation-averse central banker as a way of addressing the time-consistency problem that otherwise gives rise to inflationary bias (Rogoff 1985), then you should worry that a populist leader will appoint central bankers who are anything but conservative and inflation averse. If you think that making the central bank independent is a way of limiting the contribution of monetary policy to political business cycles (Nordhaus 1975; Berger and Woitek 2001), then you will worry that populist leaders will reinject politics into central banking, especially in the lead-up to elections. If you think that the argument for independence is that it allows central bankers to adopt long time horizons appropriate for the conduct of monetary policy (Blinder 1998), then you will worry that populist politicians

[5]Coughlin went further, advocating the elimination of member bank shareholding in Regional Reserve Banks and, indeed, elimination of the Federal Reserve System itself, which would have been replaced by a Bank of the United States governed by a board of 48 directors, one from each state, to be popularly elected. Coughlin's supporters filed suit in Philadelphia to test the constitutionality of the Federal Reserve Act, and two of his congressional supporters introduced a "Coughlin Banking and Monetary Control Bill" in both the House and Senate in 1935. See Boeckel (1936).

are temperamentally impatient and not reticent about reminding their appointees of the fact.

Central Bank Independence

These problems are by no means unique to politics and politicians with a populist bent. Binder and Spindel (2017) remind us that central bank independence, in the United States as elsewhere, has never been absolute; central banks are perennially subject to political pressure. Milton Friedman (1962), in making the case for an autonomous central bank, famously observed that the central bank is likely to retain its independence only up to the point where its objectives conflict with those of the executive. Neither Richard Nixon, who pressured Arthur Burns to keep interest rates low in the run-up to the 1972 election, nor Ronald Reagan, who (through the good offices of James Baker) did the same to Paul Volcker in 1984, is typically regarded as a populist.[6]

Alan Drazen has a thoughtful article from 20 years ago where he highlights the tension between political insulation and political responsiveness in the context of monetary policy. Both insulation and responsiveness have value, and there is a tradeoff between the two, so the task for institutional design is to identify a point on the efficient frontier that produces socially acceptable outcomes. Drazen notes that these observations are not peculiar to monetary policy: a variety of other government functions (think vaccine authorization) are delegated to expert bodies in order to ensure a degree of insulation from politics. Few consequential economic policy decisions are made via direct democracy, except in peculiar places like California and Switzerland. To take a current example, we insulate fiscal policy from partisan political pressures, partially but not entirely, by design—that is, by maintaining the 60-vote cloture rule on the filibuster in the U.S. Senate.

We go further in the direction of insulation from politics for monetary than fiscal policy. Drazen's explanation, which others share, is that monetary policy is more easily abused. An opportunistic politician need only announce a change in the central bank's policy rate, which he can do with a snap of his fingers (or by replacing the central bank

---

[6]Abrams (2006) provides evidence on the 1972 episode from the Nixon tapes. Volcker (2018:118–19) describes his recollection of the 1984 episode.

governor), whereas opportunistically changing levels of government spending or taxes is more difficult legislatively and takes longer to implement administratively.[7]

In addition, fiscal policy has more prominent distributional consequences, which makes limiting political responsiveness through delegation problematic. Different interest groups, the argument goes, should be able to agree on what constitutes a monetary policy that is not short sighted. In contrast, they will have very different views of how the structure of government spending would look under an optimal long-run fiscal policy. As Drazen (2002: 8) puts it, "The conflict of interests in fiscal policy is both across time (the investment aspect) and across groups with very divergent interests even in a long-run equilibrium, while the conflict of interests in monetary policy is primarily across time." Thus, it is only for aggregate fiscal policy (the level of spending or the size of the deficit), where the intertemporal dimension (what Drazen calls the "investment aspect") dominates, that one sees binding rules (fiscal analogs to the Taylor Rule or a fixed money growth rule in the monetary context) or delegation to an expert panel (such as an independent fiscal council analogous to the board of an independent central bank).

Distributional Consequences of Monetary Policy

The question is whether we now need to reconsider the underlying assumption, that the distributional consequences of monetary policy are second order, given the attention recently devoted to the question. If so, does this reconsideration have implications for central banking? And what does all this have to do with populism?

No doubt, there has been a sharp increase in articles, comments and speeches by critics and defenders of central banks alike (including speeches by central bankers themselves) highlighting the distributional consequences of monetary policy. Checking Google's Ngram Viewer, which tabulates all mentions of a string of words in Google's text corpora, there is no mention of the phrase "distributional effects of monetary policy" prior to 1960. There is then a first peak in 1965, a second higher peak in 1977, a third very considerably higher peak in 2002, and a fourth peak, at roughly the same level as the third,

---

[7]That's the assertion anyway, though I'm not aware of systematic evidence of the contrast.

FIGURE 1
DISTRIBUTIONAL EFFECTS OF MONETARY POLICY

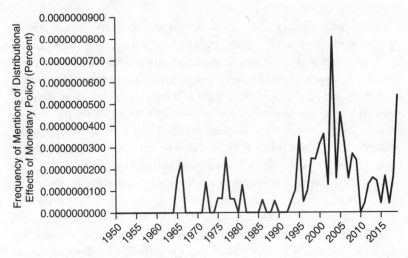

SOURCE: Google NGram data.

in 2019, when the series currently ends (Figure 1).[8] I conjecture that if we had data for 2020–2021, the fourth peak would be the highest.[9]

Already in the middle of the last decade, Ben Bernanke (2015) and Mario Draghi (2016) commented on the distributional consequences of monetary policy. At the Fed, there have been speeches and comments by Chairman Powell; Governors Bowman, Brainard, and Waller; and Presidents Bullard, Daly, and Williams, among others. Claudio Borio (2021) recently calculated the share of speeches by central bankers in advanced economies and emerging markets that mention "inequality" or "distributional consequences/impact of monetary policy," finding that these rose from negligible levels at the beginning of the century to 3 percent in 2007, 3 percent again in

---

[8]We all recall economic and monetary events around these specific times that plausibly excited questions about these distributional effects. Inflation accelerated in the mid-1960s and again, even more dramatically, in the late 1970s. The Fed took interest rates down very sharply after 9/11.

[9]Other similar strings return similar results. For example, "distributional impact of monetary policy" shows the same contours and differs mainly by returning far and away the highest frequency for 2019.

2012, and 9 percent in recent years.[10] During the 2020 presidential campaign, candidate Joe Biden proposed amending the Federal Reserve Act to add to the dual mandate responsibility for "aggressively target[ing] persistent racial gaps in jobs, wages and wealth" (Schlesinger and Siddiqui 2020). Though he has not repeated that call since assuming office, a group of Democratic members of Congress introduced a bill (the "Federal Reserve Racial and Economic Equity Act") intended to modify the Fed's mandate to minimize and eliminate "racial disparities in employment, wages, wealth, and access to affordable credit" (Long 2020).[11]

As for the distributional effects of monetary policy, there are again a large number of studies, including quite a few coming out of central banks. The IMF has recently published a compendium of such studies (Bonifacio et al. 2021). The central bankers' bank, the Bank for International Settlements, devotes a chapter of its 2021 annual report to international evidence on this question (BIS 2021).

My favorite of these studies may be that by the Sveriges Riksbank (Amberg et al. 2021), since it uses administrative data that avoids the problem of top coding incomes and focuses on monetary policy surprises. It shows that a surprise monetary loosening disproportionately benefits those at the very top of the income distribution, since they receive disproportionate amounts of capital income, and those at the very bottom of the distribution, since their income from employment is especially sensitive to monetary shocks.[12] Put another

---

[10]These earlier peaks in 2007 and 2012 of course coincided with exceptionally sharp shifts in monetary policy— first a sharp rise in the fed funds rate in 2006 and then an equally sharp fall in 2007, followed by a third round of quantitative easing (QE3) in 2012, which plausibly directed attention to the policy, including its distributional effects.

[11]The original bill, introduced in 2020, was reintroduced in April 2021. The draft is short on specific actions that the Fed might take. It adds the minimization of racial disparities to the central bank's mandate, requires the chair to discuss how the Fed is acting to address disparities in the semiannual testimony to Congress, and requires the Fed to discuss such disparities in its reporting on labor force trends. This might be taken as consistent with the idea that the Fed has the independence to choose its tactics (Congress only sets the mandate), or alternatively that the Fed has relatively little ability to affect this dimension of inequality.

[12]The surprise part is important because worsening economic conditions that would be expected to elicit a loosening of monetary policy might be correlated with increased inequality because the worsening conditions, and not the monetary policy response, was unequalizing.

FIGURE 2
ECONOMIC INEQUALITY

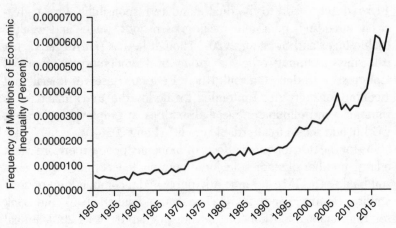

SOURCE: Google Ngram data.

way, monetary policy has both income and wealth effects, where the income effects predominate toward the bottom of the distribution, while the wealth effects predominate toward the top.[13]

So why now? Most obviously, there has been growing attention to inequality generally. Most measures of economic inequality in the United States have been trending upward since the 1980s (Saez and Zucman 2020). That more attention has been paid to the problem can again be inferred from Google Ngram data (Figure 2); the frequency of mentions begins rising in the mid-1980s. It peaks in 2014, the year that Piketty's *Capital in the Twenty-First Century* appeared in English, but remains elevated subsequently. Then the election of Donald Trump in 2016 and electoral victories of progressives like Alexandria Ocasio-Cortez raised concerns that mainstream politicians and political institutions were not doing enough to address the issue, and that their failure to do so was breeding support for unconventional, out-of-the-mainstream politicians, including of the populist variety.[14] Central bankers may not like it, but there is no reason

---

[13]These patterns are likely to generalize to other settings, although to exactly what extent is not clear.

[14]In addition, the Black Lives Matter movement trained attention on racial and structural aspects of the inequality problem.

to think that they or their institution should be exempted from this complaint.

Finally, the Fed's putative role in the development of inequality would not have become subject to the same attention had it not been required by circumstances to pursue unconventional monetary policies. There is some evidence, and widespread perception, that low interest rates and quantitative easing push up the prices of financial assets (Balatti et al. 2017), which are disproportionately held by the wealthy. There is some evidence, and widespread perception, that low interest rates have been an important factor in the rise in housing prices (Huston and Spencer 2017), which benefits homeowners relative to renters. Given this, it is logical that the Fed should come under scrutiny for its contribution to inequality trends.

Notice that there is nothing especially populist about these observations. However, these monetary policy actions took place against the backdrop of repeated bank bailouts, mounted in response to financial crises, in which the Fed was involved. The pattern encourages the perception that Fed policy, not excluding its monetary policy, favors bankers and other relatively wealthy and successful individuals. Arguments that Fed policy has distributional consequences therefore fall on receptive ears. They provide fodder for anti-elite (i.e., populist) campaigners against the central banking status quo.

What Can the Fed Do?

The trend toward increased inequality in the United States dates from the 1980s; it long predates the current period of low interest rates. Numerous studies (which I cite and describe in my book) show that this inequality trend has been mainly associated with, in descending order of importance, skill-biased technical change, globalization, taxation, education and training, and declining union density. Monetary policy is a blunt instrument for addressing this trend since its effects on the distribution of income are second order, compared to the aforementioned, and because it affects different dimensions of inequality differently. The Swedish study mentioned earlier, which finds that monetary stimulus raises the relative incomes of both the lowest and highest deciles of the distribution, is a reminder that different measures of inequality will show different associations with the stance of monetary policy. The same is true of racial inequality: a paper from the New York Fed (Bartscher et al. 2021) showed that racial inequality in the labor market was reduced by monetary stimulus—black unemployment fell by more than white unemployment—but that racial wealth inequality increased, since white households held more financial assets.

But saying that monetary policy is a blunt instrument for addressing inequality is not the same as saying that central banks can do nothing about it. As regulators, they can address predatory practices that target the disadvantaged. They can encourage competition in the provision of financial services and foster financial inclusion.

Finally, central bankers can tailor their communications strategies to the problem. They can acknowledge that inequality is of concern and talk about what government and society, as well as the central bank, can do about it. They can acknowledge the contribution of their policies, even if slight, to the development of the problem. There are those who argue that central bankers should limit their remarks to topics that bear directly on the conduct of monetary policy. They should limit the problems they discuss to those related to their core mandate, in the present context, price stability and high employment. Going beyond that mandate and acting as free-form social critics will lead politicians to question central bankers' institutional independence. Attempting to solve problems over which monetary policy has little leverage is setting the institution up for failure.

I disagree. When an issue rises to the level of an existential crisis, it is irresponsible for a central bank *not* to address it and *not* to do what it can to help solve it, even if what it is capable of doing is slight. The central bank would then appear unresponsive to political imperatives at a time when some response was essential. The central bank would be on a socially unacceptable point on Drazen's political-insulation-political-responsiveness tradeoff. And insisting on that position might engender real threats to the central bank's independent status. It would only give ammunition to the institution's populist critics.

Elsewhere (Eichengreen 2021), I've made this argument about climate change. Central banks have limited power, mainly in their capacity as financial regulators, to help meet the climate change challenge. Except insofar as it impacts inflation and employment, climate change might not seem central to the Fed's mandate. But to not address a problem that poses an existential threat to humanity would be politically unresponsive. It would give fodder to the Fed's progressive, populist critics. It could ultimately jeopardize the institution's independence.

Does inequality similarly rise to the level of an existential threat to economic, social, and political stability in the United States, thereby justifying central bank efforts to address it? That's something for each of us, and for each member of the Federal Reserve Board, to decide.

References

Abrams, B. (2006) "How Richard Nixon Pressured Arthur Burns: Evidence from the Nixon Tapes." *Journal of Economic Perspectives* 20: 177–88.

Amberg, N.; Jansson, T.; Klein, M.; and Picco, A. R. (2021), "Five Facts about the Distributional Income Effects of Monetary Policy." Sveriges Riksbank Working Paper No. 403 (May).

Balatti, M.; Brooks, C.; Clements, M.; and Kappou, K. (2017) "Did Quantitative Easing Only Inflate Stock Prices? Macroeconomic Evidence from the US and UK." Unpublished manuscript, Henley Business School (January).

Bank for International Settlements [BIS] (2021) *Annual Economic Report, June 2021: Promoting Global Monetary and Financial Stability.* Available at www.bis.org/publ/arpdf/ar2021e.pdf.

Bartscher, A.; Kuhn, M.; Schularick, M.; and Wachtel, P. (2021) "Monetary Policy and Racial Inequality." Staff Report No. 959, Federal Reserve Bank of New York (June).

Berger, H., and Woitek, U. (2001) "The German Political Business Cycle: Money Demand Rather than Monetary Policy." *European Journal of Political Economy* 17: 609–31.

Bernanke, B. (2015) "Monetary Policy and Inequality." Brookings Institution blog (June 1).

Binder, S., and Spindel, M. (2017) *The Myth of Independence: How Congress Governs the Federal Reserve.* Princeton, N.J.: Princeton University Press.

Blinder, A. (1998) *Central Banking in Theory and Practice.* Cambridge, Mass.: MIT Press.

Boeckel, R. M. (1936) "Father Coughlin vs. the Federal Reserve System." *CQ Researcher* (October 16).

Bonifacio, V. et al. (2021) "Distributional Effects of Monetary Policy." IMF Working Paper No. 2021/201 (July).

Borio, C. (2021) "The Distributional Footprint of Monetary Policy." Speech on the occasion of the Bank's Annual General Meeting, Basel (June 29).

Bruner, R., and Carr, S. (2007) *The Panic of 1907: Lessons Learned from the Market's Perfect Storm.* New York: John Wiley.

Dincer, N., and Eichengreen, B. (2014) "Central Bank Transparency and Independence: Updates and New Measures." *International Journal of Central Banking* 34: 189–253.

Dincer, N.; Eichengreen, B.; and Geraats, P. (2022) "Trends in Monetary Policy Transparency: Further Updates." *International Journal of Central Banking* (March).

Dornbusch, R., and Edwards, S. (1990) "Macroeconomic Populism." *Journal of Development Economics* 32: 247–77.

Draghi, M. (2016) "Stability, Equity and Monetary Policy." 2nd DIW Europe Lecture (25 October).

Drazen, A. (2002) "Central Bank Independence, Democracy, and Dollarization." *Journal of Applied Economics* 5: 1–17.

Eichengreen, B. (2018) *The Populist Temptation: Economic Grievance and Political Reaction in the Modern Era*, New York: Oxford University Press.

_____ (2021) "New Model Central Banks." *Project Syndicate* (9 February).

Friedman, M. (1962) "Should There Be an Independent Central Bank?" In L. Yeager (ed.), *In Search of a Monetary Constitution*. Cambridge, Mass.: Harvard University Press.

Huston, J., and Spencer, R. (2017) "Quantitative Easing and Asset Bubbles." *Applied Economics Letters* 25: 369–74.

Long, H. (2020) "Democrats Introduce Bill to Give the Federal Reserve a New Mission: Ending Racial Inequality." *Washington Post* (August 5).

Nordhaus, W. (1975) "The Political Business Cycle." *Review of Economic Studies* 42: 169–90.

Piketty, T. (2014) *Capital in the Twenty-First Century.* Cambridge, Mass.: Belknap Press for Harvard University Press.

Rajan, R. (2017) "Central Banks' Year of Reckoning." *Project Syndicate* (21 December).

Rogoff, K. (1985) "The Optimal Degree of Commitment to an Intermediate Monetary Target." *Quarterly Journal of Economics* 100: 1169–89.

Saez, E., and Zucman, G. (2020) "The Rise of Income and Wealth Inequality in America: Evidence from Distributional Macroeconomic Accounts." *Journal of Economic Perspectives* 34: 3–26.

Schlesinger, J. M., and Siddiqui, S. (2020) "Biden Urges Bigger Role for Fed in Addressing Racial Wealth Gap." *Wall Street Journal* (July 28).

Volcker, P. (2018) *Keeping At It: The Quest for Sound Money and Good Government.* New York: Public Affairs.

3
POPULISM, POLITICS, AND CENTRAL BANK INDEPENDENCE

Charles Goodhart and Rosa María Lastra

Since we wrote our paper on "Populism and Central Bank Independence" (Goodhart and Lastra 2018), the most important subsequent event has been the Covid-19 pandemic.[1] That event has reinforced the drift away from what we described as "the central liberal tenet"—namely, "that allowing the free movement of labour, capital and goods and services between nations would be both generally beneficial and desirable in almost all circumstances." Our preferred definition of a populist, therefore, is someone "wanting to restrict the movements of people, capital and goods and services between nation states" (Goodhart and Lastra 2018: 50).

Thus, the desire to protect our own population, both by limiting international travel and by ensuring that all one's residents get access to personal protective equipment and vaccines before allowing them to be exported to more vulnerable people abroad, has underlined the priority of national sovereignty over international cooperation. The same considerations, accentuated by Covid-related constraints on long supply chains and by the worsening of

Charles Goodhart is Professor Emeritus at the London School of Economics. Rosa María Lastra is the Sir John Lubbock Chair in Banking Law at the Centre for Commercial Law Studies at Queen Mary University of London. Professor Goodhart thanks Manoj Pradhan with whom he wrote: "What May Happen When Central Banks Wake Up to More Persistent Inflation?" (Goodhart and Pradhan 2021).

[1]For commentary on our earlier paper, see Agur (2018); Ferrara et al. (2021); Binder (2021); Guriev and Papaioannou (2020); Gnan and Masciandaro (2019, 2020).

Chinese-U.S. trade relationships, have further enhanced the retreat from globalization and some reversal of offshoring, back to onshoring strategic production lines.

The pandemic has redefined yet again the role of the state. Politicians of all colors, democratically elected or not, particularly in advanced economies, have come to the rescue of ailing sectors and workers with furlough schemes and other measures of fiscal support, to alleviate the economic impact of lockdown-imposed restrictions and to fund the growing demands of public health systems.[2] In this Covid crisis, central banks have not been "the only game in town," as they were during the global financial crisis (El-Erian 2016). However, their close cooperation with the fiscal authorities and the continuation of their very significant quantitative easing (QE) programs, with further expansion of the central bank balance sheets, raise important issues in terms of central bank independence.

In the UK, QE is equivalent to approximately 40 percent of annual GDP, while asset purchases programs in the United States, euro area, and Japan total around 30 percent, 32 percent, and 106 percent of GDP, respectively. While the original intent of QE in the UK in 2009 was to "unclog" the bank lending channel to the private sector and to increase the money supply, QE in response to Covid-19 started by addressing dysfunctional bond markets but soon became a measure to support the economy and economic recovery in the light of the pandemic. With QE, central banks entered uncharted territories; a policy instrument that was meant to be extraordinary and temporary has become part of the new normal (see House of Lords Report 2021).[3]

In this chapter, we first consider the return of inflation and the limits of monetary policy. We then examine the consequences for independence and accountability of the expanded central bank

---

[2]Developing countries, particularly those with limited fiscal space and external debt problems, have faced other challenges, which will not be discussed here.

[3]Rosa Lastra was a specialist adviser to the House of Lords during the inquiry that culminated in the evidence-based report. Charles Goodhart submitted oral evidence to the committee during the inquiry. As a result of QE policies, the combined balance sheets of the European Central Bank, Federal Reserve, Bank of England, and Bank of Japan expanded from around $4 trillion to around $25 trillion between 2008 and 2021. Of that increase, $10 trillion occurred after the outbreak of the pandemic.

mandates, both through the use of unconventional instruments of monetary control, in particular, QE, and through the addition of new objectives, in particular, with regard to climate change and sustainability. We finish the article with some observations about the repoliticization of central banks.

The Return of Inflation

As Goodhart and Pradhan (2020) argued, the combination of demography and globalization had led to worsening inequality within countries but less inequality between countries. Right-wing politicians jumped on the association between globalization and immigration and worsening inequality within countries, to promote a more nativist and protectionist policy, with the stated objective of "leveling up" less-skilled workers. Politically, that effort has been quite successful.

That success has led to a desire to run the economy at a hotter pace, to encourage higher minimum wages, and to accept higher wage growth, especially for those with lower incomes. But much of this agenda was conditional on the assumption that the forces that had, over previous decades, led to disinflation, and to inflation outcomes below target, would continue to operate. Indeed, there was an initial welcome for a short period of post-Covid above-target inflation, to achieve average inflation targets and to raise previously below-target expectations.

This view is still held by the mainstream: the official central bank view is that the present surge in inflation is temporary, even if slightly longer lasting than earlier expected (Ha, Kose, and Ohnsorge 2021), and due mainly to one-off supply shocks. If so, there would be no serious threat to central bank independence, since such policy would remain expansionary and accommodating as far as the eye can see, and thus fully consistent with populist desires for greater participation in employment and faster real wage growth. Indeed, with inflation assumed to remain tamed, there could be greater scope for the central bank to take on yet further objectives. Nominal interest rates might rise in due course, allowing real rates to remain gently negative, while inflation falls back to target. Meanwhile QE would cease, but arguments over the longer-run optimal level of central bank balance sheets could proceed at a much slower pace. It would be nice if the mainstream view was correct. But what if it is wrong?

What might happen if, say by mid-2022, there is little sign of CPI inflation retreating from its levels of about 4–5 percent in the United States, United Kingdom, and European Union at the end of 2021? What if expectations of future inflation trend slowly up at all horizons along with continuing shortages of labor, and if workers, even where there are no shortages, demand higher pay to compensate for both past and expected future inflation?[4]

Could it then be right to leave real interest rates at significantly negative levels, with unemployment trending downward, (who knows what the equilibrium natural rate might be), a growing need for infrastructure and green investment, and public sector deficits still historically elevated? Financial markets are currently expecting the Federal Reserve, for example, to start raising policy rates as early as March 2022, with four to five hikes of 25 bps over the course of 2022–2023. Breakeven inflation rates (the difference between nominal yields and inflation-protected securities) in the United States at the five-year horizon are hovering around 2.7 percent.[5] Thus, markets appear to be comfortable with the real policy rate remaining persistently negative over the next few years.

So how will central banks react if, and when, they begin to discover that their forecasts and models have been systematically wrong? The most worrying possibility is that central banks might reverse policies suddenly and dramatically, a 180-degree course correction—50 bps hikes and shrinking the balance sheet. One can see only too easily how this might happen. After months, some of us might say years, of getting forecasts and policies wrong, central banks might feel that their credibility is at stake. Having stated that they were supremely confident in their ability to control inflation, they might feel forced to try to demonstrate that capability quickly and suddenly. What this might mean in practice could be a rapid shift from a policy of glacially slow increases in nominal rates, plus a very slow taper of QE, to one of increases in nominal interest rates of, say, 50 bps per meeting, and no replacement of maturing central bank holdings of QE-related debt.

---

[4]See, for example, Voinea and Loungani (2021). Congdon (2021) discusses the risks of double-digit inflation in the United States, criticizing then-Fed Vice Chairman Richard Clarida.

[5]The two-year breakeven rate is higher, not lower, than the five-year, so we are being conservative with our measure of expected inflation.

But such a sudden shift of policy would be horrendously risky. Such monetary tightening would likely cause a rapid collapse in asset prices, including bringing to an end the world's most coordinated housing boom. In view of the additional debt and high leverage of the private nonfinancial corporate sector, it could cause a steep rise in bankruptcies and nonperforming loans. We could get a depression of an awe-inspiring scale. The effect on the public sector balance sheet would be devastating. Tax revenues would fall, while public sector expenditures and debt service would rise sharply.

Under these circumstances, there would be no advantage in reversing course so sharply that inflation became replaced by deflation. There are many worse outcomes than a few years of moderate inflation, say in the 4 to 5 percent range. Even if central bank credibility takes a knock, one could always blame unforeseen events or one's predecessors' policies.

So what should central banks now do against the possibility that moderate inflation becomes more persistent and increasingly engrained in the system? The first need is to have a plan about what one might do under such circumstances, even if such a scenario is still thought unlikely. The Bank of England (BOE) is to be greatly applauded for having worked out such a plan (responding to some of the recommendations of the House of Lords report on QE), and it makes sense. Indeed, it would be good to start putting that plan into operation, with a symbolic tiny increase in nominal interest rates in the immediate future.

Next, central bank economists need to start thinking about the effect of rising nominal rates as real rates remain strictly negative. With inflation having risen, and remaining persistent, it will take some time for a slow increase in nominal rates to bring real rates back to zero; but rising nominal rates on their own will have significant effects not only on financial markets but also on the real economy. In these conditions, the concentration on r^* (the real equilibrium or "natural" rate of interest) is misplaced. The rate of change of nominal interest rates will be an important factor affecting the economy on its own, even when real rates remain strictly negative. In addition, central banks may find themselves having to think harder and quicker about their balance sheet policies and the form of their monetary operations (see Cecchetti and Tucker 2021).

A floor mechanism for setting interest rates, plus QE, had many advantages during the years after the 2008 financial crisis. Not only was it easy to manipulate, but it provided commercial banks with a huge buffer of liquidity, thereby making them much more resilient in the face of the Covid-19 shock. But when nominal interest rates start to rise, the disadvantages, in some large part political, of this technique will become increasingly apparent. At a time of worsening debt service ratios, and pressure for increased taxation, the transfer of increasingly large payments from the public purse to commercial banks for holding reserves at the central bank will become increasingly unpopular, not to mention the adverse effect on central bank profitability. (You do not have to be a populist politician to see how this conjuncture could become widely unpopular and difficult to defend.)

Consequently, central banks need to consider what their balance sheet policies should become in a world of rising nominal interest rates, and whether the current structure of QE and the massive availability of additional liquidity is still going to be optimal in such a different situation.

First, central banks will have to bear capital losses on their holdings and could need recapitalization from governments. That process will have to be structured in a way that does not raise questions about central bank independence (see Allen, Chadha, and Turner 2021). Second, many of the quasi-fiscal uses of QE (such as propping up markets for mortgage-backed securities when they had assumed macroeconomic importance) will have to unwind. Finally, over a structural horizon, as age-related government debt rises, central bank balance sheets are more likely to expand than shrink. The balancing act will be about avoiding the creation of moral hazard by monetizing too much of the debt, versus doing so little that markets push interest rates higher because of concerns surrounding the financing of that debt.

Finally, through all of this, central banks need to pull these policies together in a way that convinces financial markets that an orderly evolution is not just possible but likely. In other words, fighting the right war is difficult enough. Fighting the last war would be a catastrophe.

The Expansion of Central Bank Mandates

In response to the 2008 financial crisis, financial stability considerations led to the expansion of the central bank's role as lender of last resort and new responsibilities in macro- and microprudential supervision. With the onset of the pandemic in March 2020, central banks acquired new duties as crisis managers, as monetary and fiscal authorities coordinated their efforts. More recently, the issue of climate change has been either discussed as part of the secondary mandate of the European Central Bank (ECB) or added to the mandate of the central bank, as in the case of the BOE.

The events of the last few years represent a departure from the previous central banking model, which featured one agency (the central bank), one primary objective (price stability), and one main instrument (interest rate policy). This model, which is consistent with the "Tinbergen rule," was widely adopted around the world, from the member states that signed the Maastricht Treaty in the European Union (EU) to a large number of countries that revised their central bank laws, often based on IMF recommendations. The credibility associated with this narrow mandate-based model has served countries and the global community well.

The pre-2008 model had the added benefit that it made it relatively easy to hold the central bank accountable. But beginning with the global financial crisis, then with the pandemic, and now with climate change, the mandate of central banks as crisis managers has been expanded or reinterpreted, raising important issues in terms of independence and accountability.

The intellectual justification for central bank independence developed in the 1990s is now being questioned. Otmar Issing, in oral evidence to the House of Lords (2021), told the Economic Affairs Committee: "Central banks have come closer to political decisions during the financial crisis and now in the context of the pandemic."

In the March 2021 budget, Chancellor Rishi Sunak announced that the Bank of England's mandate should support the government's efforts to make the UK economy greener and achieve net zero emissions by 2050 (Harvey and Ambrose 2021). In practice, the change means that the Bank of England will adjust its approach to corporate bond buying to take account of the impact of its acquisitions on climate change. The bank's new objective, and the tools to achieve it, is controversial, particularly when it comes to credit allocation involving picking winners and losers through green QE.

The Bank of England's Prudential Regulation Authority (PRA) is assessing the need for climate change buffers; the PRA stated on October 28, 2021, that it would examine whether changes to bank capital buffers might be necessary to manage the impact of climate change. Yet at the same time, the PRA stated that steering the move to decarbonization should be the responsibility of government, since capital requirements "seem unlikely to be the most effective tool in reducing carbon intensive activities" (Hodgson 2021).

The ECB is looking into the climate change agenda from the perspective of its mandate. The ECB, like all central banks, is a creature of history. At the time of the Maastricht Treaty, the Bundesbank model was the embodiment of the central banking model that became accepted and prevalent around the world (from New Zealand to Chile, to the EU and elsewhere). Like the Bundesbank, the independent ECB was granted independence (Article 130 TFEU) in the pursuit of the primary mandate of price stability (which is also one of the objectives of the European Union).[6] But the ECB was also given a secondary objective to support the general economic policies in the EU (Article 127 TFEU).

This secondary mandate of the ECB, forgotten or neglected for quite some time, has been the subject of much discussion during the recent strategy review of the ECB launched by President Lagarde in January 2020. But while the primary mandate is streamlined, the ECB's secondary mandate is broad and discretionary and includes employment, growth, climate change, and environmental and social sustainability (Article 127 TFEU in conjunction with Article 3 TEU; see Lastra and Alexander 2020).[7] Further, the different jurisdictional domains between centralized monetary policy and decentralized fiscal policies make it difficult to reconcile the pursuit of the primary and the secondary objectives. These difficulties notwithstanding, the current leadership at the helm of the ECB is adamant that it should aim to achieve both objectives. The debate now focuses on which instruments are best to do so, and how the ECB could be made accountable for its choices in this respect.

Given that monetary policy instruments are often a blunt tool, targeted intervention via micro- and macroprudential supervision may be more effective in addressing these challenges. For example, the ECB as bank supervisor should have an important role to play in

[6]For the full text of the "Treaty on the Functioning of the European Union" (TFEU), see https://eur-lex.europa.eu/legal-content/EN/TXT/?uri=LEGISSUM %3A4301854.

[7]For the full text of the "Treaty on European Union" (TEU), see https://eur-lex .europa.eu/legal-content/EN/TXT/?uri=celex%3A12012M%2FTXT.

ensuring that authorized firms are identifying and managing adequately the risks from climate change. Prudential authorities can help banks design stress tests based on forward scenarios that will help the industry judge what its capital and liquidity requirements should be in the face of future threats to stability caused by environmental or social phenomena.

Climate change and risks from unsustainable environmental and social activities not only impact the secondary objective; they also affect the central bank primary objective through monetary conditions and financial stability risks (Lastra and Alexander 2020).[8]

In any case, at the EU level, the main locus of the authority for mitigating environmental and social sustainability risks should always be at the level of EU institutions (i.e., the Council, Commission, and Parliament) and member state governments, which, unlike the ECB, control legislation, taxation, and expenditure programs and have overall responsibility for regulatory frameworks and direct economic interventions. And not to be excluded are private-sector market participants who are the main agents for implementing governmental policies—and who are the source of most of the risks and have the greatest potential for managing risks and steering the economy to a more sustainable path (Lastra and Alexander 2020).

Repoliticization?

The primacy given to price stability in the traditional central banking model reflected the consensus that stable prices are essential to achieve a favorable economic environment and a high level of employment, and that an independent central bank is the best institutional arrangement to keep inflation under control. Like Ulysses at the mast, political authorities can resist the inflationary sirens under a delegated depoliticized monetary policy. But how does one reconcile this model with the new political realities? Are we witnessing a repoliticization of central banks and with it a decline in independence? And, in broader terms, is a new social contract in economic policymaking emerging?

---

[8]Based on the experience of the 2008 financial crisis and the 2020 pandemic, it can be observed that the resources of governments and central banks are likely to become devoted to short-term crisis management.

Politicians (in particular, populist leaders) could easily clash with "expert" central bankers in the pursuit of much broader policies such as climate change, fighting crises or pandemics.

The 2021 House of Lords Report questioned the potential politicization of the Bank of England in the light of the expansion of the size of the central bank balance sheet, the effects of combining loose monetary and fiscal policies, the relationships between the Bank of England and the Treasury, the risks to the public finances, the allegations of monetary financing, the impact of QE on debt management and debt sustainability, the effects on independence, financial stability and wealth inequality, and the future of QE. With QE, the contours of what constitutes depoliticized monetary policy and what constitutes politicized fiscal policy become blurred. The House of Lords held the Bank of England to account by asking these challenging questions (House of Lords Report 2021).

What is certain is that with expanded mandates, central banks require commensurate mechanisms of accountability.[9] As the mandate has become broader or multifaceted (encompassing a variety of goals, which can be conflicting at times, for example "green inflation"), the consensus that surrounded the goals is questioned and with it the importance of independence diminishes (given its instrumental nature). Accountability is not simply an "add on" to justify independence (Lastra 1992; 1996: chap. 1). Accountability (ex ante and ex post) is a constitutive part of the design of an independent agency in a democratic system.[10] An accountable central bank should be judged for the reasonableness of its actions, by Parliament, by the executive, by the public, and by the Courts of Justice.

In line with the dynamic nature of central banks, the broadening of their objectives—through legal revision or reinterpretation—and the expansion of the range of tools needed to address such objectives require adjustments to their status of independence and accountability.

---

[9]Balls, Howat, and Stansbury (2016) advocated the preservation of operational independence, while sacrificing a certain degree of political independence for the sake of legitimacy and accountability.

[10]See https://transparency.eu/wp-content/uploads/2017/03/TI-EU_ECB_Report _DIGITAL.pdf.

References

Agur, I. (2018) "Populism and Central Bank Independence: Comment." *Open Economies Review* 29: 687–93.

Allen, W.A.; Chadha, J.; and Turner, P. (2021) "Quantitative Tightening: Protecting Monetary Policy from Fiscal Encroachment." Available at VoxEU.org (October 21).

Balls, E.; Howat, J.; and Stansbury, A. (2016) "Central Bank Independence Revisited: After the Financial Crisis, What Should a Model Central Bank Look Like?" M-RCBG Associate Working Paper No. 67, Harvard Kennedy School of Government.

Binder, C. (2021) "Political Pressure on Central Banks." *Journal of Money, Credit and Banking* 53 (4): 715–44.

Cecchetti, S., and Tucker, P. (2021) "Understanding How Central Banks Use Their Balance Sheets: A Critical Categorisation." Available at VoxEU.org (June 1).

Congdon, T. (2021) Institute of International Monetary Research Newsletter (October). Available at https://mailchi.mp/9a432 b620575/which-economic-thoughtcomes-out-best-from-the-last -decade-1336447?e=152dd21677.

El-Erian, M. (2016) *The Only Game in Town.* New York: Random House.

Ferrara, F. M.; Masciandaro, D.; Moschella, M.; and Romelli, D. (2021) "Political Voice on Monetary Policy: Evidence from the Parliamentary Hearings of the European Central Bank." Baffi Carefin, Centre for Applied Research on International Markets Banking Finance and Regulation Working Paper No. 21159. Milan: Bocconi University. Forthcoming in *European Journal of Political Economy.*

Gnan, E., and Masciandaro, D. (2019) *Populism, Economic Policies and Central Banking.* Vienna: SUERF (The European Money and Finance Forum).

_____ (2020) "Populism, Economic Policies, and Central Banking: An Overview." SUERF Policy Note Issue No. 131. Vienna: SUERF (The European Money and Finance Forum).

Goodhart, C., and Lastra, R. M. (2018) "Populism and Central Bank Independence." *Open Econ Review* 29: 49–68.

Goodhart, C., and Pradhan, M. (2020) *The Great Demographic Reversal: Ageing Societies, Waning Inequality, and an Inflation Revival.* New York: Palgrave Macmillan.

_____ (2021) "What May Happen When Central Banks Wake Up to More Persistent Inflation?" Available at VoxEU.org (October 25).

Guriev, S., and Papaioannou, E. (2020) "The Political Economy of Populism." Available at https://ssrn.com/abstract=3542052.

Ha, J.; Kose, M. A.; and Ohnsorge, F. (2021) "Inflationary Pressures: Likely Temporary but Challenging for Policy Design." Available at VoxEU.org (July 14).

Harvey, F., and Ambrose, J. (2021) "Bank of England Given Green Remit to Aid Net Zero Carbon Goal." *The Guardian* (March 3).

Hodgson, C. (2021) "Bank of England Considers Capital Rules for Banks to Cover Climate Risks." *Financial Times* (October 28).

House of Lords Report, Economic Affairs Committee (2021) "QE: A Dangerous Addiction?" (July). Available at https://committees.parliament.uk/publications/6725/documents/71894/default.

Lastra, R. M. (1992) "The Independence of the European System of Central Banks." *Harvard International Law Journal* 33 (2): 475–519.

_____ (1996) *Central Banking and Banking Regulation*. London: Financial Markets Group, London School of Economics.

Lastra, R. M., and Alexander, K. (2020) "The ECB Mandate: Perspectives on Sustainability and Solidarity." Monetary Dialogue Papers Requested by the ECON Committee of the European Parliament. Available at www.europarl.europa.eu/RegData/etudes/IDAN/2020/648813/IPOL_IDA(2020)648813_EN.pdf.

Voinea, L., and P. Loungani, P. (2021) "Predicting Inflation Using Cumulative Wage Gaps." Available at VoxEU.org (August 16).

4

TECHNOPOPULISM AND CENTRAL BANKS

Carola Binder

In recent years, warnings of a populist threat to central bank independence have proliferated. Rajan (2017), for example, describes central bankers, "with their PhDs, exclusive jargon, and secretive meetings," as the "rootless global elite the populist nationalists love to hate." But populist sentiment in the United States and elsewhere has *not* led to a more restricted role for central bankers. Instead, central bankers increasingly combine technocratic and populist appeals as they gain greater power and discretion. My argument is that the broader political logic of technopopulism (Bickerton and Accetti 2021) can help us understand central banking today and points to a stronger case for rule-based monetary policymaking to preserve the democratic legitimacy of central banks.

Democracy, Delegation, and Central Bank Independence

Tension around the role of expertise and expert power in a democracy is as old as democracy itself (Turner 2001). Delegation of power to experts, or technocrats, can reduce myopic or capricious behavior on the part of elected officials, but may not reflect the will of the public. This tension is inherent in central banking. In one of the earliest essays on central bank independence (CBI), Milton Friedman (1962: 177–78) noted that "The device of an independent central bank embodies the very appealing idea that it is essential to prevent monetary policy from being a day-to-day plaything at the mercy of every

Carola Binder is an Associate Professor of Economics at Haverford College.

whim of the current political authorities." But Friedman (1962: 180) asked, "Is it really tolerable in a democracy to have so much power concentrated in a body free of democratic control?"

Friedman's question was rhetorical; he argued for a legislated money growth rule rather than an independent central bank. But in the decades that followed, as this question continued to be posed in academic and policymaking circles, a different consensus emerged—that "the goals of monetary policy should be established by the political authorities, but that the conduct of monetary policy in pursuit of those goals should be free from political control" (Bernanke 2010). According to this consensus, political independence was made tolerable in a democracy by the use of transparency as an accountability mechanism (Bernanke 2007; Dincer and Eichengreen 2014).

Today, this consensus is on shaky grounds. The Great Recession and global financial crisis simultaneously increased public reliance on, and eroded trust in, central banks and other authoritative institutions—and populist movements gained ground (Roth 2009; Wälti 2012; Braun 2016; Binder 2020a). Reichlin (2017) warns that "To the populist bull, unelected technocrats wielding policies that have political and distributional consequences may as well be waving a red cape."

The Technopopulist Age

These and many other warnings of a populist threat to central bank independence are based on a deep-seated antagonism between technocracy and populism. This antagonism is worth questioning. As political scientist Christopher Bickerton argues:

> We cannot understand the contemporary political moment if we stick to this opposition between populism and technocracy. Political competition in advanced democratic states today is increasingly ordered around appeals to both 'the people' and to competence and expertise. Far from clashing with one another, these appeals are combined in multiple and complex ways [Bickerton 2020].

Both technocracy and populism are predicated upon a critique of representative democracy (Bickerton and Accetti 2017; Caramani 2017; James 2019; Berger 2020). Bickerton's recent book with Carlo Invernizzi Accetti—*Technopopulism: The New Logic of Democratic*

Politics (2021)—explains how a new "technopopulist" age is arising out of dissatisfaction with representative democracy and its institutions. Bickerton and Accetti (2021: 2) note that, "Even though appeals to the popular will and to competence are often rhetorically deployed against each other, there is also a deep affinity between them, which consists in the fact that they are both unmoored from the representation of specific values and interests within society and therefore advance an *unmediated conception of the common good.*"

Bickerton and Accetti focus on technopopulism across Western Europe, where it has taken a wide variety of forms, but with some important common features. All share a highly contested and politicized role of experts and expertise. Policy debates take the form of "'my expert versus yours'" (Bickerton 2020). A breakdown of trust in official information and institutional authority (Bennett and Livingston 2021) leads to appeals to "new forms of expertise from below" (Grundmann 2017). Policy disputes are "spectacularized" and "deeply confrontational," and "personal qualities . . . tend to assume center stage" (Bickerton and Accetti 2021: 12). In the next section, I argue that we can observe these features of technopopulism in both the pressures that central banks face and in the ways central bankers respond to these pressures.

Central Banks in the Technopopulist Age

In previous research, I have shown that political pressure on central banks is prevalent regardless of legal central bank independence, and that populist or nationalist politicians are more likely to apply such pressure (Binder 2020b, 2021a). In the United States, presidents have pressured Fed officials and influenced Fed policy to varying extents throughout the central bank's history (Cargill and O'Driscoll 2013; Dorn 2019). The logic of technopopulism can help us understand the nature of political pressure on central banks in recent years.

The influence of technopopulism was evident in President Trump's relationship with the Fed. He was more vocal and confrontational in his criticisms and attempts to influence Fed policy than were other recent presidents. President Trump took his opinions directly to Twitter, where he urged the "boneheads" at the Fed to cut interest rates using nationalist and populist language, while appealing to his own expertise. For example, on December 14, 2020, he tweeted, "It is incredible that with a very strong dollar and virtually no inflation, the outside world blowing up around us, Paris is burning and China way down, the Fed is even considering yet another interest rate hike. Take the Victory!"

Technopopulist pressures on the Fed come from both the right and the left. Many of President Biden's core group of economic advisers are prominent members of "#EconTwitter," where "'very online' economists have been pushing from the outside for the federal government and the Federal Reserve to pursue big spending and slightly higher inflation in their bid to help the labor market fully recover from the Covid-19 pandemic" (Guida, Thompson, and Meyer 2021). The monetary policy discourse on Twitter combines technocratic and populist appeals in a public, sometimes spectacularized, arena that allows visible votes of confidence in the forms of likes, retweets, comments, and even gifs. Commentators on monetary policy brandish not only their models and their professional credentials, but also their networks and their carefully cultivated public personas to establish themselves as "your expert."

The *Financial Times* editorial board urges central bankers to "remain calm and tell the unvarnished truth" in the face of populist pressures (*Financial Times* 2019). But central bankers also recognize the contested nature of expert knowledge and the lack of trust in official statistics, and this is reflected in their rhetoric as they ramp up their efforts to communicate with the general public (Binder 2017a, 2017b). In February 2021, San Francisco Fed President Mary Daly tweeted, "What is the real unemployment rate? Not 6.3 percent. How can we know? Look around." Similarly, Chairman Powell recently followed a discussion of economic statistics by noting that, "These encouraging statistics were reaffirmed and given voice by those we met and conferred with . . . during the 14 Fed Listens[1] events we conducted in 2019" (Powell 2021).

The technopopulist influence is reflected in central banks' communication strategies more broadly—so much so that we can describe the

---

[1]The "Fed Listens" events, a series of meetings in 2019 with union members, small business owners, residents of low-income communities, retirees, and others, are reminiscent of Emmanuel Macron's "Great March," a "fact-finding mission" across France conducted by policy specialists and public opinion experts. Bickerton and Accetti (2021) point to the Great March as a salient manifestation of technopopulism in France.

past few years as a new technopopulist wave of the communications revolution in central banking. In the first wave, central banks increased the transparency of their communication to make more precise information available and improve monetary policy predictability. Transparency also aimed to facilitate monetary policy transmission and promote accountability to elected representatives (Bernanke 2007). Dincer and Eichengreen (2010: 78) explain that central bank transparency works as an accountability mechanism "only if those deciding monetary policy cannot claim that their policy decisions are, in fact, in the public interest for reasons that only they understand."

But monetary policymakers *do* now claim—sometimes explicitly—that their decisions are in the public interest for reasons only they understand. When Neel Kashkari took office as president of the Minneapolis Fed, he urged the Fed to act on "economic anger" and said that "You are not going to have the population as a whole understand all the nuances of what we are talking about here. They need to trust us" (Fleming and Donnan 2016).

This technopopulist pursuit of popular trust is why, as a recent headline puts it, "Reggae. Puppies. Whatever It Takes, Central Banks Want Attention" (Smialek 2019). Trust, according to Cochrane (2020), "must be earned by evident competence and institutional restraint. . . . But a popular movement wants all institutions of society to jump into the social and political goals of the moment, regardless of boring legalities." Central banks are taking this jump (Skinner 2021). For example, in November 2021, the Minneapolis Fed's website featured traditionally populist language embodying Kashkari's call to act on anger. On both November 11 and 28, the following banner appeared on the website: "Pursuing an economy that works for all of us." In the first case, the boldface text reads: "As the richest Americans get richer, the price of college soars." That text was followed by: "Minneapolis Fed research explores how rising income inequality pushes tuition ever higher." On November 28, the boldface type noted a second strand of Fed research: "Racism and the Economy: Focus on Financial Services."

One can find a similar technopopulist tilt when viewing the website for the European Central Bank, which, in 2021, carried a large, colorful photo of ECB President Christine Lagarde—consistent with technopopulist emphasis on leaders' personalities and their need to establish themselves as "the people's expert." In line with this, ECB communications have become more populist and charismatic in recent years (Tortola and Pansardi 2018; Lokdam 2020).

The Federal Reserve Bank of New York website, among others, has undergone similar aesthetic changes. Many central bank websites in 2021 also featured more content related to salient political and social issues like inequality, mobility, racism, inclusion, global warming, and climate change, which have also become more prominent topics in central bankers' speeches (e.g., Powell 2019; Daly 2020; and Skinner 2021) and in Federal Reserve Bank working papers (see Binder and Skinner 2021a).

What will come of this increasing central bank activism? It seems likely to exacerbate what Cochrane (2020) describes as "a crisis of trust in our institutions, a crisis fed by a not-inaccurate perception that the elites who run such institutions don't know what they are doing, are politicized, and are going beyond the authority granted by accountable representatives."

Some evidence comes from a recent online survey in which Christina Skinner and I asked respondents who they thought should be most responsible for various policy areas: elected officials, the Fed, other unelected officials, or others (Binder and Skinner 2021b). We found interesting divides: for instance, 17 percent of college-educated respondents but almost no respondents without a college degree want the Fed to be primarily responsible for climate change. More generally, people with a college degree and people who get their economic news on social media want a more activist role for the Fed and are more likely to want the Fed to be responsible for policies related to inequality, climate change, and even gender. When central banks communicate on Twitter, these college-educated, social media users are the primary audience and are more likely to support a larger role for technocrats in the most politically salient policy areas. But this misses a big share of people who are not comfortable handing these things over to unelected officials. This not only politicizes the Fed, it also exacerbates democratic discontent, and exacerbates the sense of failure of political representation.

Bickerton and Accetti (2021: 157) warn that a consequence of technopopulism is that "Increasingly atomized individuals are bound to get a sense that political representation is being hollowed out, even if—or indeed precisely because—political actors claim to represent the substantive interests of society as a whole in a 'direct' and 'unmediated way.'" This is exactly what central bankers are claiming to do.

A prime example came on August 27, 2020, when the Fed amended its Statement on Longer-Run Goals and Monetary Policy Strategy. With these amendments, the Fed adopted an average inflation targeting (AIT) strategy and began to refer to "shortfalls of employment from its maximum level" rather than "deviations from its maximum level." The AIT amendments are vague enough to leave monetary policymakers enormous flexibility. For example, the strategy does not specify a time horizon over which average inflation will be computed. Cleveland Fed President Loretta Mester said that AIT "isn't really tied to a formula," leading Marte and Schneider (2020) to report that Fed policymakers will "do their own math on 'average' inflation . . . a complication for investors or households setting expectations about the future."

The Fed's repeated claims to competence, claims to representing the interests of "the people," and efforts to build trust attempt to justify and legitimatize this additional discretion. The chairman's explanation for the amendments themselves includes both technocratic and populist elements. He provides technical motivations, like the decline in the equilibrium real interest rate, and cites dozens of academic papers and technical reports. But he also repeatedly cites how "the Fed Listens events helped us connect with our core constituency, the American people" (Powell 2020).

This claim to represent "the people" as a whole, in a direct and unmediated way, is the populist appeal to legitimacy. And the choice of the word "constituency" is especially interesting. This word has several different definitions, but the first in Merriam-Webster is "a body of citizens entitled to elect a representative." Federal Reserve officials are not our representatives; we do not elect them. Members of Congress represent their constituencies. There is something gone awry, some failure of representation, that is leading central banks to take on more discretion in exchange for greater responsiveness to the supposed popular will, and to let such responsiveness be conflated with or even replace accountability. This will only have a ratchet effect. Central banks will continue to be awarded greater discretion in exchange for greater responsiveness, and will double down in their appeals to the people and to their own expertise in hopes of preserving legitimacy.

Conclusion

The logic of technopopulism provides a useful lens for understanding the pressures on central banks and their responses. In particular, as populist movements have gained strength, they have not seized power from central bankers, as might be expected given the traditional equating of populism with "anti-expert and anti-technocratic sentiment" (Buiter 2016). Rather, the more technocratic discretion central banks have, the more populists will rely on them to translate their causes into policy (Guasti and Buštíková 2020; Krein 2020).

Where does this leave us? As Friedman asked, is this really tolerable in a democracy? It is certainly getting less tolerable. I think this trend points to a stronger case for a rule-based monetary policy, such as a nominal GDP level target. A well-defined, quantitative target clarifies the meaning of accountability and helps distinguish accountability from responsiveness. Reducing technocratic discretion in this way reduces the impetus to work through the central bank to achieve a variety of policy goals that are better left to the political process. This is our best hope of achieving Friedman's (1962) goal of "converting monetary policy into a pillar of a free society rather than a threat to its foundations."

References

Bennett, W. L., and Livingston, S. (2021) "A Brief History of the Disinformation Age: Information Wars and the Decline of Institutional Authority." In W. L. Bennett and S. Livingston (eds.), *The Disinformation Age*, 3–40. New York: Cambridge University Press.

Berger, E. (2020) "From Technocracy and Populism to Technopopulism." *American Affairs Journal* IV (2).

Bernanke, B. S. (2007) "Federal Reserve Communications." Speech at the Cato Institute's 25th Annual Monetary Conference, Washington, D.C. (November 14). Available at www.federal reserve.gov/newsevents/speech/bernanke20071114a.htm.

_____ (2010) "Central Bank Independence, Transparency, and Accountability." Speech at the Institute for Monetary and Economic Studies International Conference, Bank of Japan, Tokyo, Japan (May 25). Available at www.federalreserve.gov /newsevents/speech/bernanke20100525a.htm.

Bickerton, C. J. (2020) "The Rise of the Technopopulists: The Politics of the People and a New Age of Emptiness." *The New Statesman* (October 23–29).

Bickerton, C. J., and Accetti, C. I. (2017) "Populism and Technocracy: Opposites or Complements?" *Critical Review of International Social and Political Philosophy* 20 (2): 186–206.

_____ (2021) *Technopopulism: The New Logic of Democratic Politics*. New York: Oxford University Press.

Binder, C. (2017a) "Fed Speak on Main Street: Central Bank Communication and Household Expectations." *Journal of Macroeconomics* 52: 238–51.

_____ (2017b) "Federal Reserve Communication and the Media." *Journal of Media Economics* 30 (4): 191–214.

_____ (2020a) "NGDP Targeting and the Public." *Cato Journal* 40 (2): 321–42.

_____ (2020b) "De Facto and De Jure Central Bank Independence." In E. Gnan and D. Masciandaro (eds.), *Populism, Economic Policies, and Central Banking*. Vienna: SUERF, the European Money and Finance Forum.

_____ (2021a) "Political Pressure on Central Banks." *Journal of Money, Credit, and Banking* 53 (4): 715–44.

_____ (2021b) "Presidential Antagonism and Central Bank Credibility," *Economics and Politics* 33 (2): 244–63.

Binder, C., and Skinner, C. (2021a) "Laboratories of Central Banking." SSRN Working Paper. Available at https://papers.ssrn .com/sol3/papers.cfm?abstract_id=3956845.

_____ (2021b) "The Legitimacy of the Federal Reserve." SSRN Working Paper. Available at https://papers.ssrn.com/sol3 /papers.cfm?abstract_id=3956847.

Braun, B. (2016) "Speaking to the People? Money, Trust, and Central Bank Legitimacy in the Age of Quantitative Easing." *Review of International Political Economy* 23 (6): 1064–92.

Buiter W. H. (2014) "Central Banks: Powerful, Political and Unaccountable." CEPR Discussion Paper Series No. 10223.

Caramani, D. (2017) "Will vs. Reason: The Populist and Technocratic Forms of Political Representation and Their Critique to Party Government." *American Political Science Review* 111 (1): 54–67.

Cargill, T. F., and O'Driscoll, G. P. Jr. (2013) "Federal Reserve Independence: Reality or Myth?" *Cato Journal* 33 (3): 417–35.

Cochrane, J. (2020) "Central Banks and Climate: A Case of Mission Creep." *Defining Ideas* (November 13).

Daly, M. (2020) "Is the Federal Reserve Contributing to Economic Inequality?" Speech at the University of California, Irvine (October 13).

Dincer, N. N., and Eichengreen, B. (2010) "Central Bank Transparency: Causes, Consequences and Updates." *Theoretical Inquiries in Law* 11 (1): 75–123.

_____ (2014) "Central Bank Transparency and Independence: Updates and New Measures." *International Journal of Central Banking* (10) (1): 189–259.

Dorn, J. (2019) "Myopic Monetary Policy and Presidential Power: Why Rules Matter." *Cato Journal* 39 (3): 577–95.

Financial Times Editorial Board (2019) "How Central Bankers Can Survive Populist Attacks: Rate-Setters Should Remain Calm and Tell the Unvarnished Truth." *Financial Times* (August 30).

Fleming, S., and Donnan, S. (2016) "Fed Must Act on 'Economic Anger', Says Official." *Financial Times* (February 16).

Friedman, M. (1962) "Should There Be an Independent Monetary Authority?" In L. B. Yeager (ed.), *In Search of a Monetary Constitution*. Cambridge, Mass.: Harvard University Press.

Grundmann, R. (2017) "The Problem of Expertise in Knowledge Societies." *Minerva* 55: 25–48.

Guasti, P., and Buštíková, L. (2020) "A Marriage of Convenience: Responsive Populists and Responsible Experts." *Politics and Governance* 8 (4): 468–72.

Guida, V.; Thompson, A.; and Meyer, T. (2021) "#EconTwitter Makes It to the Oval." *Politico* (March 9).

James, H. (2019) "What's Behind the Crisis of Democracy?" *Project Syndicate* (December 4).

Krein, J. (2020) "Trump Needed the 'Boneheads' More Than He Knew." *New York Times* (December 7).

Lokdam, H. (2020) "'We Serve the People of Europe': Reimagining the ECB's Political Master in the Wake of Its Emergency Politics." *Journal of Common Market Studies* 58 (4): 978–98.

Marte, J., and Schneider, H. (2020) "Fed Policymakers Do Their Own Math on 'Average' Inflation." *Reuters* (August 28).

Powell, J. (2019) "Welcoming Remarks." Speech at the 2019 Federal Reserve System Community Development Research Conference on "Renewing the Promise of the Middle Class." Washington,

D.C. (May 9). Available at www.federalreserve.gov/newsevents /speech/powell20190509a.htm.

_____ (2020) "New Economic Challenges and the Fed's Monetary Policy Review." Speech at "Navigating the Decade Ahead: Implications for Monetary Policy," an Economic Policy Symposium sponsored by the Federal Reserve Bank of Kansas City, Jackson Hole, Wyoming (August 27). Available at www.federal reserve.gov/newsevents/speech/powell20200827a.htm.

_____ (2021) "Getting Back to a Strong Labor Market." Speech at the Economic Club of New York (February 10). Available at www.federalreserve.gov/newsevents/speech/powell 20210210a.htm.

Rajan, R. (2017) "Central Banks' Year of Reckoning." *Project Syndicate* (December 21).

Reichlin, L. (2017) "Populism and the Future of Central Banking." *Project Syndicate* (January 19).

Roth, F. (2009) "The Effect of the Financial Crisis on Systemic Trust." *Intereconomics* 44 (4): 203–08.

Skinner, C. (2021) "Central Bank Activism." *Duke Law Journal* 71 (2): 247–328.

Smialek, J. (2019) "Reggae. Puppies. Whatever It Takes, Central Banks Want Attention." Bloomberg Economics. Available at www.bloomberg.com/news/articles/2019-01-29/reggae-puppies-whatever-it-takes-central-banks-want-attention.

Tortola, P. D., and Pansardi, P. (2018) "The Charismatic Leadership of the ECB Presidency: A Language-Based Analysis." *European Journal of Political Research* 58 (1): 96–116.

Turner, S. (2001) "What Is the Problem with Experts?" *Social Studies of Science* 31 (1): 123–49.

Wälti, S. (2012) "Trust No More? The Impact of the Crisis on Citizens' Trust in Central Banks." *Journal of International Money and Finance* 31: 593–605.

5

CAPTURE THE FED

Christina Parajon Skinner

It is gradually dawning upon the average man that the most important public question is the control of money and credits.

—Senator Elmer Thomas (1933)

There is today a palpable struggle for control of the Fed's vast power. There are those in Congress, academia, and the executive branch that now seek to capture the Fed's balance sheet, or its regulatory and supervisory might, to accomplish various social and economic policy goals—concerning climate change, inequality in the labor market, financial inclusion, and U.S. competitiveness with China. As this chapter will argue, those who wish to push the Fed beyond its classic technocratic purview appear to perceive the Fed's power as a valuable commodity ripe for capture.

While I have elsewhere written about popular pressure on the Fed to engage in activism, and the risks such pressure presents to the Fed's independence (Skinner 2021a), I have yet to offer a theory of what precisely incentivizes or invites such pressure in the first place. Why does the Fed's power seem capable of capture? This chapter takes that step back and offers a theory of what makes the Fed susceptible to ongoing popular efforts at capture. Specifically, it argues that Congress has played a significant role in the way that it has delegated various responsibilities to the Fed.

Christina Parajon Skinner is an Assistant Professor at the Wharton School of the University of Pennsylvania.

To that end, I examine the Fed's mandates that have recently been the target of capture and offer a (partial) explanation by looking to the structure of the law. Within the employment arm of the Fed's mandate, Congress introduced an indefinite and not well-bounded fiscal policy goal. Where the financial stability goal is concerned, Congress left that key term undefined and not time-bounded, thereby leaving it to future policymakers to shoehorn any number of hypothetical risks into the definition. And by giving the Treasury secretary the power to add items to the bucket category of "financial stability risk," Congress provided a back-door way for the popular views of the president's party to influence that Fed mandate. The price stability mandate, meanwhile, had for quite some time seemed less vulnerable to popular conscription. Possibly, the price stability mandate has been more robust to capture because Congress always perceived that goal as the core of technocratic central banking. That status quo may, however, change in coming months or years. Accordingly, the balance of this chapter sketches the basic outline of a theory of mandate capture and will be a launchpad for future work.

Captured Mandates

As a starting point, legally (constitutionally) Congress may not delegate any manner of its legislative duties to other agencies. Indeed, as Congress itself has recognized in the context of delegating power to the Fed, the U.S. Constitution enables Congress only to delegate "definite power within a limitation" to the Federal Reserve—and, importantly, "limitations must be fixed definitely on the upper and lower side" (Hearings 1937: 219). At face value, this prohibition against overly broad or unlimited delegations should protect the Fed from popular (i.e., extra-legislative) pressure to expand its responsibilities and goals. Yet fidelity to principles of nondelegation—which eschews, as unconstitutional, overly broad delegations of power to administrative agencies—fell out of fashion after 1935. Consequently, many of the Fed's key mandates, which Congress added after that period, were significantly less airtight than the Congress of 1913 might have imagined possible. As this chapter suggests, because the Fed's current mandates do not clearly establish upper, lower, or time-delimited bounds, they can become political prizes to be captured.

This chapter examines the statutory reasons why several of the Fed's main mandates—in particular, its responsibility for full employment, financial stability, and bank safety and soundness—have been or are being sought for capture. The Fed's responsibility over payments systems is not yet captured, but this chapter indicates why it may yet be vulnerable. Further, this chapter suggests that price stability has remained surprisingly resistant to capture, likely because of the deep history and convention shrouding price stability as the essence of technocratic central banking. Still, like these others, price stability too may become vulnerable.

Employment

Section 2A of the Federal Reserve Act of 1977 instructs the Fed "to promote effectively the goals of maximum employment, stable prices, and moderate long-term interest rates."[1] The third goal here was effectively incorporated into the price stability side of the mandate (FOMC 2012), and the 2A language has come to be known as the Fed's "dual mandate." It establishes the Fed's monetary policy goals.

The employment arm of the dual mandate has, over the past several years, become a focus for Fed expansionists. In August 2020, as part of the Fed's monetary policy framework overhaul, the Federal Open Market Committee (FOMC) announced ever so slight a shift in the framing of its employment goal as one that would be "broad-based and inclusive" (Powell 2020). This interpretation has changed the Fed's policy conversation in two important ways.

First, this shift in interpretation of the employment mandate appears to justify consideration of certain segments of the economy and how different groups fare in the labor markets. Fed Governor Lael Brainard, for example, asserts that pursuant to a "broad-based and inclusive goal," the Fed must "assess the strength of the labor market" by "studying geographic areas and demographic groups that are not faring as well." Moreover, the Fed should lean into "insight" gained from "the disaggregation of unemployment by different racial and ethnic groups" (Brainard 2021a).

That the Fed should focus on employment and labor market conditions for certain groups now appears to be the dominant view of the

[1]See www.federalreserve.gov/aboutthefed/section2a.htm.

Fed's employment objective across Fed leadership (Hatzius et al. 2021; Powell 2020).[2] For some Fed leaders, this also means recasting the employment objective as one aimed at "reduc[ing] racial inequities and bring[ing] about a more inclusive economy" (Siegel 2020). Such power to identify economic policy winners and losers (and tailor policy in response) seems quite valuable to capture.

Arguably, this interpretive stretch did not happen in a vacuum. Rather, Congress created the incentives to capture the employment arm for such economic justice–oriented goals when it made the fiscal goal of maximum employment into a monetary policy mandate for the Fed. The notion that the federal government should be an "employer of first resort" arose among politicians and policymakers around the end of World War II. In his 1944 State of the Union Address, President Franklin Delano Roosevelt set out an Economic Bill of Rights, establishing as its first right, the right to full employment. His vision for a new America was centrally based on "economic security, social security, [and] moral security," which he saw as inseparable (Roosevelt 1944).

Together with the president, there were various special interests that supported full employment legislation. For one, there was the National Farmers Union, an organization "grounded in a neopopulist ideology that celebrated the small family farmer and found most of its membership in the Rocky Mountain and Plains states" (Wasem 2013: 80). This group bound together with urban advocates for full employment policy. The "merger of rural and urban working people under the banner of a full employment economy created potent imagery that was distinctively American. This basis of support for full employment was an effective shield against subsequent charges of socialism and communism" (Wasem 2013: 80).

Two years later after FDR's address, Congress passed the Employment Act of 1946. Although the legislation did not offer the guarantees its original sponsors had wished for, it did fundamentally cast employment as a fiscal-governmental promise (Harvey 2005;

---

[2]Chairman Powell (2020) does not appear to espouse this interpretation as clearly as others. However, in November 2021, he stated: "While monetary policy does not target any particular group of people, when we assess whether we are at maximum employment, we purposely look at a wide range of indicators, and we are attentive to disparities in the labor market, rather than just the headline numbers" (Powell 2021).

Wasem 2013). Two decades later, employment again became bound up in social justice issues during the Civil Rights Era (Ginsburg 2012).

The Keynesian ethos of the Employment Act of 1946 was again carried forward into the 1970s (Santoni 1986). By that time, by some accounts, the Employment Act had fallen short of its proponents' intended outcomes. A new bill, sponsored by Senator Hubert Humphrey and Representative Augustus Hawkins, was introduced in 1976—the Full Employment and Balanced Growth Bill of 1976. With little doubt, that bill was meant to amplify the ideas of the Employment Act (Steelman 2011).[3]

The bill gave the president responsibility for establishing numerical targets for employment, production, and purchasing power as set out in an annual Economic Report (Roth 1976: 5). It would have made the Federal Reserve Board an instrumentality of the president's fiscal economic goals, requiring the Board to:

> make an independent report in conjunction with the Economic Report setting forth its intended policies for the year and the extent to which those policies support the President's economic goals. Any substantial variations from the President's goals would have to be justified by the Board. If the President determines that the Board's policies are inconsistent with the achievement of his economic targets, he is to make recommendations to the Board and to the Congress to assure closer conformity with the purposes of the Act [Roth 1976: 6].

Although the legislation would not formally require the Fed to change its policies to align with presidential feedback, if unhappy with Fed policy, the president could use the process to propose new monetary legislation that would better promote his goals, "thus giving both the President and the Congress additional influence in the setting of monetary policy" (Roth 1976: 6).

---

[3]In March 1976, Senator Humphrey commented on the floor of Congress: "It is my judgment that [the Employment Act of 1946] has, from time to time, been conveniently ignored . . . [such that] Congress had to adopt new legislation to achieve 'full employment with reasonable price stability'" (Meltzer 2010: 986–87). With similar spirit, Representative Hawkins addressed the House of Representatives regarding the bill, stating that "assuring continuing full employment is the single most important step in the national interest at this time" (Congressional Record 1974: 21278–83).

Fed leaders at the time observed that the bill radically elevated the fiscal goal of employment over the monetary goal of stable prices. As one member of the Board, Charles Partee, remarked at the time:

> The prescribed procedures would alter the traditional relationship between Congress, the Federal Reserve, and the executive branch in a way that might be detrimental to the economic well-being of the Nation, and the procedures would "seriously impair" the operational flexibility which the Board currently has and needs in the formulation and conduct of monetary policy . . . . [For one] the Act would open up monetary policy to short-run political pressures leading to excessive Government spending which historically has led to serious inflation [Roth 1976: 23].

With similar reaction, Henry Wallich said on record, "If you contemplate what Humphrey-Hawkins implies, if anybody abroad thought this would be taken seriously, we would be disavowing all our anti-inflation effort" (Thornton 2012: 119).[4]

The bill was debated for two years, and the version that passed in 1978 was substantially watered down. While the act imposed various reporting requirements on the Fed and stipulated what the Fed should consider in formulating monetary policy ("employment, unemployment, production, investment, real income, productivity, international trade and payments, and prices"), it did not expressly give the president power to dispute the Fed's targets or Congress a means to overturn them.[5]

The timeline is important. In the intervening years while the Humphrey-Hawkins bill was being debated, Congress revised the Federal Reserve Act, adding section 2A. Again, with 2A, Congress gave the Fed two main jobs: to promote stable prices and maximum employment. But the design choice here was somewhat curious. Congress gave the Fed a two-legged mandate (that is, two goals) without any specification as to the priority among those goals.

---

[4]According to one former director of the Bureau of the Budget, "the issue among economists is not whether enactment of the act will lead to inflation, but whether 'the resultant inflation would be a high but steady rate or an ever-accelerating rate'" (Roth 1976: 19).

[5]See Full Employment and Balanced Growth Act of 1978, Pub. L. No. 95–523, 92 Stat. 1887 (1978).

And these were two very different goals—one fiscal and the other monetary; one political and value laded, the other largely technocratic. Clearly, conflicts would be inevitable at some point down the line (Brainard 2021a).

Notably, the Fed is the only leading central bank with an employment mandate. In the 1990s, when the U.K. Parliament was devising the Bank of England's mandate, the Labour Party's Gordon Brown would have liked such a mandate very much! In his words, "I wanted the Bank to have a dual mandate to keep inflation low and employment high—one that was similar to that of the American Federal Reserve. But the lawyers advised that it was too difficult legally to have two primary objectives" (Brown 2017: 121). Prescient words indeed.

Safety, Soundness, Financial Stability

Like monetary authority, supervision is an awesome power of the Fed (Tahyar 2019: 3). Yet the law of Fed supervision is gray, unspecific, and indeterminable.[6] General language surrounding a bank's "safety and soundness" provides the basis for most microprudential supervision of bank balance sheets, governance, and operations.[7] The Fed's mandate to supervise and regulate on financial stability grounds is also rather vague. Unlike other central banks, like the Bank of England, the Fed does not in fact have an explicit financial stability mandate.

In 2010, the Dodd-Frank Act solidified the financial stability mandate for the Fed a bit more, at least insofar as "systemically important" institutions and activities were concerned.[8] In particular, Title I of the Dodd-Frank Act required that the Board supervise and regulate with heightened standards any financial institution (bank or nonbank) that was determined to pose a financial stability risk in the United States. Title I also required the Fed to stress test the banking system, again cementing the Fed's responsibility to supervise the

---

[6]The "word supervision, although longstanding, appears nowhere in the legal framework governing the banking sector. The only public source is the explanations published in agency reports and on agency websites. These explanations are not helpful to understanding the theory of banking supervision beyond logical extensions of the traditional banking examination" (Tahyar 2019).
[7]See Bank Holding Company Act, *U.S. Code 12* (1965) §§ 1841 et seq.
[8]See www.congress.gov/111/plaws/publ203/PLAW-111publ203.pdf.

financial system's overall stability. And since the passage of Dodd-Frank, the Fed has leaned into its newly acquired financial stability role in developing its stress testing capability and, for the first time in its history, publishing annual assessments of financial stability risks in the U.S. financial system.[9]

But while the Dodd-Frank Act assigned the Fed to this manner of financial stability assessment and control, it left the definition of "financial stability risk" wide open. Further, Congress gave the Treasury secretary considerable latitude to shape that key definition though the newly created Financial Stability Oversight Council (FSOC).[10] The FSOC has the power to decide which nonbank financial institutions present bank-like financial stability risks (Skinner 2017: 1379, 1384). It also has the power to decide which financial "activities" are financial stability risks. In both cases, the Fed's mandate would be triggered. In the former case, it expands the Fed's perimeter—that is, when an institution receives a systemically important financial institution (SIFI) designation, it is ported into the Fed's jurisdiction. In the latter case, the FSOC can recommend the Fed to take action with regard to any activities it deems to be financial stability risks.

But what qualifies as a financial stability risk is a moving target. From 2010, the Fed more or less operated on one definition of financial stability risk—namely, credit-related risk that, if manifest, would threaten the solvency of the banking system (or one bank) and hence present a macroeconomic threat. Indeed this is precisely why the stress tests have focused on bank capital and the capital planning process (Board of Governors 2013: 1).

Now, however, these definitions—"safety and soundness" and "financial stability"—are at risk of capture. Climate change is the signature issue in this regard. Over the past few years, numerous academic voices have positioned climate change as a financial stability risk and therefore something for the Fed to act on (Steele 2020: 109). Treasury Secretary Janet Yellen has also used her position on FSOC to pressure the Fed to tackle climate change. In March 2021, she referred to climate change as "an existential threat to our environment," and warned that "it poses a tremendous risk to our country's

---

[9]See www.federalreserve.gov/publications/financial-stability-report.htm.
[10]Title I of Dodd-Frank created the FSOC.

financial stability" (Yellen 2021). Officially, as of October 2021, the FSOC's position is that "climate-related financial risks . . . [are] an emerging threat to the financial stability of the United States" (FSOC 2021: 1–2).

This pressure from academia and the executive branch appears to have had some bite. Recently, the Fed formed two committees to study the possibility of supervising climate risk from a microprudential ("safety and soundness") and macroprudential ("financial stability") stance, respectively (Brainard 2021b). But the claim that climate change is a financial stability risk depends on a very different (and much expanded) interpretation of that term, beyond what was understood under Dodd-Frank (Skinner 2021b).

Problematically, the text of the Dodd-Frank Act did not set out a definition of what constitutes a financial stability risk. Congress did not specify how hypothetical the risk could be or how far into the future the Fed could look for it. That manner of drafting imprecision is, arguably, what has rendered the Fed's financial stability mandate vulnerable to popular pressure. The same may be said of the Fed's microprudential "safety and soundness" supervisory mandate, given the longstanding ambiguity around what circumstances qualify under that descriptor (Tahyar 2019). It has long been a relatively open secret among Fed experts and lawyers that the Bank Holding Company Act gives the Fed considerable latitude to exercise its judgment as to whether any given bank activity or investment will implicate its "safety and soundness."

Price Stability

On its face, the goal of price stability is also a broad delegation of Congress's legislative power, namely, its constitutional authority to "regulate the value" of money (Article I). Again, as with Congress's other delegations to the Fed, Congress neither expressly defined the term "price stability" nor established a process by which the Fed should construct a definition. Interestingly, however, at least until quite recently, the price stability goal seemed relatively more robust to efforts at popular capture. One possible reason for this is that Congress had so clearly—and for such a long time—considered price stability as the core of the Fed's technocratic purpose.

Although the original Federal Reserve Act did not give the Fed a price stability mandate, it was certainly on the table at the time.

At least one of the Federal Reserve Act's framers, Senator Robert Owen, had favored language requiring the powers of the Reserve Banks be employed to "promote a stable price level" (Hearings 1937: 155). But the language was taken out by the House of Representatives and Owen found it too politically onerous to reinsert the drafting at the later stage of negotiation and compromise (Hearings 1937: 155). The intellectual environment in 1913 was also a key factor to consider. At the time, the so-called real-bills doctrine dominated the conceptual debate around the role of the Fed.[11] Given that the doctrine's core tenet assumed levels of money and credit would automatically adjust according to the needs of business and commerce (and alongside an international gold standard), instructing the Fed to actively steer price levels was probably seen as moot—at least for the influential real-bills adherents in Congress (Mehrling 2002: 207).

A paradigm shift in the 1920s inspired the Fed's early experimentation with price stability pursuits. At that time, the president of the New York Federal Reserve Bank, Benjamin Strong, challenged the real-bills viewpoint by actively using monetary policy tools (first, open market operations, and later, discount window policy) to steer price levels and manage inflows of gold to accomplish certain policy aims abroad (namely, helping Europe to return to the gold standard) (Skinner 2021a: 305).

Strong embraced a different intellectual framework. In his view, the Fed could effect changes in the price level by actively adjusting the money supply. Thus, he developed the Federal Reserve System's first foray into active price-level management, albeit without the congressional mandate to do so (Humphrey 1997; Mehrling 2002: 211).[12]

[11]One notable proponent of the real-bills doctrine was J. Lawrence Laughlin. Together with Parker Willis, their real-bills views became hard-wired into the Federal Reserve Act, which used language that would commit the Federal Reserve to the goal of "accommodating commerce and business," but only by passively providing reserve credit for "agricultural, industrial, or commercial purposes" (Mehrling 2002: 207; Selgin 1989: 489).

[12]Irving Fisher held influential views at the time and developed the so-called quantity theory of money and the accompanying $MV = PT$ equation. Fisher believed that M (money) could be adjusted to achieve any (P) price level. Strong, meanwhile, though a proponent of actively managing monetary policy, believed that there was much noise created by the velocity of money that the Fed could not control (Hetzel 1985: 3, 7–8).

On several occasions during the Strong era, Congress considered whether it should formalize the Fed's responsibility to target stable prices. The debate in Congress fell along the lines of whether, "in place of the existing discretionary power in a majority of the eight commissioners on the Federal Reserve Board to bring on falling prices, they should be obliged by law to hereafter operate the great Federal reserve system to maintain stability in the index number of general prices—the price level" (Congressional Record 1926: 4302). But Congress was not successful in passing any of the myriad price stability bills that were introduced and debated, and after Strong's death, the balance of power shifted from the New York Reserve Bank to the Board and back into the hands of real-bills proponents. This power shift led the Federal Reserve to adopt a passive posture during the Great Depression, an utterly suboptimal policy stance amid a disastrous macroeconomic event.

In light of the Fed's failure to act during the Great Depression, it was not surprising that the idea of a formal mandate for price stability came back on the congressional agenda in the mid-1930s. In 1937, Congress debated the Monetary Authority Act that would have made the Fed Board into a monetary authority proper "for the express purpose of regulating the value of money" (Hearings 1937: 5). The real-bills doctrine was recognized a failure: "Whatever its merits in theory, the old pattern of monetary system, with its presumed reliance on automatic operation, can hardly be said to have promoted the foregoing objectives" (Hearings 1937: 116).

Many thought that the responsibility to maintain stable prices, previously implicit, simply needed to be made explicit. In one exchange, Senator Frazier asked one of the testifying experts, George L. LeBlanc, "Wasn't . . . one of the intentions of the Federal Reserve law, that the Federal Reserve Board should have that authority[?]" Frazier added, "Perhaps not in the law in just so many words, but I think Senator Owen will agree that was the intention of the law when it was passed, that the Federal Reserve Board and their system should stabilize."

Even as early as 1937, most in Congress agreed that, regardless of whether a formal mandate should be added, the Fed's role in price stability should not be political. During the hearings on that act, the Senate heard from one expert that a monetary authority should in all cases be designed as an apolitical institution much like the Supreme Court, "because their power and responsibility to the people would be fully as great as the Supreme Court" (Hearings 1937: 114).

Senator Owen apparently believed a price stability mandate would in fact serve as an anti-populist check (at least if coupled with robust accountability):

> I am of the opinion that in order to prevent the Federal Reserve Board from being misled by people who are concerned in influencing our economic and financial life, and who would have every means of access to them to persuade, in order to prevent the Federal Reserve Board from being influenced by such forces, as they were on May 18, 1920, and as they were later on when the panic of 1921 and the panic of 1933 took place, I think there should be a positive mandate from Congress of the United States requiring them to use the powers of their system to promote the economic stability of this country, and that more than that, the House of Representatives and the Senate of the US should have independent power by a simple resolution to remove from power if they don't achieve that goal [Hearings 1937: 116].

Ironically, it was also fear of populist interventions that gave opponents reason to resist the bill. One such expert economist, Walter E. Sphar, stated:

> Section 2 converts the Board of Governors of the Federal Reserve System into the proposed monetary authority which would be a governmental agency with practically unlimited powers over our currency and banking. The lessons of good central banking will not support this type of proposal; instead, these are to the effect that the best central banking exists when the central banking authority is free from all pressure, both governmental and private, and is thus better able to operate the currency and banking structure in the interests of the general welfare [Hearings 1937: 235].

In any case, the question of a formal price stability mandate for the Fed lay dormant for several decades after that. It was not until a 1975 concurrent resolution that Congress would again consider such a mandate (U.S. Congress 1975).

This brief history suggests that since the Fed's founding in 1913, Congress assumed that the Fed's price stability goal—whether de facto or de jure—was necessarily premised on apolitical technocracy; this legislative understanding may have buffered the mandate against popular efforts at capture over the decades.

Still, the conclusion regarding price stability's vulnerability to populism is not yet written. When the Fed shifted to average inflation targeting in August 2020, it may have leaned too far into the open-ended nature of its mandate, thereby introducing opportunity for popular pressure going forward. By relinquishing its 2 percent inflation target in favor of an average of 2 percent, the Fed did not specify how far beyond 2 percent it would allow inflation to rise or for how long (Skinner 2021a: 282–83). By introducing ambiguity into the heretofore relatively apolitical goal, the Fed may have—whether purposefully or not—eroded some of the political and cultural norms against popular pressure to enlist the price stability mandate toward broader social or economic justice goals.

Conclusion

This chapter has, on the whole, suggested that imprecise and broad mandates invite popular attempts at capture. In particular, the chapter identified at least four features that make a Fed mandate most vulnerable to popular maneuvers: (1) the lack of a clear time frame for anchoring the goal; (2) the lack of parameters or definitions to give content to a goal; (3) the conflation of a fiscal for a monetary goal; and (4) the lack of clear instructions regarding how to prioritize or resolve conflicts among goals.

To be sure, debate over whether—and how broadly—Congress can delegate its legislative power has existed since the founding of America.[13] Madison and others were concerned that any legislative delegations would run afoul of the separation-of-powers that was the lodestar of the Constitution. Of this view, Supreme Court Justice Marshall would prohibit delegations in 1825. But over time, as the administrative state expanded and Congress depended more and more on technocratic expertise, the nondelegation doctrine became whittled down to mere formality. Even so, debate around the dangers and costs of overly broad delegations continue. In discussing the ways that certain kinds of broad or ambulatory delegations to the Fed create openings for popular pressure on the central bank, this chapter has also shed some further light on the larger debate on delegation.

[13]There is a rich legal literature on the so-called nondelegation doctrine, impossible to canvas here.

Finally, this chapter has offered a theory of what makes the Fed vulnerable to populism. It suggests that the answer lies largely in Federal Reserve law—namely, the way in which Congress has left particular mandates ill-defined, used mandates to import fiscal goals into the Fed, and introduced conflicts among a mandate's means and ends. There are lessons here for the present and the future.

As one closing example, let us consider briefly the Fed's payments authority. Currently underway are popular and academic efforts to press the Fed to adopt a central bank digital currency (CBDC). What will be the interpretive fate of Federal Reserve Act, Sections 16 and 11, which authorize the Fed to operate in the wholesale payments space? These provisions do not expressly obligate or authorize the Fed to engage in retail digital payments for the sake of customer convenience, financial sector competition, or economic inclusivity. But will the desire for expedience win out? Whether the Fed's legal authority in the payments space will be pressed to expand outside the legislative process, to address these extra-textual currency goals, will unfold in coming years.

References

Board of Governors (2013) "Capital Planning at Large Bank Holding Companies: Supervisory Expectations and Range of Current Practice" (August). Available at www.federalreserve.gov/bankinfo reg/bcreg20130819a1.pdf.

Brainard, L. (2021a) "How Should We Think about Full Employment in the Federal Reserve's Dual Mandate?" Speech at Principles of Economics Class, Harvard University (February 24). Available at https://www.federalreserve.gov/newsevents/speech /brainard20210224a.htm.

_____ (2021b) "Financial Stability Implications of Climate Change." Speech at Transform Tomorrow Today Conference, Ceres (March 23). Available at https://www.federalreserve.gov /newsevents/speech/brainard20210323a.htm.

Brown, G. (2017) *My Life, Our Times*. New York: Random House.

Congressional Record (1926) 69th Cong., 1st Sess., vol. 67, pt. 4, 4302.

_____ (1974) 93rd Cong., 2nd sess.,vol. 120: 21278–83.

Federal Open Market Committee [FOMC] (2012) "Statement on Longer-Run Goals and Monetary Policy Strategy." Available at

www.federalreserve.gov/monetarypolicy/files/fomc_longer
rungoals.pdf.

Financial Stability Oversight Council [FSOC] (2021) *FSOC Report on
Climate Related Financial Stability Risk*. Available at https://
home.treasury.gov/system/files/261/FSOC-Climate-Report.pdf.

Ginsburg, H. L. (2012) "Historical Amnesia: The Humphrey-
Hawkins Act, Full Employment and Employed as a Right."
Review of Black Political Economy 39 (1): 121–36.

Harvey, P. (2005) "The Right to Work and Basic Income Guarantees:
Competing or Complementary Goals?" *Rutgers Journal of Law
and Urban Policy* 2 (1): 8–59.

Hatzius, J. et al. (2021) "The Fed's Broad and Inclusive Maximum
Employment Goal." Goldman Sachs (March 22).

Hearings (1937) U.S. Congress, Senate Subcommittee on the
Committee on Agriculture and Forestry. "Hearings on the
Monetary Authority Act." 75th Cong., 1st Sess. (August).

Hetzel, R. L. (1985) "The Rules versus Discretion Debate over
Monetary Policy in the 1920s." *Federal Reserve Bank of Richmond
Economic Review* (November/December): 3, 7–8.

Humphrey, T. M. (1997) "Fisher and Wicksell on the Quantity
Theory." *Federal Reserve Bank of Richmond Economic
Quarterly* 83 (Fall).

Mehrling, P. (2002) "Economists and the Fed: Beginnings." *Journal
of Economic Perspectives* 16 (4): 207–18.

Meltzer, A. H. (2010) *A History of the Federal Reserve: Volume 2,
Book 2, 1970–1986*. Chicago: University of Chicago Press.

Powell, J. H. (2020) "New Economic Challenges and the Fed's
Monetary Policy Review." Speech at Navigating the Decade
Ahead: Implications for Monetary Policy Symposium, Federal
Reserve Bank of Kansas City (August 27).

_____ (2021) "Opening Remarks." Speech at the Conference
on Diversity and Inclusion in Economics, Finance, and Central
Banking, Bank of Canada et al. (November 9).

Roosevelt, F. D. (1944) "State of the Union Message to Congress."
Franklin D. Roosevelt Presidential Library and Museum
(January 11).

Roth, D. M. (1976) "The Humphrey-Hawkins Bill: Summary, Major
Issues, and Contending Arguments." Washington: Congressional
Research Service.

Santoni, G. J. (1986) "The Employment Act of 1946: Some History Notes." *Federal Reserve Bank of St. Louis Review* 68 (9): 5–16.

Selgin, G. A. (1989) "The Analytical Framework of the Real-Bills Doctrine." *Journal of Institutional and Theoretical Economics* 145 (3): 489–507.

Siegel, R. (2020) "To Narrow Racial and Economic Disparities, Atlanta Fed Chief Raphael Bostic Is Rethinking What the Fed's Mandate Means." *Washington Post* (August 21).

Skinner, C. P. (2017) "Regulating Nonbanks: A Plan for SIFI Lite." *Georgetown Law Journal* 105 (5): 1379–432.

_____ (2021a) "Central Bank Activism." *Duke Law Journal* 71 (2): 247–328.

_____ (2021b) "Central Banks and Climate Change." *Vanderbilt Law Review* 74 (5): 1301–64.

Steele, G. (2020) "Confronting the 'Climate Lehman Moment': The Case for Macroprudential Climate Regulation." *Cornell Journal of Law and Policy* 30 (1): 109–57.

Steelman, A. (2011) "The Federal Reserve's 'Dual Mandate': The Evolution of an Idea." Federal Reserve Bank of Richmond, Economic Brief No. 11–12 (December).

Tahyar, M. E. (2019) "Testimony of Margaret E. Tahyar before the U.S. Senate Committee on Banking, Housing and Urban Affairs" (April 30). Available at www.banking.senate.gov/imo/media/doc /Tahyar%20Testimony%204-30-19.pdf.

Thomas, E. (1933) "How Far Inflation? A Reply by Thomas." *New York Times* (July 16).

Thornton, D. L. (2012) "The Dual Mandate: Has the Fed Changed Its Objective?" *Federal Reserve Bank of St. Louis Review* 94 (2): 117–33.

U.S. Congress (1975) "Concurrent Resolution to Lower Interest Rates." H Res. 113, 94th Cong., 1st sess. Conference Report Filed in House (March 19). Available at www.congress.gov/bill/94th-congress/house-concurrent-resolution/133.

Wasem, R. E. (2013) *Tackling Unemployment: The Legislative Dynamics of the Employment Act of 1946.* Kalamazoo, Mich.: W. E. Upjohn Institute for Employment Research.

Yellen, J. (2021) "Remarks by Secretary Janet L. Yellen at the Open Session of the Meeting of the Financial Stability Oversight Council." Press Release (March 31). Available at https://home .treasury.gov/news/press-releases/jy0092.

6

CENTRAL BANK INDEPENDENCE WITH PRINCIPLED ALLOCATION

Robert C. Hockett

This chapter critiques contemporary understandings of the doctrine of central bank independence and their implicit correlate—the dogma that central banks can and must engage only in what I call "credit modulation" (i.e., adjusting monetary aggregates), without engaging in what I call "credit allocation" (i.e., guiding the direction of monetary flows). The latter belief is wrong-headed as to both the premise on which it appears to be based—that public allocation is infeasible—and the conclusion it seems to encourage—that public allocation should not be attempted. The premise is shaky in that macroallocation in favor of productive, as distinguished from merely speculative, credit flows is no more difficult to manage (technically and politically) than is credit modulation itself. The conclusion is shaky both for its grounding in a false premise and for its overlooking that sound credit modulation itself is impossible without sound allocation. This impossibility is in turn rooted in the nature of endogenous Wicksellian credit money, which, through the dynamics of what I call "recursive collective action problems," inevitably fuels

Robert C. Hockett is the Edward Cornell Professor of Law at Cornell University, an Adjunct Professor of Finance at Georgetown's McDonough School of Business, Senior Counsel for Westwood Capital, LLC, and a Fellow at the New Consensus. He thanks Blanca Braun, Jeff Madrick, Paul McCulley, Sarah Bloom Raskin, and colleagues at New Consensus for inspiration and helpful suggestions.

inescapable bubbles and busts.[1] Privately ordered production, I conclude, requires at least partly publicly ordered finance. That will of course ring surprising, but I'll make my case carefully, step by step.

Public Capital and the Twin Scissors of Public Finance

Let's begin with the institutional and implicit intellectual roots of the contemporary dogma that I wish to refute. Where public finance in a decentralized exchange economy with endogenous credit money is concerned, there appear to be two broad public functions that both have to be, and indeed tend to be, carefully discharged at least partly by public instrumentalities. This is so notwithstanding—indeed, even because of—market exchange's primarily decentralized, privately ordered character.

The first such function is the money modulatory task, while the second is the money allocative task. Central banks discharge the first task, while private sector business firms and public finance ministries jointly discharge the second task. These tasks are seldom specifically identified, let alone considered at length or in relation to one another, in popular discourse. Yet they seem to be at least tacitly recognized as necessary, for all modern states maintain both monetary and fiscal authorities.[2]

It is tempting to believe that the modulatory and allocative tasks go barely remarked in popular discourse precisely because, with fiscal and monetary authorities in place, the functions have now long been taken for granted. Perhaps for the same reason, what goes more perniciously unremarked is that these two functions are necessitated by credit money's endogeneity, and that this same endogenity renders the functions both theoretically and operationally inseparable.

---

[1]Endogenous credit money, which Wicksell dubbed "bank money," is credit extended in the form of spendable deposits, the monetary nature of which is rooted in bank transaction accounts' integration into national payments systems. A salient consequence of credit money's endogeneity is its susceptibility to over-issuance during booms. See Wicksell ([1898] 1936).

[2]Two exceptions are economist Charles Plosser and monetary historian George Selgin, who recognize the importance of both functions but, unlike myself, think them separable.

The modulatory and allocative functions accordingly constitute, we might say, two blades of one scissors of public finance. I'll elaborate these claims more fully and further explain them in due course. But first a bit more on money endogeneity and the blades individually, along with their links to central bank independence and what I call "recursive collective action predicaments" (Hockett 2015). For only when we are fully clear on the blades' purposes and full operational environments can we grasp their full structures and functional inseparability.

Endogenous Central Bank Credit Money: Publicly Generated, Privately Allocated Investment Capital

There has been much written on credit money's endogenous character, so there is no need to be tedious here. The essentials, however, must be grasped firmly to understand the inseparability of modulation and allocation.

Contemporary polities publicly license private-sector banks and other financial institutions to generate and allocate monetary aggregates without falling afoul of anti-counterfeiting laws. This they do by authorizing these institutions to extend spendable credit in fiduciary account form—the credit feature of credit money. They also publicly recognize payments made out of such accounts as discharging commercial obligations via legal tender laws and associated public administration of national payments systems—the monetary feature of credit money.[3] This amounts to public outsourcing of the public's own money issuance authority to private-sector lending institutions, presumably on the theory that they are in all cases better at productive allocation than is the public sector. Hence, Wicksell's dubbing this money form "bank money," which I generalize to issuance by

---

[3]A concrete example might aid intuition: If you seek a loan from your publicly licensed local bank and your loan application is approved, a typical form for your loan proceeds to take will be a simple crediting of your preexisting transaction account held at the bank. The bank doesn't "transfer" the money from a vault or some other account to your account, it simply credits your account with the lent amount, while booking your corresponding liability—your promissory note—as an asset on its own balance sheet. Because payment cards and paper checks associated with your newly credited account "count" as payment media in the national payments system, in turn, your newly credited account effectively adds newly issued endogenous money to "the money supply."

additional financial institutions through use of the broader term "credit money" (Hockett 2019–2020, 2021a).

There are three characteristics of endogenous Wicksellian credit money that bear noting for present purposes. First, as data like that compiled in the Federal Reserve's quarterly flow of funds reports regularly indicates, it represents by far the greater portion of contemporary economies' money supplies. Second, the only limitation on this form of money's generation by private-sector institutions, apart from public guidance, is the prospective profitability of lending—a prospective profitability that in stratified financial markets includes loans not just for productive purposes, but also for speculative purposes. Third, publicly licensed endogenous credit money is publicly issued, yet privately allocated investment capital. In this very hybridity of contemporary investment capital lies the (thus far unrecognized) inseparability of credit modulation and allocation as essential public functions.

First Blade of the Scissors: Modulation, Technocracy, and Independence

Public finance's modulatory task is necessitated by the endogeneity of credit money. The task is to retain variation in the quantity of money, rooted in the indefinite extensibility and contractibility of bank-issued credit money, within a tolerable band. In finance parlance, this is a "collaring" function. Variable credit money availability, made possible by money endogeneity, opens the door to aggregate over- or underextension of credit relative to goods, services, and financial assets purchasable with credit money. This, in turn, renders credit-fueled inflation, hyperinflation, deflation, and Fisherian debt deflation ever-present dangers.

Because credit money endogeneity also renders inflations and deflations potentially self-perpetuating—amplifying them into what I long ago christened "recursive collective action problems" (Hockett 2015), centralized management of endogenous credit money supplies is imperative if decentralized market finance, and with it decentralized market exchange (including markets for productive inputs) generally, is to be sustained over time. Money supply management is, accordingly, one minimal degree of centralized jurisdiction that must be retained if otherwise decentralized market exchange is to be possible over time.

That bears repeating in production-focused form: continued private ordering of production requires, at a minimum, a high degree of public ordering of finance (Hockett 2019–2020, 2021a). What is overlooked, however, is that this also means public *allocation*, not just public modulation.

Now the populations of many contemporary polities seem at least partly or semiconsciously aware of the public modulatory imperative. For they all exercise some degree of collective agency where endogenous credit money aggregates are concerned. They do so through public instrumentalities tellingly labeled *"central* banks" or *"monetary authorities,"* the italicized components of these phrases suggesting collective agency and corresponding centralizations of authority. Polities then task these instrumentalities with collaring price instability.

Now comes a crucial move in the way of thinking that I'm reconstructing. The modulatory task as I have characterized it is inherently counter-majoritarian, in what lawyers will recognize as the Bickelian sense, as a theoretical matter.[4] And it is inherently technical, in a straightforward sense, as a practical matter. And this is the justification—fully appreciated or not—of modern central banks' independent and technocratic characteristics alike, in the sense that celebrants and critics alike seem to have in mind.

The modulatory task is countermajoritarian because it has to be countercyclical within any environment of decentralized market exchange. It has to be countercyclical because it is rooted in an environment where inflation and deflation are endogenous and recursive collective-action problems.

Endogeneity's Achilles Heel: Recursive Collective Action Problems

A collective action problem is of course simply a choice situation in which multiple individually rational decisions aggregate into collectively irrational outcomes. It is accordingly tragic in the classical Greek ("damned if you do, damned if you don't") sense of the word. Commons tragedies, arms races, bubbles, and busts are all cases in point. A recursive collective action problem (ReCap) is just such a

---

[4]The reference is to Alexander Bickel (1986).

tragedy: it is an ongoing collective action predicament with feedback effects.

Markets in which endogenous publicly generated, privately allocated credit money figures as a medium of exchange are rife with predicaments of this sort—a fact that continues to go surprisingly unremarked. In an inflation or hyperinflation (a.k.a. "bubble"), for example, individuals rationally buy now in anticipation of prices rising later. In so doing they collectively drive prices higher, leading to more purchasing, more price rises, and so on. In a deflation or bank-run or "bust," the same happens in reverse once the upswing is exhausted in what is frequently labeled an "inflection point."

In all such cases, individual agents collectively and indeed tragically drive collectively irrational cycles simply by making individually rational decisions. Only a collective agent, acting in the name of all, can prevent such decisions aggregating into collectively irrational outcomes. The agent does so by short-circuiting the recursion cycle itself—crucially, by *countering the crowd*, by acting contrarian. More specifically, the agent does so by rendering participation in the relevant crowd no longer individually rational—for example, by raising borrowing costs (e.g., interest rates or margin requirements), taxing away asset price capital gains, taxing speculative short-swing or churning transactions, or the like. The aim is to close the spreads between low credit costs and rising goods, services, or asset prices.

It is easy to see why some degree of insulation from crowd preferences—some form and degree of independence—will be necessary if this contrarian task of countercyclical collective agency is to be discharged effectively. Countermajoritarian action is possible only when short-term majoritarian preferences can be temporarily disregarded; hence when democratic accountability is lagged (e.g., through staggered central bank appointment terms) rather than immediate.

Here, then, is the independence piece of the modulatory task. The technocratic bit enters through what is required to discharge the role not so much at all, as competently and effectively. Central banks have to modulate endogenous money supplies relative to anticipated resource, goods, services, and asset supplies that money purchases. This involves massive data collection, aggregation, estimation, and prediction. So does the task of deploying the tools used to vary money availability relative to those projections. These are technical tasks in which technical expertise, though not sufficient to discharge the task, is in any event necessary.

Second Blade of the Scissors: Allocation, Democracy, and Accountability

The allocative task is the second blade of the scissors. Here we speak less in quantitative than in qualitative terms where endogenous credit money is concerned. We are highlighting not how much or how fast money is flowing or changing hands so much as *where* it is flowing. The first question to ask about allocation is whether and why it is really an objective of public finance at all. Is collective agency as obviously necessary here as it is in the case of modulation?

It takes some, but not much, reflection to see that the answer has to be "yes." Polities do things and act on decisions about what collectively should be done. Indeed, that is all that collective agency and collective action are—decisions made and executed jointly by or on behalf of multiple deciders acting as one. What anyone does (public officers and other collective agents included) always involves some use of resources through money expenditures.

But this is just allocation. It is money allocation for purposes of resource use in pursuit of public objectives. Polities and other associations also typically take interest, for purposes of maintaining some degree of social or juridical cohesion if not actual justice, in distributions of advantage and disadvantage among their constituent members. This too is just an interest in resource allocation, with resources now understood broadly as materials used, not by publics in pursuit of public objectives, but by private citizens and subsovereign associations of citizens in pursuit of privately conceived plans and projects.

Because resource allocation (including money) produces comparative winners and losers in connection with literally every decision, polities actuated by democratic values will tend to view the allocative character of a collective decision as best subject to democratic accountability. The apocryphal war cry of the American Revolution, "no taxation without representation," is but one dramatic example of the idea at work here. We accordingly tend to vest the more overtly money allocative authority of our polity in institutions that we endeavor to keep less technocratic and insulated, more democratic and accountable.

We resort, in other words, to legislatures subject to regular elections, and to finance ministries subject in turn to continuous legislative oversight. Here, again with varying cognizance of the fact, is the basis for contemporary jurisdictions maintaining finance ministries or treasuries separate from their central banks and other monetary authorities. Here also, accordingly, is the basis for running aspirationally separate fiscal and monetary policies via these institutions, with each institution issuing its own monetary or quasi-monetary financial instruments in furtherance of its mission (e.g., in the United States, Federal Reserve notes or dollar bills in the one case, and Treasury notes, bills, or bonds in the other).

The idea, implicit or otherwise, is that the one institution will only neutrally *modulate* supplies of, and accordingly be authorized to issue, explicitly monetary instruments and their fiduciary (e.g., bank account) equivalent. The other institution will instead overtly *allocate* and accordingly be able to monetize only such of its own financial instruments as the legislature authorizes for particular purposes and the independent central bank or public will purchase to convert into spendable money. Hence, we have central bank independence and finance ministry accountability in modern public finance.

Scissors Need Two Blades: No Modulation without Allocation

Now, even granting the intuitive tractability and provisional usefulness for some purposes of (1) the modulation-allocation distinction as just elaborated, and (2) its modern institutional embodiment, recent events confront us with a set of questions that we can either duck, as we have done for five decades now, or instead finally address. The questions are:

- Is the modulation-allocation distinction as crisp as I have just made it sound?
- Has it always been strictly observed, tacitly or otherwise?
- And if it isn't or hasn't, is the way of thinking that latently and therefore uncritically relies upon the distinction, and that complex's current institutional embodiment, salvageable?

I think the answer to the first two queries is "no," while that to the third query is "yes," with revision. That is, the distinction partly dissolves under scrutiny and has often been at least tacitly rejected, at least in part and for brief periods, in consequence. But it is also partly salvageable if we attend carefully to its actual contours and respond institutionally by reconstructing our principal organs of public finance—that is, our central banks and finance ministries. And, crucially, this need not imply any objectionable form of nonneutrality or, therefore, independence. My reasons for saying these things are rooted in the very phenomenon that leads us to recognize the urgency of the modulatory task itself—credit money endogeneity.

Credit money's endogeneity, which necessitates modulation as a collective task in the first place, also renders effective modulation impossible absent a certain definable range of forthright collective allocation—a range I'll define momentarily in principled fashion. This means that more thoroughgoing fiscal and monetary coordination or consolidation, which always intensifies during crises but then recedes once the crises appear to be past, must become a "new normal." At least that is so if ever-deeper, more frequent, and more devastating crises are not themselves to remain a new normal.

Credit-fueled bubbles develop as overissuances of speculative credit money to traders who spot and then trade upon fads in the making. The objects of these fads can be virtually anything: junk bonds, subprime mortgages, cryptocurrencies, and so on.

Once a boom in the prices of such objects begins to attract momentum traders, a decentralized monetary exchange economy with endogenous credit money and deep secondary financial and tertiary derivatives markets—what I elsewhere dub "stratified" or "meta" markets—generates the most formidable of all known recursive collective action predicaments: the credit-fueled asset price bubble and subsequent bust (Hockett 2021a). For indefinitely extensible credit can be borrowed cheaply to purchase assets whose prices are rising at rates higher than borrowing rates—a transaction type that for a while will be profitable for lender and borrower alike.

Under boom conditions of this sort, it becomes individually rational for investors to borrow in order to buy in order either to sell on the secondary markets or to hedge on the tertiary markets. But everyone's acting thus rationally aggregates into irrational outcomes as prices are driven to points at which even the most profligate lenders at last balk. Ensuing reversals then culminate in busts as intemperate as their antecedent booms, leaving debt overhang and hence negative net worth in the wake since debt obligations are fixed while asset prices are variable.

These reactive debt deflations (i.e., "depressions"), which are themselves recursive collective action problems of the same sort, are of course the bane of macroeconomic stability; hence, of sustained productive activity and full employment. They must accordingly be defused collectively. But this is just the modulation challenge that I sketched above, begun in an allocation challenge as are all endogenity-rooted modulation challenges.

What, then, can we do? Must all endogenous credit money allocation be independently and technocratically managed just as must modulation? Must fiscal and monetary policy be collapsed into one another—fully consolidated? And what then of all of that picking of winners and losers, and of the intolerable democratic deficit that doing this technocratically and independently of politics would seem to entail?

Production and Speculation: More Distinguishable than Modulation and Allocation

The quandary is not as acute as it first looks. The key is to revive the distinction between *productive* investment and merely *speculative* betting, and then draw the implications for how we govern primary investment markets versus secondary and tertiary betting markets.

The United States mistakenly abandoned this distinction in 1935 owing to a false lesson drawn from the first years that followed the 1929 crash, but can retrieve it in new and improved form both theoretically and operationally—without even changing the law.

Start with the distinction itself. While investment and speculation overlap at the margin, paradigmatic cases of the former are readily identified cases in which producers and suppliers of material goods and services, or of material inputs to productive processes, are tapping the lending or capital markets. We can call the markets in which all of this happens the "primary markets."

Paradigmatic cases of merely speculative betting are cases in which the *claims* generated by primary market investment are themselves bought, sold, or bet upon or against, with the speculators borrowing in order to purchase those claims with a view either to selling them at higher prices in secondary markets or capitalizing on such secondary market price changes in other ways through tertiary market derivative instruments. The markets in which these purchases and sales occur are accordingly what I call the "secondary," "tertiary," and iteratively through time what I call "n-ary" or "meta-" markets (Hockett 2021a).

Primary markets in decentralized exchange economies with endogenous credit money do not typically generate serious recursive collective action predicaments of the kind that I highlighted above. For they are ultimately grounded in, anchored by, or tethered to, something that nature or physics themselves more or less exogenously modulate—namely, potentially profitable material production. But where credit money is endogenous and profitability is not immediately tethered to material production but can also include the winning of short-term bets, metamarkets have to be *artificially* modulated if there is to be any exogenous constraint upon endogenous credit dissemination. And this means that modulation will require at least a broad, macro form of allocation—steering money broadly from speculative metamarkets to productive primary markets.

Meanwhile, the exogenous modulation in question will still have to be done collectively—both in the manner, and for the reasons, elaborated earlier. But if the latter is partly allocative, at least as between productive primary markets on the one hand and speculative metamarkets on the other hand, is it politically viable to do that technocratically and independently? Are we faced with yet another tragedy that is the flip side of that tragedy that is the ReCap itself, in the sense that modulation requires independent collective agency while also requiring allocation, which then requires an accountable collective agency?

The answer is "no"! This needn't be tragic. For the production-speculation distinction is itself technically tractable and universally appreciable as critical to macroeconomic sustainability (i.e., to the avoidance of Marxian "contradiction" and terminal crisis), while at the same time there is sufficient variety under each heading to allow for a great deal of private ordering where allocation under them is concerned. Hence, we can afford a degree of independence to certain forms of central bank allocation and concomitant fiscal-cum-monetary consolidation without resorting to comprehensive state planning or objectionably insulating the pickers of winners and losers from desirable democratic accountability. All we need do is keep public capital—again, endogenous credit money—out of the metamarkets. Let public capital flow only to primary markets, while restricting secondary and tertiary markets solely to preaccumulated private capital.

We can see how to do this both in early Fed history, prior to the Banking Act of 1935, and in my proposal for an updated version of pre-1935, "Spread Fed" discounting alike (Hockett 2020).

The Scissors in Retrospect: The "Spread Fed" of 1913–1935

What I have just been saying used to be, perhaps surprisingly, unsurprising. As I have written extensively elsewhere (Hockett 2020, 2021a), the founders of the Federal Reserve System in 1913 designed a network of forthrightly allocative regional development finance institutions. The Fed was what I call "productively spread." This entailed unabashed cross-regional allocation, much as calls for the Fed to address wealth gaps and climate risk now would do. Each of the 12 regional Federal Reserve District Banks provided short-term funding directly or indirectly (through local banks) to developing businesses that needed it. This they did by discounting—in effect, directly or indirectly purchasing—commercial paper issued by those businesses.

The eligibility criteria that the Fed applied in determining what kinds of paper to discount rendered the regime yet more forthrightly allocative in character. The Federal Reserve Act was—and ironically remains—quite explicit about this: discount lending is solely for productive, not speculative purposes. The Fed even employed an index developed by the World War I–era War Industries Board (WIB) to assess the productivity of this statutorily mandated productive lending, and housed offices of the WIB's financing arm, the forthrightly allocative War Finance Corporation (WFC), in its regional District Banks to assist with productive development nationwide.

So what happened? Well, it all boils down to a tragic conflation of necessity with sufficiency—both before and then after the critical year 1935.

The allocative Fed as originally founded reflected the influence of a once popular, half-right idea known as the "Real Bills Doctrine" (RBD). Prominent among the Fed's founders were the RBD adherents Paul Warburg and Carter Glass (the latter of course better known now for the Glass-Steagall Act). The RBD in its crude form suggested that productively lent credit money could not fuel inflation or deflation. For the productivity requirement would ensure that lent funds stayed in primary market investment, not metamarket speculation.

But in fact there are other possible sources of monetary disturbance than mere fad investment and metamarket speculation, the effects of which demand-responsive endogenous lending can then procyclically amplify, pursuant to the recursive dynamic, as readily as if they were the latter. A sudden petroleum price hike by OPEC nations as in the 1970s, for example, or an influx of New World silver into Spain 400 years earlier, can quickly alter the money-goods balance, commencing a self-amplifying inflationary or deflationary episode. In effect, exogenous factors can spark endogenous self-amplification.

In effect, this is the "cumulative process" that Wicksell identified in the late 19th century, but of which Anglo-Americans, notwithstanding Adam Smith's having also spotted it, tragically didn't take systematic heed until decades later when Wicksell was translated into English. Something much like it happened in the early 1930s after the twinned real estate and stock market crashes of the late 1920s. Exogenous money supply changes were amplified by endogenous lending and contacting before and after 1929 (Hockett 2009).

A savvy Fed after 1929 would thus have supplied a countercyclical exogenous money infusion, a boost to the by-then only transaction-driven money supply, to counteract the contraction in the money supply wrought by the Crash and ensuing Fisher-style debt deflation. But the Fed of the time, mistaking productive lending's necessity to monetary stability for sufficiency to the same end, assumed that the money supply must by definition be right. It accordingly took no countercyclical corrective action. (The gold standard didn't help either.)

So how did this lead to our separating modulation and allocation, monetary and fiscal policy, Fed and Treasury? We overreacted. We effectively decided that, since productive allocation was not sufficient to afford optimal modulation, it was not necessary either. This was only half right, just as the crude form of the RBD had been half right. The upshot was the Banking Act of 1935.

Under the influence of Irving Fisher's rendition of the quantity theory of money, the Banking Act focused almost exclusively on monetary modulation, eschewing credit allocation. The act accordingly established an independent Federal Open Market Committee in Washington to formulate and execute monetary policy (good), while sidelining the Federal Reserve District Banks and their discounting role (bad). It switched out, in other words, one blade of the scissors for the other.

This change opened the door for the Fed to massively enter the credit markets and thus to misallocate endogenous credit money. Glass-Steagall prevented, for a time, this misallocation by restricting speculative bank lending, and other parts of USC Title 12 (the Banking Code) limited interstate banking and branching. Fed Chairs who understood their modulatory roles, and a very actively allocating fiscal state operating through many institutions, especially the Reconstruction Finance Corporation (RFC) and its progeny—the Federal Housing Authority, Fannie Mae, and the Small Business Administration prominent among them—up to the 1990s, kept markets relatively stable during the so-called Great Moderation. But when those fell away over the 1990s, we fell into continual private misallocation of endogenous public credit money. Multiple life-, wealth-, and polity-destructive crises have been the upshot.

Must we continue this way? Is it just crises henceforth, followed by temporary fiscal-monetary coordinations, followed by ever-worse crises? Not at all. The key is to recover what was right in the Real Bills Doctrine, while leaving what was wrong on the ash heap. The key is, in other words, to restore the pre-1935 blade of the scissors while keeping the post-1935 blade.

The Scissors in Prospect: The Post-Covid "Spread Fed"

We can still have the modulating with a once again allocating Fed—call it the "both scissors blades Fed." This will be what elsewhere I call a "Spread Fed" that modulates from Washington and New York against exogenous shocks, while allocating in endogenously productive, counterspeculative manners from each of its 12 district Reserve Banks (Hockett 2020). I'll limit myself here to a schematic description and accompanying links to my InvestAmerica Plan, which I've also put out as a draft bill—the "National Reconstruction and Continuous Development Act of 2021" (Hockett 2021b). The plan features four planks.

First, create within the White House cabinet a National Reconstruction and Development Council (NRDC), analogous to the WIB (and later WPB), to formulate and regularly update a National Development Strategy (NDS) analogous to the National Security Council's regularly updated National Security Strategy. The NDS identifies ongoing national development imperatives and accordingly determines what counts as *productive investment* in a democratically accountable manner. It is a counterpart to the WIB's old Production Index.

Second, upgrade Treasury's existing Federal Financing Bank into a full financing arm of the NRDC analogous to the WFC (and later RFC). It would be tweaked to draw and disburse funds in multiple ways, including through sales of hybrid financial instruments and the taking of debt and equity stakes, to jumpstart infrastructures and heavy industries.

Third, once again "spread" the Fed over its regional district Reserve Banks to resume lending to local and startup businesses, but only for projects that count as productive by the NRDC. This will effectively replicate the use to which the Fed used to put the old WIB production index used to determine discounting before 1917.

Fourth, enable the Fed and Treasury to disburse funds through a new universal digital savings and payments platform on which all citizens, legal residents, and businesses have peer-to-peer digital wallets— my "Digital Greenbacks plan." (Hockett 2021c) This liability-side counterpart to the asset-side upgrades that are planks one through three will streamline and universalize fund flows nationwide, thereby optimizing not only public finance as just prescribed, but also private finance and commerce.

I have designed all four planks of the plan to be implementable even without House or Senate majorities—that is, pursuant to law already on the books. The Biden administration (or any later administration) could, in other words, do all of these things under existing authority. But since we have those majorities, why not mandate what would otherwise be discretionary and go big? It's the easiest way to get Fed and Treasury collaboration, and hence central bank independence and finance ministry accountability, permanently right. It is the way, that is, to restore the scissors of public finance in the manner our forebears came close to doing but didn't complete.

Allocating, Hence Modulating, Independently by Allocating Productively

We can anticipate the usual skepticism about the production-speculation distinction on which my arguments and proposals rest. Some will ask, how do you tell these apart? Others will go helpfully further by noting that many investments bear both productive and speculative elements—precisely because risk attends all investment—and that multiple motives can be at work in any decision.

These arguments at best will be unwarranted counsels of despair, and at worst will be bad faith rhetorical clichés. First, categories that overlap are nonetheless tractable as distinct categories. Some people are manifestly bald, while others are manifestly not, even while others are not clearly yet one or the other. To think that the latter deprive the word "bald" of meaning or use is no more than a crude Sorites error.

Second, what renders an investment productive or speculative for policy purposes is not motive, but likely effect. Projects more likely than not to produce profitably saleable primary goods and services, or to improve the productivity of such, are actuarially identifiable without any regard to motive. Motive at most is a clue that itself is derived from more objectively observable clues such as churn in the secondary and tertiary markets. So mixed-motive investing is irrelevant to what I am advocating.

Finally, even assuming that there are hard cases, in respect of which it isn't immediately clear whether a prospective investment would be more productive than speculative or vice versa, it is easy enough simply to resolve doubt in favor of the former when monetary expansion seems called for as a modulatory matter, and of the latter when contraction is more prudent. The distinction is policy driven in the first place, so of course it will be policy driven in application.

Conclusion: Privately Ordered Production Requires Publicly Ordered Finance

John Maynard Keynes ended his epoch-making *General Theory* of 1936 with the unelaborated observation that a "socialization of investment" might be requisite to modern capitalism's long-term survival. People have puzzled over what he might have meant ever since. But the answer is found in works written nearly a decade earlier by Keynes himself (Liberal Party 1928), but also 30 or more years earlier by acute observers who should have made the epochs that Keynes is now credited with. I refer to Rosa Luxemburg (1913), Rudolf Hilferding (1910), and to a lesser extent Keynes's more forthright successor Joan Robinson (1956).

What these observers all seem to have recognized, with varying degrees of clarity, is that privately ordered production is not compatible with altogether privately ordered finance (Hockett 2019–2020, 2021a). This recognition has awaited detailed explication ever since. That is tragic, because clear exposition and explication show how logically inexorable the point is. It also shows that a publicly ordered institutional response need not entail public micromanagement of all productive activity; it only requires a pre-1935 Federal Reserve. Finally, it shows how to use existing law to commence that response.

It is entirely feasible broadly to allocate, via regionally sensitive Federal Reserve Banks, in favor of production over speculation, even while leaving as many investment decisions as we wish under the broad heading of production to be taken privately by firms and (bona fide) entrepreneurs alike. This is what I mean by "principled allocation."

All we need do now is recognize at long last that much high finance ceased to be truly entrepreneurial (i.e., more productive than speculative) a century ago, and retake control of our own public investment capital—our endogenously issued central bank credit money—for public purposes. Modulate and allocate that productively, and you'll have the only form of capitalism that is both sustainable and worthy of sustaining.

References

Bickel, A. M. (1986) *The Least Dangerous Branch: The Supreme Court at the Bar of Politics.* 2nd ed. New Haven, Conn.: Yale University Press.

Hilferding, R. ([1910] 1981) *Finance Capital: A Study of the Latest Phase of Capitalist Development.* Edited by T. Bottomore from translations made by M. Watnick and S. Gordon. London: Routledge & Kegan Paul.

Hockett, R. (2009) "A Fixer-Upper for Finance." *Washington University Law Review* 87 (6): 1213–91.

_____ (2015) "Recursive Collective Action Problems: The Structure of Procyclicality in Money Markets, Macroeconomies, and Formally Similar Contexts." *Journal of Financial Perspectives* 3 (2): 113–28.

_____ (2019–2020) "The Capital Commons: Digital Money and Citizens' Finance in a Productive Commercial Republic." *Review of Banking and Financial Law* 39: 345–498.

_____ (2020) "Spread the Fed: Distributed Central Banking in Pandemic and Beyond." *Virginia Law & Business Review* 15 (1): 89–122.

_____ (2021a) "The Wealth of Our Commonwealth: Money and Capital in the Productive Republic." Cornell Legal Studies Research Paper No. 21-48. Available at https://papers.ssrn.com/sol3/papers.cfm?abstract_id=3808790.

_____ (2021b) "The National Reconstruction and Continuous Development Act of 2021." Draft bill. Available at https://papers.ssrn.com/sol3/papers.cfm?abstract_id=3775616.

_____ (2021c) "Digital Greenbacks." *Journal of Technology Law & Policy* 25 (1): 1–39.

Keynes, J. M. (1936) *The General Theory of Employment, Interest, and Money.* London: Palgrave Macmillan.

Liberal Party of Great Britain (1928) *Britain's Industrial Future: Report of the Liberal Industrial Inquiry of 1928.* London: Ernest Benn.

Luxemburg, R. (1913) *The Accumulation of Capital.* Available at www.marxists.org/archive/luxemburg/1913/accumulation-capital.

Robinson, J. (1956) *The Accumulation of Capital.* London: Macmillan.

Wicksell, K. ([1898] 1936) *Interest and Prices: A Study of the Causes Regulating the Value of Money.* Available at https://mises-media.s3.amazonaws.com/Interest%20and%20Prices_2.pdf.

7

MYOPIC MONETARY POLICY AND PRESIDENTIAL POWER: WHY RULES MATTER

James A. Dorn

Independence is central to the Federal Reserve's ability to choose policy actions that achieve price stability. Sacrificing much of its independence, as the Fed often has, permits others to pressure the Fed to achieve other objectives, usually short-term objectives. That is one reason that the Fed responds to short-term events often at the cost of failing to achieve longer-term objectives.

—Allan H. Meltzer (2013: 405)

The Fed's Vulnerability to Political Pressure

In the absence of a monetary rule, a central bank is vulnerable to politicization. In the case of the United States, Congress delegated monetary authority to the Federal Reserve in 1913 and has increased the scope of that authority over time, especially following crises. However, Congress has never enacted an explicit rule to guide Fed policy, and it has used the Fed as a scapegoat when things go awry.

James A. Dorn is Vice President for Monetary Studies and a Senior Fellow at the Cato Institute. This chapter is an updated version of his article in the *Cato Journal*, Vol. 39, No. 3 (Fall 2019). He thanks Kevin Dowd, Thomas M. Humphrey, and George Selgin for helpful comments.

By law, the Federal Reserve has a triple mandate to "promote effectively the goals of maximum employment, stable prices, and moderate long-term interest rates." In doing so, the Federal Open Market Committee (FOMC) is instructed to "maintain long-run growth of the monetary and credit aggregates commensurate with the economy's long-run potential to increase production" (Section 2A, Federal Reserve Act).[1] That congressional mandate, however, is a weak reed upon which to rest sound monetary policy in a world of government fiat money not subject to any enforceable monetary rule.

In 1978, the Humphrey-Hawkins Act required the Fed to set targets for monetary aggregates and report those benchmarks to Congress twice a year. There was no penalty if the FOMC failed to hit its targets, but the Fed would have to explain why (P.L. 95–523, Sec. 108 (a)). The reporting requirements expired in May 2000 and the Fed no longer pays much attention to the money supply. Instead, the Fed's main policy instrument since the mid-1980s has been the fed funds rate (i.e., the overnight rate at which member banks lend to each other).[2]

This chapter examines the relationship between Fed policy and presidential power in a fiat money regime in which Congress has delegated significant power and discretion to the Fed. By making the Fed responsible, but not accountable, for achieving full employment and price stability, Congress can shift blame to the Fed when it fails to meet those objectives. In their study of the political history of the relationship between the Fed and Congress, Binder and Spindel (2017) argue that the relationship is one of "interdependence" and that Fed independence is a "myth."

The fact that Congress has given the Fed increased power and discretion means that Congress is evading its constitutional duty to safeguard the value of money and, at the same time, opening the door for presidential jawboning. As Robert Weintraub, staff director for the House Subcommittee on Domestic Monetary Policy from 1976 to 1980, argued: By sanctioning "short-run money market myopia"—that is, lowering the short-run policy rate by expanding the

---

[1] See www.federalreserve.gov/aboutthefed/section2a.htm.
[2] The Fed now sets a target range for the fed funds rate, using interest on excess reserves as the upper limit and the Fed's overnight reverse repo rate as the lower limit. For a discussion of the Fed's new operating system, see Federal Reserve Bank of New York (2008) and Selgin (2018).

money supply—"Congress weakened its own hand in supervising monetary policy and strengthened the hand of the Executive." Moreover, "money market myopia fitted harmoniously with administration concerns about financing the government's deficits" (Weintraub 1978: 359). He concluded that, without a credible monetary rule, "the President's objectives and plans will continue to be the dominant input in the conduct of monetary policy" (p. 360).

Consequently, in the absence of a credible/enforceable rule, money supply targets are insufficient to overcome presidential ambitions to push for accommodative monetary policy, keeping rates low to finance deficits and stimulate production, at least in the short run. Of course, a strong leader in the White House could push for sound money, as did President Eisenhower; and a strong leader at the Fed, such as Paul Volcker, could do likewise.

From President Clinton through President Obama, criticism of Fed policy was usually in private. But there was a sea change with President Trump, who was highly critical of Fed Chairman Jerome Powell for raising rates in December 2018 (see Smialek 2019). With rising inflation and deficits, tension between the White House and the Fed may increase as rates move up and the Fed trims its bloated balance sheet, which now stands at nearly $9 trillion. As such, it is an appropriate time to revisit the case for Fed independence, the relationship between the Fed and the president, and the case for a monetary rule to guide Fed policy and reduce the uncertainty inherent in a discretionary government fiat money regime.

Legally, the Fed is independent, but in practice, that independence is continuously tested by political pressures for using accommodative monetary policy and credit allocation to win votes. An examination of the evidence reveals that presidents tend to get the monetary policy they desire. The adoption of a rules-based monetary regime could help limit interference in the conduct of monetary policy and improve economic performance.

Fed Policy and Presidential Power: An Uneasy Relationship

In considering the relationship between the government and the Fed, Allan Sproul (1948), then president of the New York Federal Reserve Bank, distinguished between "independence from government and independence from political influence." Most people, he said, accept the idea that the Fed should be held accountable by the government/Congress. However, from a narrow political viewpoint, "The powers of the central banking system should not be a pawn of any group or faction or party, or even any particular administration" (quoted in Meltzer 2003: 738).

That sentiment was recently endorsed by Fed Chairman Jerome Powell when he stated:

> The Fed is insulated from short-term political pressures—what is often referred to as our "independence." Congress chose to insulate the Fed this way because it had seen the damage that often arises when policy bends to short-term political interests. Central banks in major democracies around the world have similar independence [Powell 2019: 1].

History, however, does not bear out this view of Fed "independence." The fact is that, in a purely discretionary fiat money regime, with little congressional guidance, the door is open for presidential power/jawboning to influence Fed policy. We have seen that in the past and see it now.

In his monumental *History of the Federal Reserve*, Meltzer (2003, 2010a, 2010b) provides ample evidence that monetary policy is not free from political influence. Likewise, Cargill and O'Driscoll, in their review of that history, and based on Ferrell's (2010) diary of Arthur F. Burns, conclude:

> The Fed was appropriately constrained by fiscal dominance in both great wars. It was independent under the modified gold standard in the 1920s because of a rule. It gained operational independence after the 1951 Accord, but lost that independence starting with William McChesney Martin in the early 1960s and especially Burns in the 1970s. Paul Volcker and Alan Greenspan reestablished de facto independence in terms of focusing on price stability with an implicit adoption of the Taylor Rule. It has surely lost any meaningful independence under Ben Bernanke [Cargill and O'Driscoll 2013: 431].

It is well known that President Truman continued to pressure the Fed for low interest rates after the 1951 Accord. He disliked Fed Chairman Thomas B. McCabe, who was adamant about ending the pegging of U.S. bond rates and was pressured to step down shortly after the Accord was signed (Meltzer 2003: 712). His replacement, William McChesney Martin, became the longest serving Fed chairman (1951–1970). He believed in Fed independence and survived in office under five presidents by largely following their preferences. For example, under President Dwight D. Eisenhower, the Fed pursued a stable money policy with low inflation and moderate long-term interest rates. But under President Lyndon B. Johnson, the Fed was pressured to pump up money growth and achieve lower short-run interest rates.

In October 1955, Martin gave his famous "punch bowl speech," in which he argued that the job of the Fed was to take away the punch bowl (i.e., slow money growth and raise interest rates) when the economy was at peak performance.[3] In that speech, he emphasized the importance of an independent central bank and the limits of monetary policy.

> In framing the Federal Reserve Act great care was taken to safeguard this money management from improper interference by either private or political interests. That is why we talk about the over-riding importance of maintaining our independence. . . . While money policy can do a great deal, it is by no means all powerful. . . . If we ask too much of monetary policy we will not only fail but we will also discredit this useful, and indeed indispensable, tool for shaping our economic development [Martin 1955: 3–4].

As Fed chairman under Eisenhower, Martin spoke out against central planning and price controls. He supported free enterprise and monetary stability:

> The answers we sought to the massive problems of the 1930s increasingly emphasized an enlarging role for Government in our economic life. That role was greatly extended again in the

---

[3]The "punch bowl" line was really taken from another writer whom Martin doesn't identify. The exact quote is: "The Federal Reserve, as one writer put it, after the recent increase in the discount rate, is in the position of the chaperone who has ordered the punch bowl removed just when the party was really warming up" (Martin 1955: 12).

1940s when the emergency of World War II led to direct controls over wages, prices, and the distribution of goods ranging from sugar to steel. That experience led to growing concern over the effect of a straitjacket of controls on the economy's productive capacity, and the price that would be exacted in terms of individual liberty if the harness of wartime economic controls were carried over into the postwar years. Such a strait jacketing of the economy is wholly inconsistent with our political institutions and our private enterprise system. The history of despotic rule, of authoritarian rule, not merely in this century but throughout the ages is acutely repugnant to us. It has taken a frightful toll in human misery and degradation.

. . . The advantages of a system where supply capacities and demand wants and needs are matched in open markets cannot be measured in economic terms alone. In addition to the advantages of efficiency in the use of economic resources, there are vast gains in terms of personal liberty. Powers of decision are dispersed among the millions affected instead of being centralized in a few persons in authority [Martin 1955: 4–5].

On the idea that a little inflation is the path to lower unemployment, Martin was clear:

Allan Sproul, president of the Federal Reserve Bank of New York, put his finger on the fallacy in this contention in testifying before a congressional committee earlier this year when he said: "Those who would seek to promote 'full employment' by creeping inflation, induced by credit policy, are trying to correct structural maladjustments, which are inevitable in a highly dynamic economy, by debasing the savings of the people" [Martin 1955: 8].

While monetary policy during the Eisenhower administration (1953–1961) was characterized by low inflation, the Johnson administration (1963–1969) leaned heavily on Martin to keep rates low and maintain the economic expansion via adequate money growth. President Johnson warned that "it would be self-defeating to cancel the stimulus of tax reduction by tightening money" (*Economic Report* 1964: 11).

However, Martin increased the discount rate in December 1965 against the president's wishes and Johnson lashed out at him when they met at LBJ's ranch, even pushing Martin around (Granville 2017). With continued growth in the money supply relative to real output, the Martin Fed helped usher in the Great Inflation (1965–1984).[4] As Meltzer (2005: 168) points out, "Martin's acceptance of policy coordination with the [Johnson] administration prevented the Federal Reserve from taking timely actions and contributed to more expansive policies than were consistent with price stability."[5]

When Martin's term ended on January 31, 1970, President Nixon nominated Arthur Burns who served as Fed chairman until 1978. From 1971 to 1973, inflationary pressures grew as Burns accommodated Nixon's demands for lower interest rates and expansionary money growth. In August 1971, President Nixon instituted wage and price controls by executive order in an attempt to contain rising inflation, and he put Burns in charge of the Committee on Interest and Dividends (CID). The primary purpose of CID was to maintain low interest rates. With the cap on wages and prices, Burns could use the Fed's power to create base money to pump up the money supply while not worrying about inflation and give Nixon the low interest rates he wanted to help him win the election in 1972. Weintraub (1978: 356) correctly calls the combination of wage-price controls and CID "an invitation to disaster."

The gears shifted in 1974 when President Gerald Ford called for tighter monetary policy. But in 1977, President Carter thought inflation was much less an issue than unemployment and called for Burns to shift to easy money once more. It was not Congress that

---

[4]It should be noted that, in January 1965, Johnson urged Congress "to eliminate the arbitrary requirement that the Federal Reserve Banks maintain a gold certificate reserve against their deposit liabilities" (*Economic Report* 1965: 12). As Robert Weintraub (1978: 355) notes, removing that constraint would allow domestic monetary policy to be more accommodative, providing cover for Johnson's Great Society programs and the Vietnam War. Congress obliged by passing a bill in March 1965 eliminating the gold requirement for deposits/reserves held at the Federal Reserve Banks, and in March 1968 removed the gold requirement for Federal Reserve notes (Ramage 1968: 8). When President Nixon closed the gold window in August 1971, the last vestige of the gold standard was gone.

[5]Meltzer (2005: 145) blames the persistence of inflation on "political choices, analytic errors, and the entrenched belief that inflation would continue." He notes that, under the sway of simple Keynesian models, those calling for policy coordination accepted the practice of monetizing the debt—that is, having the Fed help finance fiscal deficits.

pressured the Fed to accelerate M1 growth in 1977; it was the administration. As Weintraub (1978: 358) argues, "It is not unfair to conclude that the Federal Reserve accelerated M1 growth in 1977 above its own target range because it perceived its 'assignment' in the new administration's economic game plan to be to resist upward pressures on short-term rates."

It was left to Paul Volcker, whom Carter nominated in 1979 and who remained as Fed chairman until 1987, to restore Fed independence and crack down hard on inflation by raising rates and slowing money growth. In October 1979, Volcker met with the FOMC and changed the Fed's operating system. Instead of managing the day-to-day fed funds rate, Volcker decided to focus on controlling the volume of bank reserves directly, which meant that there would be more variability in the funds rate but better control of the money supply. He stood his ground and pushed the Fed funds rate to a peak of 20 percent in late 1980. Money growth slowed and by 1983, inflation came down from double digits to less than 4 percent (Medley 2013).

Alan Greenspan became Fed chairman in 1987 and followed in Volcker's footsteps, adding credibility to the Fed. When President George H. W. Bush failed to get the Fed to accommodate his wishes for an expansionary monetary policy, he blamed Greenspan for his defeat in the 1992 election, saying: "I think that if the interest rates had been lowered more dramatically that I would have been re-elected president because the [economic] recovery that we were in would have been more visible. . . . I reappointed him, and he disappointed me" (Wall Street Journal 1998).

Greenspan prolonged the "Great Moderation," which began under Volcker in 1983 and lasted until 2003. It was a period of relative macroeconomic stability in which the variability of both inflation and output decreased. John B. Taylor (2009) attributed that stability to Fed policy that approximated the Taylor rule.[6] When the Greenspan Fed departed from that rule in mid-2003, the fed funds rate fell to 1 percent and remained at that level until mid-2004, far below the rate prescribed by the Taylor rule (see Taylor

[6]William Niskanen (2001) found that the Greenspan Fed adhered to a de facto demand rule from early 1992 to early 1998 by keeping total spending on a steady growth path of about 5.5 percent per year.

2009: 3, Fig. 1). Although the Greenspan Fed increased the fed funds rate, it continued to be below the Taylor-rule rate until 2006. Consequently, Taylor (2009) argued that, by holding rates too low for too long, the Greenspan Fed encouraged risk taking and helped fuel the housing bubble.

Likewise, Anna Schwartz (2009: 19–20) has argued:

> The Fed was accommodative too long from 2001 on and was slow to tighten monetary policy, delaying tightening until June 2004 and then ending the monthly 25 basis point increase in August 2006. . . . The rate increases in 2004 were too little and ended too soon. This was the monetary policy setting for the housing price boom.

She concludes that, "if monetary policy had been more restrictive, the asset price boom in housing could have been avoided" (p. 23).

Greenspan's policy reversal could have been influenced by the need to accommodate President George W. Bush's 2001 tax cut and the deficit that followed. Identifying whether he did it for political reasons under pressure from the administration, however, is difficult.

The global financial crisis greatly increased the power and discretion of the Fed and other central banks. Ben Bernanke, who took over as Fed chairman in 2006, worked closely with the G. W. Bush administration, especially Treasury Secretary Hank Paulson, to restore financial stability and stimulate the economy by unconventional monetary policy—including lowering the fed funds rate to near zero, engaging in large-scale asset purchases (credit allocation), and using forward guidance to encourage risk taking and prop up asset prices. Monetary policy drifted into fiscal policy as the Fed bought trillions of dollars of U.S. debt and mortgage-backed securities. The policy coordination that was evident under Arthur Burns was super-charged under Bernanke.[7] The Fed, of course, had an obligation to provide liquidity to the banking/financial system, but its emergency lending programs and bailouts stretched its powers considerably. The rule of law gave way to the rule of central bankers (White 2010; see also Humphrey 2010).

---

[7]The president and CEO of the Federal Reserve Bank of New York, Timothy Geithner, was also a key player in the policy coordination process.

In light of the available evidence, it is fair to say that without a credible rule, monetary policy is likely to be more myopic and open to politicization than would be the case with either an implicit or explicit rule. As Cargill and O'Driscoll (2013: 429) observe:

> Central bank independence is intimately tied to rules that constrain the central bank to focus on price stability, preferably a legislated rule. Focus on the short term inevitably leads the central bank into the political thicket and the loss of de facto independence. Central bank independence is more easily lost than restored.

President Trump wanted an accommodative monetary policy from the Fed to keep the expansion going and asset prices rising. He called Fed policy "very destructive" and demanded a cut in the fed funds rate (Salama 2019). The Trump administration's tax cuts and regulatory reforms had positive effects on private investment and real economic growth. However, with large increases in spending and no long-run solution to slow entitlement spending, fiscal deficits deepened. Financing those deficits at higher interest rates would be very costly. Thus, the White House tried to pressure Fed Chairman Jerome Powell to keep rates lower for longer and not engage in quantitative tightening. Nevertheless, Powell maintained his distance from President Trump.

However, in July 2019, Powell pivoted when the Fed lowered its policy rate (for the first time since December 2008) in response to a sluggish economy, trade conflicts, and below-target inflation (Cox 2019; Domm 2019). The lesson here is that, even if the Fed acts in the direction wanted by the president, that decision doesn't necessarily mean a loss of independence, if the policy move is correct—that is, consistent with the Fed's independent pursuit of its mandate.

From our brief review of the politics of Fed behavior, it seems safe to say that the Fed is neither independent within government nor outside the fray of day-to-day politics. It is also questionable whether, as Weintraub (1978: 349) contends, "the dominant guiding force behind monetary policy is the President." Congress may only play a "watchdog role," but presidents don't always get the monetary policies they want. More important, without a guiding monetary rule, and with multiple mandates, both the White House and the Fed will be more focused on the short run than the long run, and politics will play an oversized role.

Reducing Monetary Uncertainty: Toward a Rule-Guided Regime

Monetary rules matter because they help focus monetary authorities on what they can do—influence nominal spending and the price level in the long run—not on what they can't do—permanently raise the level of real income. Without the guidance of a credible rule, monetary authorities face two major problems, as pointed out by Meltzer (2013: 406, 411–12): (1) "Excessive concern for short-term changes causes the Fed to respond to events over which it has little control and largely ignore longer-term changes that it can influence"; and (2) "Excessive attention to short-term changes neglects the distinction between permanent and temporary changes that is central to standard economic analysis."

The introduction of money-growth targets for a brief period in the late 1970s and early 1980s set some limits on the Fed, but they were not sufficiently implemented as a long-term constraint to depoliticize the Fed. Although the Federal Reserve Reform Act of 1977 required the Fed to set targets for "the ranges of growth or diminution of monetary and credit aggregates" and report those ranges to Congress, the legislation lacked real teeth to enforce a monetary growth rule:

> Nothing in this Act shall be interpreted to require that such ranges of growth or diminution be achieved if the Board of Governors and the Federal Open Market Committee determine that they cannot or should not be achieved because of changing conditions [P.L. 95–188, Sec. 2A].

Nonetheless, setting a framework for the conduct of monetary policy (e.g., by requiring the Fed to report money supply targets) helped provide information that allowed fiscal policymakers to better plan their budgets. For example, in July 1977, pursuant to House Concurrent Resolution 133, which was adopted in March 1975 to require the Fed to report money growth targets, Rep. Parren J.

Mitchell (D-MD), chairman of the House Subcommittee on Domestic Monetary Policy, held hearings to inquire why the Fed had let money growth exceed the announced target ranges. In questioning Fed Governor J. Charles Partee, Mitchell stated:

> What we have done in this Congress in an effort to get a handle on Government spending is to establish a Committee on the Budget which works in concert with Ways and Means, Appropriations, and all the other major committees. Key to that working relationship is the understanding of monetary policy established early in the year.
>
> . . . If there is a commonly agreed on monetary growth policy at the beginning of the year, then all of us—banking, budget, all of Congress—operate roughly within those guidelines established by you and accepted by the Congress. To the extent and degree that you move away from those guidelines, you throw this whole delicate balance out of whack.
>
> . . . This is, indeed, in my opinion, disruptive to the fiscal policy planning process and to business and consumer planning as well [U.S. Congress 1977: 50–51; quoted in Weintraub 1978: 357–58].

The 1983–2003 experiment with a Taylor rule helped guide Fed policy under Volcker and Greenspan and gave the Fed more space from the White House and more confidence in its independence. But we can do better. Formal adoption of a legislated rule and effective implementation of a rule would further separate day-to-day politics from monetary policy. The failure of Congress to legislate a rule-based monetary regime, or for Congress or the president to establish a commission to examine Fed performance and alternative monetary rules, is disappointing but not surprising.

The Fed has little incentive to bind itself to a rule and lose discretionary power. Congress and the executive branch, meanwhile, have little incentive to put the Fed on auto pilot and deprive themselves of influencing monetary policy or placing blame for economic instability on the Fed. An example suffices to illustrate the difficulty of reforming the monetary regime or even taking the first step by establishing a presidential commission to consider alternatives to the present discretionary government fiat money regime.

After Ronald Reagan was elected president in 1980, Martin Anderson, a key member of Reagan's campaign staff and later appointed as chief domestic policy adviser, reached out to several influential economists for ideas on what policy actions President Reagan should take during his first 100 days in office. One of those contacted was James M. Buchanan, a pioneer in public choice and constitutional economics, who recommended that Reagan "appoint a presidential commission that would look into the whole structure of our monetary authority" (Buchanan 1988: 32–33).

As Buchanan observed:

> What we have now is a monetary authority that essentially has a monopoly on the issue of fiat money, with no guidelines to amount to anything; an authority that never would have been legislatively approved, that never would have been constitutionally approved, on any kind of rational calculus, no matter what political system. We have an authority that just happened to get there and happened to be in place when we demonetized gold totally and completely over this half century. So I thought it was a good idea to use that presidential commission-type device to get a little publicity, to get a discussion going about the legitimacy of this authority [Buchanan 1988: 33].

After sending Anderson a letter in early December, Buchanan heard back from Reagan's "Kitchen Cabinet" expressing interest in the idea for a presidential commission and asking Buchanan to consider chairing it. He then wrote a "position paper" that he sent to the Western White House, but he never heard anything back (ibid.: 33–34). Here's the way Buchanan described it:

> Nothing happened. Absolutely nothing happened. I never heard a word, not one word, from them. I found out months later, that they did seriously consider the idea, but Arthur Burns shot it down. Arthur Burns totally and completely rejected it, and would not have anything to do with any proposal that would challenge the authority of the central banking structure—you don't even question, you don't even raise it as an issue to be discussed [Buchanan 1988: 34].

In other words, Burns, a former chairman of the Fed, "had taken it as his mission to defend the institution as it is, independently of any question. It became a sacrosanct institution to Arthur Burns, and he prevailed in the Reagan councils" (Buchanan 1988: 34).

Official resistance to establishing a commission to explore alternative monetary regimes persists to this day, as attested by the fact that Congress failed to enact the Centennial Monetary Commission Act of 2015 (H.R. 2912), introduced by Rep. Kevin Brady (R-TX).[8]

Without a transparent and credible rule to guide monetary policy, there is much uncertainty. As Karl Brunner (1980: 61) noted:

> The products emerging from our professional work reveal a wide range of diffuse uncertainty about the detailed response structure of the economy. . . . A nonactivist [rules-based] regime emerges under the circumstances . . . as the safest strategy. It does not assure us that economic fluctuations will be avoided. But it will assure us that monetary policymaking does not impose additional uncertainties . . . on the market place.

A rule-guided monetary policy would help depoliticize the Fed, shift resources to more productive uses than "Fed watching," and reduce regime uncertainty by concentrating on long-run stability of nominal income and the price level rather than trying to fine-tune the economy or cater to Wall Street. Moreover, a "hard" rather than "soft" rule (i.e., one fudgeable by the Fed) would end the "ambiguous and chaotic" state of monetary law that Clark Warburton referred to when noting that "Monetary law in the United States . . . does not contain a suitable principle for the exercise of the monetary power held by the Federal Reserve System, and has caused confusion in the development of Federal Reserve policy" (Warburton 1966: 316).

The Federal Reserve Act of 1913 sought to provide "an elastic currency" and to have reserve banks set discount rates "with a view of accommodating commerce and business." Those were vague guidelines, however. The Fed failed to provide a quantity of money sufficient to maintain monetary equilibrium in the early 1930s, as Friedman and Schwartz (1963) and Warburton (1966) have shown. Weintraub (1978: 341–42) sums up the situation nicely:

> In the crucible of reality, the [1913] Act was found wanting. It contained no meaningful operational standard for the conduct of monetary policy. Aside from the constraints imposed

---

[8]See www.congress/gov/bill/114th-congress/house-bill/2912/text.

by the gold standard and the gold backing requirement on Federal Reserve notes and deposits, the Federal Reserve was free to do as it wanted, when it wanted, for whatever reasons it might have.[9]

The myopic nature of monetary policy stems from the lack of a rules-based monetary regime that would give credence to Section 2A of the Federal Reserve Act. As we have seen, the Fed never really adhered to a money supply target regime, and the link between money, income, and prices was severed by financial innovation beginning in the 1990s (see Labonte and Makinen 2008).[10] Thus, in July 1991, at a congressional hearing, Fed Chairman Alan Greenspan noted:

> The historical relationships between money and income, and between money and the price level, have largely broken down, depriving the aggregates of much of their usefulness as guides to policy. At least for the time being, M2 has been downgraded as a reliable indicator of financial conditions in the economy, and no single variable has yet been identified to take its place [Federal Reserve Bank of New York 2008: 2].

Since the 2008 financial crisis, the Fed's balance sheet has exploded, and, with the payment of interest on excess reserves (IOER) since October 2008, the increased demand for reserves has mitigated the monetary transmission mechanism whereby an increase in base money leads to a multiple increase in money and credit, and boosts nominal income (see Selgin 2018).

By separating its balance sheet from administering interest rates under the so-called floor system, the Fed has been able to avoid run-

---

[9]Humphrey and Timberlake (2019) argue that the Fed's adherence to the Real Bills Doctrine led it to misdiagnose the causes of the Great Contraction. The idea that limiting the discount window to commercial paper would bring about an optimal quantity of money was proven to be a poor guide to stable money and prices.

[10]Meltzer (2013: 410) has questioned the breakdown in the money-nominal income linkage: "The Federal Reserve rejects use of any monetary aggregate by claiming that monetary velocity is unstable. This conclusion comes from tests based on quarterly data. This is another example of the dominant role of myopia. . . . For the United States, annual data on monetary base velocity and a bond rate for nearly 80 years show reasonable stability." Using a Divisia (weighted) measure of the broad money supply (M4) also shows that money matters in shaping the path of income and prices (see Hanke 2018).

away inflation even as it suppresses interest rates—and it is more open to political manipulation. Indeed, the floor system allows for more administrative and congressional abuse of the Fed's balance sheet (Selgin 2017). As former Philadelphia Fed President Charles Plosser (2018: 15) argues, "A large balance sheet untethered to the conduct of monetary policy creates the opportunity and incentive for political actors to exploit the Fed's balance sheet to conduct off budget fiscal policy and credit allocation." Nevertheless, the Fed's new operating system need not expose the Fed to any greater tendency to set its rate targets according to presidential whims.

The Fed has sought to use "forward guidance" to steer monetary policy, but there is little certainty about the future course of monetary policy. Forecasting the macroeconomy and interest rates is notoriously difficult. Demands on forecasts could be significantly reduced by moving to a rule-based monetary regime. There are many rules to choose from, including ones based on convertibility of the dollar into some commodity or basket of commodities, a constant money growth rule, an inflation or price level rule, a nominal GDP rule designed to keep total spending on a steady path, a Taylor rule, and so on.[11]

Conclusion

In thinking about the Fed's strategy and communications, we should not forget two important points: (1) independence is necessary for the Fed to do its stabilization job well, free of presidential meddling; and (2) adopting a monetary rule can help achieve independence. Moreover, the Fed needs to be open to a rational discussion of alternative monetary rules in attempting to improve the monetary regime. The problem is not too little inflation but too much discretion.

There needs to be a better understanding of why rules matter in reducing myopic monetary policy and in insulating the Fed from presidential power and day-to-day politics. Ultimately, the Fed must be bound by a constitution that protects the value of money and safeguards individual freedom under a rule of law. The current monetary regime is far from that ideal.

---

[11]On alternative monetary rules, see Dorn (2017) and Salter (2017). For a summary of the literature on the case for rules versus discretion, see Dorn (2018).

Creating a monetary commission to evaluate the Fed's performance and consider alternatives to the current discretionary fiat
money regime would be a step in the direction of securing sound
money.

References

Binder, S., and Spindel, M. (2017) *The Myth of Independence: How
Congress Governs the Federal Reserve.* Princeton, N.J.: Princeton
University Press.
Brunner, K. (1980) "The Control of Monetary Aggregates." In
Controlling Monetary Aggregates III, 1–65. Boston: Federal
Reserve Bank of Boston.
Buchanan, J. M. (1988) "Comment by Dr. Buchanan." *Economic
Education Bulletin* 28 (6): 32–35. Special issue on "Prospects for a
Monetary Constitution," Proceedings of the Progress
Foundation's International Monetary Conference, Lugano,
Switzerland, May 27, 1988.
Cargill, T. F., and O'Driscoll, G. P. Jr. (2013) "Federal Reserve
Independence: Reality or Myth?" *Cato Journal* 33 (3): 417–35.
Cox, J. 2019) "Fed Cuts Rate by a Quarter Point, Cites 'Global
Developments,' 'Muted Inflation.'" *CNBC.com* (July 31).
Domm, P. (2019) "Federal Reserve's Quick Pivot to Easier Policy
Started with a Trump Tweet on Trade." *CNBC.com* (June 20).
Dorn, J. A. (2017) *Monetary Alternatives: Rethinking Government
Fiat Money.* Washington: Cato Institute.
_____ (2018) "Monetary Policy in an Uncertain World: The Case
for Rules." In J. A. Dorn (ed.), *Monetary Policy in an Uncertain World:
Ten Years after the Crisis*, 179–206. Washington: Cato Institute.
Economic Report of the President (1964) Available at https://
fraser.stlouisfed.org/title/45/item/8135.
_____ (1965) Available at https://fraser.stlouisfed.org/files
/docs/publications/ERP/1965/ERP_1965.pdf.
Federal Reserve Bank of New York (2008) "The Money Supply."
Available at www.newyorkfed.org/aboutthefed/fedpoint/fed49.html
(July 2008).
Ferrell, R. H., ed. (2010) *Inside the Nixon Administration: The Secret
Diary of Arthur Burns, 1969–1974.* St. Lawrence, Kans.:
University Press of Kansas.

Friedman, M. and Schwartz, A. J. (1963) *A Monetary History of the United States, 1867–1960*. Princeton, N.J.: Princeton University Press for the National Bureau of Economic Research.

Granville, K. (2017) "A President at War with His Fed Chief, 5 Decades before Trump." *New York Times* (June 13).

Hanke, S. (2018) "The Fed's Misleading Money Supply Measure." *Forbes.com* (October 21).

Humphrey, T. M. (2010) "Lender of Last Resort: What It Is, Whence It Came, and Why the Fed Isn't It." *Cato Journal* 30 (2): 333–64.

Humphrey, T. M., and Timberlake, R. H. (2019) *Gold, The Real Bills Doctrine, and the Fed: Sources of Monetary Disorder, 1922–1938*. Washington: Cato Institute.

Labonte, M., and Makinen, G. E. (2008) "Monetary Policy and the Federal Reserve: Current Policy and Conditions." *CRS Report for Congress*. Washington: Congressional Research Service (April 30).

Martin, W. M. (1955) "Address before the New York Group of the Investment Bankers Association of America" (October 19). Available at https://fraser.stlouisfed.org/title/448/item/7800.

Medley, B. (2013) "Volcker's Announcement of Anti-Inflation Measures." *Federal Reserve History* (October). Available at www.federalreservehistory.org/essays/anti_inflation_measures.

Meltzer, A. H. (2003) *A History of the Federal Reserve: Vol. 1: 1913–1951*. Chicago: University of Chicago Press.

_____ (2005) "Origins of the Great Inflation." Federal Reserve Bank of St. Louis *Review* 87 (2, Part 2): 145–75.

_____ (2010a) *A History of the Federal Reserve: Vol. 2, Book 1: 1951–1969*. Chicago: University of Chicago Press.

_____ (2010b) *A History of the Federal Reserve: Vol. 2, Book 2: 1970–1986*. Chicago: University of Chicago Press.

_____ (2013) "What's Wrong with the Fed? What Would Restore Independence?" *Cato Journal* 33 (3): 401–16.

Niskanen, W. N. (2001) "A Test of the Demand Rule." *Cato Journal* 21 (2): 205–09.

Plosser, C. (2018) "The Risks of a Fed Balance Sheet Unconstrained by Monetary Policy." In M. D. Bordo, J. H. Cochrane, and A. Seru (eds.), *The Structural Foundations of Monetary Policy*, 1–16. Stanford, Calif.: Hoover Institution Press.

Powell, J. H. (2019) "Economic Outlook and Monetary Policy Review." Speech at the Council on Foreign Relations, New York (June 25).

Ramage, J. C. (1968) "The Gold Cover." *Federal Reserve Bank of Richmond Monthly Review* (July): 8–10.

Salama, V. (2019) "Trump Says Fed Policy Makers Have Become 'Very Disruptive.'" *Wall Street Journal* (June 10).

Salter, A. W. (2017) "Some Political Economy of Monetary Rules." *The Independent Review* 21 (3): 443–64.

Schwartz, A. J. (2009) "Origins of the Financial Market Crisis of 2008." *Cato Journal* 29 (1): 19–23.

Selgin, G. (2017) "Interest on Reserves: A Secret Fiscal Weapon We're Better Off Without." *Alt-M* (January 25).

_____ (2018) *Floored! How a Misguided Fed Experiment Deepened and Prolonged the Great Recession*. Washington: Cato Institute.

Smialek, J. (2019) "Trump's Feud with the Fed Is Rooted in Presidential History." *New York Times* (June 25).

Sproul, A. (1948) "Letter to Robert R. Bowie" (September 1). Files of Allan Sproul, Box 2, "Memorandums and Drafts." Federal Reserve Bank of New York.

Taylor, J. B. (2009) *Getting Off Track: How Government Actions and Interventions Caused, Prolonged, and Worsened the Financial Crisis*. Stanford, Calif.: Hoover Institution Press.

U.S. Congress, Subcommittee on Domestic Monetary Policy (1977) "Recent Monetary Developments and Future Economic Performance." Hearings, 95th Cong., 1st sess. (July).

Wall Street Journal (1998) "Bush Pins 1992 Election Loss on Fed Chair Alan Greenspan." *Wall Street Journal* (August 25).

Warburton, C. (1966) *Depression, Inflation, and Monetary Policy: Selected Papers, 1945–1953*. Baltimore: The Johns Hopkins University Press.

Weintraub, R. E. (1978) "Congressional Supervision of Monetary Policy." *Journal of Monetary Economics* 4: 341–62.

White, L. H. (2010) "The Rule of Law or the Rule of Central Bankers?" *Cato Journal* 30 (3): 451–63.

PART 2

FISCAL DOMINANCE AND THE RETURN OF INFLATION

8

FISCAL INFLATION

John H. Cochrane

From its inflection point in February 2021 to November 2021, the CPI rose 6 percent (278.88/263.161), an 8 percent annualized rate. Why?

Starting in March 2020, in response to the disruptions of Covid-19, the U.S. government created about $3 trillion of new bank reserves, equivalent to cash, and sent checks to people and businesses. (Mechanically, the Treasury issued $3 trillion of new debt, which the Fed quickly bought in return for $3 trillion of new reserves. The Treasury sent out checks, transferring the reserves to people's banks. See Table 1.) The Treasury then borrowed another $2 trillion or so and sent more checks. Overall federal debt rose nearly 30 percent. Is it at all a surprise that a year later inflation breaks out? It is hard to ask for a clearer demonstration of fiscal inflation, an immense fiscal helicopter drop, exhibit A for the fiscal theory of the price level (Cochrane 2022a, 2022b).

What Dropped from the Helicopter?

From December 2019 to September 2021, the M2 money stock also increased by $5.6 trillion. This looks like a monetary, not a fiscal intervention, Milton Friedman's (1969) classic tale that if you want inflation, drop money from helicopters. But is it monetary or fiscal policy? Ask yourself: Suppose the expansion of M2 had been entirely

John H. Cochrane is the Rose-Marie and Jack Anderson Senior Fellow at the Hoover Institution. He is also a Research Associate of the National Bureau of Economic Research and an Adjunct Scholar of the Cato Institute.

TABLE 1
FEDERAL DEBT, RESERVES, AND M2, 2019–2021
(BILLIONS OF DOLLARS)

	Q4 /Dec 2019	Q3 /Sep 2021	Difference
Federal debt held by Federal Reserve Banks	$2,637	$5,644	$3,007
Federal debt held by public	$17,187	$22,353	$5,166
Reserves of depository institutions	$1,698	$4,193	$2,495
M2	$15,460	$21,209	$5,749
CPI	258.6	274.1	6.0%

SOURCES: Federal Reserve Bank of St. Louis, FRED.

financed by purchasing Treasury securities. Imagine Treasury debt had declined $5 trillion while M2 and reserves rose $5 trillion. Imagine that there had been no deficit at all, or even a surplus during this period. The monetary theory of inflation, MV=PY, states that we would see the same inflation. Really? Similarly, ask yourself: Suppose that the Federal Reserve had refused to go along. Suppose that the Treasury had sent people Treasury bills directly, accounts at Treasury.gov, along with directions how to sell them if people wished to do so. Better, suppose that the Treasury had created new mutual funds that hold Treasury securities and sent people mutual fund shares. (I write mutual fund as money market funds are counted in M2.) The monetary theory of inflation says again that this would have had no effect. These would be a debt issue, causing no inflation, not a monetary expansion. Really?

Clearly, overall debt matters, not the split of government debt between interest-paying reserves or monetary base and Treasury securities. The Federal Reserve itself is nothing more than an immense money market fund, offering shares that are pegged at $1 each, pay interest, and are backed by a portfolio of Treasury and mortgage-backed securities. (Plus, an army of regulators and a huge staff of economists who are supposed to help forecast inflation.)

Milton Friedman's (1969) helicopter drop is a powerful parable. But a helicopter drop is a *fiscal* policy, not a monetary policy.

The U.S. Federal Reserve may not legally drop money from helicopters; it may not write checks to voters. The Fed may even less vacuum up money; it may not tax people. Helicopter drops and money vacuums are fiscal operations. The Fed may only lend money, or buy and sell assets. To accomplish a helicopter drop in the United States, the Treasury must issue debt, the Fed must buy it with newly printed money, and then the Treasury must drop that money from helicopters, writing it down as a transfer payment. And that is pretty much exactly what happened.

Ask yourself: If, as Friedman's helicopter is dropping $1,000 on each household, the Fed sends burglars who remove $1,000 of Treasury securities from the same households, would we still see inflation? That's monetary policy. If Friedman's helicopter were followed by the Treasury secretary with a bullhorn, shouting "Enjoy your $1,000 in helicopter money. Taxes are going up $1,000 tomorrow," would we still see inflation?

Friedman's helicopters are not a monetary change, a substitution of money for debt, an increase in the liquidity of a given set of household assets. They are a "wealth effect" of government debt. Dropping debt from helicopters is a brilliant psychological device for convincing people that the government debt raining down on them will not be repaid by future taxes or spending restraint. It will be left outstanding, so they had better spend it now. Indeed, we just witnessed a "helicopter drop." But a helicopter drop is fiscal policy.

Why did fiscal inflation not happen sooner? The government has been borrowing money like the proverbial drunken sailor, for decades. The Fed has been buying Treasury securities and turning the debt into reserves for a decade. Why now?

Inflation comes when government debt increases, *relative* to people's expectations of what the government will repay. If the Treasury borrows, but everyone understands it will later raise tax revenues or cut spending to repay the debt, that debt does not cause inflation. It is a good investment and people are happy to hold on to it. If the Fed prints up a lot of money, buys Treasury debt, and the Treasury hands out the money, as happened, but everyone understands the Treasury will pay back the debt with future surpluses, the extra money causes no inflation. The Fed can always soak up the money by selling its Treasury securities, and the Treasury repays those securities with surpluses (i.e., taxes less spending).

The 2020–2021 borrowing and money episode was distinctive because, evidently, it came without a corresponding increase in expectations that the government would, someday, raise surpluses by $5 trillion in present value to repay the debt. Looking into people's heads is hard, but why? We can at least find some plausible speculations.

One may look to politicians' statements. Even in the Obama-era "stimulus" spending, the administration emphasized promises of eventual debt reduction. One may chuckle and sneer at promises to repay debts decades after an administration leaves office, but at least they went through the motions to make that promise! Nobody went through any motions about long-run fiscal planning, long-run deficit reduction, and entitlement and tax reform in 2020–2021. It was the era of modern monetary theory (MMT), of costless "fiscal expansion" made possible, or so it was claimed, by the manna from heaven that interest rates would stay low forever.

The manner of fiscal expansion matters too. When the Treasury borrows in the usual manner, it borrows from established long-term investors, who view Treasury debt as debt that will be repaid and not defaulted or inflated. They view it as a savings or investment vehicle, not as cash to be spent. They save, or invest, based on long and so far mostly successful experience. This time, following canary-in-the-coal-mine disruptions in Treasury markets during March 2020, the Federal Reserve immediately bought new Treasury debt with newly created money, before it even touched these investor's portfolios. The effect of the operation was to print new money and send people checks, so the debt issue is now held as bank deposits flowing into reserves, rather than as Treasury securities. People holding this new money are likely to spend it rather than regard it as a long-term investment. In our simplest economic models, it does not matter who holds the debt. But in just a little more nuanced view, who holds the debt matters.

In our simplest economic models, interest-paying reserves and Treasuries are equivalent securities. But people likely do see a difference between reserves and short-run Treasuries. Treasuries may well carry a reputation that they will be repaid, while people assume reserves will not be repaid by larger surpluses. Then issuing lots of reserves rather than Treasuries is inflationary, but not because the reserves are "money," but rather because they convey a different set of fiscal expectations, just as dropping money or debt from helicopters sends a different signal about repayment than issuing debt at a Treasury auction.

Most of the previous operations financed government spending or government worker salaries, counting on higher incomes to slowly filter through the economy. This one sent checks directly to people.

Finally, this fiscal stimulus was enormous, and carried out on a deep misdiagnosis of the state of the economy. Even in simplistic hydraulic Keynesian terms, $5 trillion times any multiplier is much larger than any plausible GDP gap. And the Covid recession was not due to a demand deficiency in the first place. A pandemic is, to the economy, like a huge snowstorm. Sending people money will not get them to go out to closed bars, restaurants, airlines, and businesses.

"Stimulus," "accommodation," "easing" was the point. This method finally worked, where previous stimulus efforts failed. One can see several suggestive differences, which amount to important economic lessons.

What about "supply shocks"? What about a shift of demand from services to durables? Much analysis misses the difference between relative prices and inflation, in which all prices and wages rise together. A supply shock makes one good more expensive than others. Only demand makes all goods rise together. There wouldn't be "supply chain" problems if people were not trying to buy things like mad! A shift in demand from services to durables can make durables prices go up. But it would make services prices go down. And let us not even go down the ridiculous path of blaming inflation on a sudden contagious outbreak of "greed" and "collusion" by businesses from oil companies to turkey farmers, needing the administration to send the FTC out to investigate.

It is telling that inflation was a complete surprise to the Federal Reserve. The Federal Reserve's job is supposed to be to monitor the supply capacity of the economy and to make sure demand does not outstrip it. The Fed failed twice. First, the economy did not need demand-side stimulus. Insurance was wise, and forestalling a financial crisis was necessary. But sending money to every citizen to stoke demand was not. Second, the Fed being surprised by supply shocks is as excusable as the Army losing a battle because its leaders are surprised that the enemy might attack. As we see by the outcome, the Fed's understanding of supply, largely based on statistical analysis of labor markets, is rudimentary.

Will Inflation Continue?

If the government borrows or prints $5 trillion, with no change in its plan to repay debt, on top of $17 trillion outstanding debt, then the price level will rise a cumulative 30 percent, so that the $22 trillion of debt is worth in real terms what the $17 trillion was before. In essence, absent a credible increase in future surpluses, the deficit is financed by defaulting on $5 trillion of outstanding debt, via inflation. By this calculation, the 6 percent or so cumulative inflation we have seen so far leaves a way to go. But people may think some of the debt will be repaid. If they think half will eventually be repaid, then the price level need only rise 15 percent overall.

But then it stops. A one-time unbacked debt increase leads to a one-time price-level increase, not continuing inflation. Whether inflation continues or not depends on future monetary policy, future fiscal policy, and whether people change their minds about overall debt repayment.

Fiscal policy may not be done with us yet. If unbacked fiscal expansions continue—that is, borrowing when people do not expect additional repayment—then additional bouts of fiscal inflation will occur. Untold trillions of spending, including new entitlements, with no realistic hope of raising tax revenues commensurately to cover them are certainly high on the Biden administration's agenda. (Higher tax rates do not necessarily mean higher revenues, if economic growth falters; and even so, the proposed taxes do not cover the proposed spending increases even with static scoring.) The mentality that borrowed money need never be repaid, because the MMT fairy or $r<g$ magic makes debt free, remains strong in Washington. But the failure of the so-called Build Back Better plan may augur well for budget seriousness and a limit to ill-constructed social policies with strong supply disincentives.

The most troublesome question remains: Do people, having decided that at least some of our government's new debt will not be repaid, so they should spend it now and inflate it away, now think that the government is less likely to repay its existing debts, or less likely to repay future borrowing? If so, even more inflation can break out, seemingly (as always) out of nowhere.

Fiscal Constraints on Monetary Policy

Fiscal and monetary policies are always intertwined in causing or curing inflation. Even in a pure fiscal theory of the price level, monetary policy (setting interest rates) can control the path of expected future inflation. Thus, whether inflation continues or not also depends on how monetary policy reacts to this fiscal shock and its consequences.

Whether the Fed *will* do something about it is an obvious concern. The Fed's habits and new operating procedures, formed before 2019 in a Maginot Line against perpetual below-target inflation, look remarkably like the Fed of about 1971: let inflation blow hot to march down the Phillips curve to greater employment, wait for inflation to exceed target for a while before doing anything about it, talk about "transitory" and "supply" shocks to excuse each error. The Fed understands "expectations" now, unlike in 1971, but seems to view them as a third force amenable to management by "forward guidance" speeches rather than formed by a hardy and skeptical experience with the Fed's concrete actions. The Fed likes to say it has the tools to contain inflation, but never dares to say just what those tools are. In recent U.S. historical experience, the Fed's tool is to replay 1980: 20 percent interest rates, a bruising recession hurting the disadvantaged especially, and the medicine applied for as long as it takes. Will our Fed really do that? Will our Congress let our Fed do that? Can you deter an enemy without revealing what's in your arsenal and whether you will use it?

If the Fed needs to fight inflation, fiscal constraints on monetary policy will play a large and unexpected role. In 1980, the debt-to-GDP ratio was 25 percent. Today it is 100 percent, and rising swiftly. Fiscal constraints on monetary policy are four times larger today—and counting.

For a rise in interest rates to lower inflation, fiscal policy must tighten as well. Without that fiscal cooperation, monetary policy cannot lower inflation. There are two important channels of this interconnection.

First, the rise in interest rates raises interest costs on the debt. The government must pay those higher interest costs, by raising tax revenues and cutting spending, or by credibly promising to do so in the future. At 100 percent debt to GDP, 5 percent higher interest rates mean an additional deficit of 5 percent of GDP or $1 trillion, for every year that high interest rates continue.

This consideration is especially relevant if the underlying cause of the inflation is fiscal policy. If we are having inflation because people don't believe that the government can pay off the deficits it is running to send people checks, and it will not reform the looming larger entitlement promises, then people will not believe that the government can pay off an additional $1 trillion deficit to pay interest costs on the debt. In a fiscally driven inflation, it can happen that the central bank raises rates to fight inflation, which raises the deficit via interest costs, and thereby only makes inflation worse. This has, for example, been an analysis of several episodes in Brazil.

Second, if monetary policy lowers inflation, then bondholders earn a real windfall. Fiscal policy must tighten to pay this windfall. People who bought 10-year Treasury bonds in September of 1981 got a 15.84 percent yield, as markets expected inflation to continue. From September 1981 to September 1991, the CPI grew at a 3.9 percent average rate. By this back-of-the-envelope calculation, those bondholders got an amazing 12 percent annual real return. That return came completely and entirely courtesy of U.S. taxpayers. The 1986 tax reform and deregulation, which allowed the United States to grow strongly for 20 years, eventually did produce fiscal surpluses that nearly repaid U.S. federal debt. At 100 percent debt-to-GDP ratio, each 5 percentage point reduction in the price level requires another 5 percent of GDP fiscal surplus.

Ask yourself, if inflation gets built into bond yields, and the Fed tries to lower inflation, will our Congress really raise tax revenues or cut spending in order to finance an unexpected (by definition) and undeserved (it will surely be argued) windfall profit to wealthy investors, foreign central bankers, and fat cats on Wall Street? If it does not do so, the monetary attempt at disinflation fails.

We state too casually that the United States will always repay its debts and prioritize that repayment over all else. We should not take such probity for granted. For example, in the 2021 debt ceiling discussion, it stated as fact by all concerned, from the Treasury to Congress to the White House, that hitting the debt ceiling must trigger a formal default. That is untrue. The United States could easily prioritize its tax revenues to repaying interest and principal on outstanding debt, by cutting other spending instead. Painful, yes. Impossible, no. That the U.S. contingency plan for a binding debt ceiling is formal default tells you that the spirit of Alexander Hamilton, preaching the sanctity of debt repayment to build reputation so we can borrow in the future, is truly dead. And with inflation, we are not even talking about formal default. The question is, will the United States undertake sharp fiscal austerity to support monetary policy in the fight against inflation, by paying higher interest costs on the debt and by repaying bondholders in more valuable money? Or will the government just repay as promised, but in dollars that are worth more than expected? If the government does the latter, monetary policy fails.

There is a third troublesome requirement for higher nominal interest rates to produce lower inflation. One needs an economic model in which this is true, that model needs to be correct, and its preconditions need to be met. It's not as easy as it sounds, because in the long run, when real interest rates settle down, higher nominal interest rates must come with higher, not lower inflation. So you need an understanding of how and when things work the other direction in the short run.

In standard new-Keynesian models, used by all central banks, for example, higher interest rates only produce lower inflation if the higher interest rate is unexpected—that is, a shock to the economy— and if there is a sharp contemporaneous fiscal contraction, for the above reasons.[1] A widely expected rise in nominal interest rates *raises* inflation. A rise in interest rates without the corresponding "austerity" *raises* inflation. Both preconditions are questionable today. More complex ingredients, such as long-term debt or financial frictions, can allow a higher nominal rate to temporarily lower inflation. But reliance on more complex ingredients and frictions is also dangerous.

The Future

The future is not hopeless. Inflation control simply requires our government, including the central bank, to understand classic lessons of history. Forestalling inflation is a joint task of fiscal, monetary, and microeconomic policy. Stabilizing inflation once it gets out

---

[1]See Cochrane (2022b: chap. 17), "The Fiscal Underpinnings of new-Keynesian Models," for analysis.

of control is a joint task of fiscal, monetary, and microeconomic policy. Expectations are "anchored" if people believe such policy is in place, and politicians and Fed officials are ready to act if needed.

I add "microeconomic," as it is perhaps the most frequently overlooked adjective. Fiscal surpluses do not result from sharply higher tax rates, especially of a tax system so riven with economic distortions as ours. Fiscal surpluses can come from spending restraint, but that too is difficult. The best road to fiscal surpluses is strong economic growth, which increases the tax base and lowers the need for social spending.

In the conundrum between taxes and spending, there is a way out: raise long-term economic growth. And there is only one way to do that: increase the supply-side capacity of the economy. That is, however, just as politically controversial as the first two options. Most of the job is to get out of the way. Most economic regulation is designed to transfer incomes, to protect various interests, or to push on the scales of bilateral negotiation, to undo the harsh siren of economic incentives, in a way that stifles economic growth. Many interests hate progrowth legislation and regulation just as much as they hate taxes and spending cuts. The $r<g$ crowd has a point, but increasing g is the answer.

Much of the "supply shocks" of 2021 come down to the "great resignation"—that is, the puzzling decline in labor force participation despite a labor shortage. The work disincentives of social programs— paying people not to work, bluntly—are laid bare.

All successful inflation stabilizations have combined monetary, fiscal, and microeconomic reforms. I emphasize *reforms*. In most cases the tax *system* is reformed to provide more revenue with less distortion. The *structure* of spending programs is reformed to help people in need more efficiently without work disincentives. Regulations are *reformed*, though they hurt the profits of incumbents, to increase entry, competition, and innovation. The policy *regime* is changed, durably. Reversible decisions and pie-crust promises do not do much to change the present value of surpluses, to raise the government's ability to pledge a long stream of surpluses to support debt.

The United States did not succeed in 1980 from monetary toughness only. Supply-side deregulation took place and was quickly followed by tax reforms in 1982 and 1986. The economy took off, so by the late 1990s, economists were seriously writing papers about what to do when the federal debt had all been repaid.

Many monetary stabilizations have been tried without fiscal and microeconomic reform. They typically fail after a year or two. The history of Latin America is littered with them (Kehoe and Nicolini 2021). The high interest rates of the early 1980s likely represented a fear that the United States would suffer the same fate. The 1970s were not just a failure of monetary policy. The deficits of the great society and Vietnam War contributed, while the supply shocks and productivity slowdown did their part.

These points are especially important if the 2021 inflation turns into a sustained 2020s inflation, as the 1971 inflation turned into a sustained 1970s inflation. For this time, the roots of inflation will most likely be fiscal, a broad change of view that our government really will not eventually reform and repay its debt. The only fundamental answer to that question will be, to reform and set in place a durable structure that will repay debt. Monetary machination will be pointless.

A small bout of inflation may be useful to our body politic. Inflation is where dreams of costless fiscal expansion, flooding the country with borrowed money to address every perceived problem, hit a hard brick wall of reality. A small bout of inflation and debt problems may reteach our politicians, officials, and commentariat the classic lessons that there are fiscal limits, fiscal and monetary policy are intertwined, and that a country with solid long-term institutions can borrow, but a country without them is in trouble, and one must allow the golden goose to thrive if one wants to tax her eggs. A small bout of inflation may reteach the same classes that supply matters, incentives matter, and sand in the gears matters. The 1980s reforms only happened because the 1970s were so painful.

In the meantime, however, there is one technical thing the Fed and Treasury can do to forestall a larger crisis: borrow long. Interest costs feed into the budget as debt rolls over. U.S. debt is shockingly short maturity, rolled over on average about every two years. If the United States borrows long term, then higher interest rates do not raise interest costs on existing debt at all. Shifting to long-term debt would remove one of the main fiscal constraints on monetary policy. The Federal Reserve has not helped this fiscal constraint, by transforming a fifth of the federal debt to overnight, floating-rate debt. The 30-year Treasury rate is, as I write, 2 percent, about negative 1 percent in real terms. Okay, the 1-year rate is 0.13 percent. As long as this lasts, the government seems to pay lower interest costs. But a

1.87 percent insurance premium to wipe out the danger of a sovereign debt crisis and to buy huge fiscal space to fight inflation seems like a pretty cheap insurance policy. The window of opportunity will not last long, however, as interest rates are already creeping up.

References

Cochrane, J. H. (2022a) "The Fiscal Theory of the Price Level: An Introduction and Overview." Manuscript, in preparation for *Journal of Economic Perspectives*. Available at www.johnhcochrane.com /research-all/fiscal-theory-jep-article.

_____ (2022b) *The Fiscal Theory of the Price Level*. Princeton, N.J.: Princeton University Press. Manuscript available until publication at www.johnhcochrane.com/research-all/the-fiscal-theory -of-the-price-level-1.

Friedman, M. (1969) "The Optimum Quantity of Money." In M. Friedman, *The Optimum Quantity of Money and Other Essays*, 1–50. Chicago: Aldine.

Kehoe, T. J., and Nicolini, J. P. (2021) *A Monetary and Fiscal History of Latin America, 1960–2017*. Minneapolis: University of Minnesota Press.

9
THE RETURN OF INFLATION?
Fernando M. Martin

The economic challenges presented by the Covid-19 pandemic prompted the U.S. government to respond in a manner that was unprecedented in speed, scope, and size. These actions resulted in soaring deficits and debt levels, as well as an accommodative monetary policy. The aggregate price level declined early on, but afterward, as the economy recovered, started growing at an accelerated pace. Higher rates of inflation were initially deemed transitory and the result of a few outliers.[1] However, high inflation has proved more persistent and broad based than anticipated, raising concerns for future inflation risk.

A central question of this article is to what extent higher rates of inflation, observed and expected, have a fiscal origin. I begin by briefly reporting on the current economic and policy context. Then, I describe how economic theory links fiscal policy to inflation and the interplay between the fiscal and monetary authorities. Next, I analyze how the fiscal response may have contributed to inflation during Covid-19 and how the fiscal outlook may pose a risk to future inflation. Finally, I discuss the credibility of the Federal Reserve in the present context and the risks posed by the adoption of the new monetary policy framework.

Fernando M. Martin is Assistant Vice President, Federal Reserve Bank of St. Louis. The views expressed in this paper do not necessarily reflect official positions of the Federal Reserve Bank of St. Louis, the Federal Reserve System, or the Board of Governors.

[1]This was the prevailing view at the Federal Reserve by the end of summer 2021. For example, see Powell (2021).

Economic and Policy Context

The Covid-19 pandemic implied a sharp drop in output, mostly driven by public policy and private mitigation strategies that disrupted normal economic activity. The economy rebounded quickly, and by the second quarter of 2021, real output surpassed its prepandemic level, though it has remained below its prepandemic trend. Figure 1 below shows real gross domestic product (GDP) per capita, including the two previous recessions for reference.

At the onset of the pandemic, the U.S. federal government enacted massive programs to assist households and businesses, mostly from April to June 2020. The fiscal expansion continued over the following year as the pandemic persisted. These increases in expenditure were not financed with new revenues. The deficit was $3.1 trillion in fiscal year 2020 and $2.8 trillion in 2021, roughly 14 percent of GDP.[2] Correspondingly, debt held by the public rose

FIGURE 1
REAL GDP PER CAPITA
(DOLLARS, SEASONALLY ADJUSTED ANNUAL RATE)

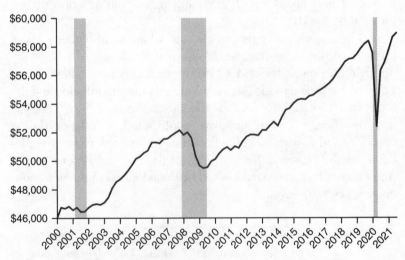

SOURCES: Bureau of Economic Analysis and author's calculations. Shaded areas indicate recessions.

[2]In the United States, the fiscal year runs from October 1 to September 30. Fiscal years are referenced by their end date.

FIGURE 2
INTEREST RATES AND FED'S BALANCE SHEET

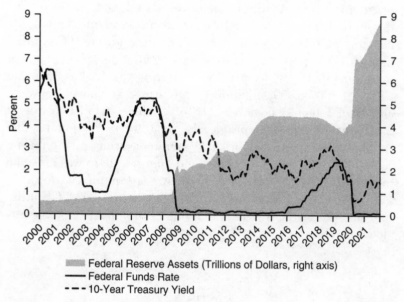

Federal Reserve Assets (Trillions of Dollars, right axis)
Federal Funds Rate
10-Year Treasury Yield

SOURCES: Board of Governors of the Federal Reserve System and author's calculations.

sharply, surpassing 100 percent of GDP for the first time since World War II.[3]

At the same time, the Federal Reserve lowered its policy rate back to near zero, opened a series of temporary credit facilities designed to support the functioning of financial markets, and restarted its asset-buying programs. Figure 2 shows the federal funds rate, the yield on 10-year Treasuries, and the total assets held by the Federal Reserve. Since the start of the pandemic in March 2020 and up to December 2021, the Federal Reserve bought about $3.2 trillion of U.S. Treasuries and $1.2 trillion of mortgage-backed securities. The Treasuries bought by the Federal Reserve account for 56 percent of the debt issued by the federal government to the public since the start of the pandemic.

[3]Debt held by the public excludes holdings by federal agencies (mainly, the Social Security trust funds), but includes holdings by the Federal Reserve System.

During the initial months of the pandemic, characterized by lockdowns and production and trade disruptions, the aggregate price level fell. As these measures eased and the economy rebounded, prices started to grow at an accelerated pace. By November 2021, personal consumption expenditure (PCE) inflation was 5.7 percent year-over-year. Inflation spikes are not unique to this episode; previously, during the Global Financial Crisis of 2007–2009, inflation temporarily rose above 4 percent and then fell into negative territory before stabilizing around 2 percent. During that episode, the volatility in inflation was due to fluctuations in energy prices. When measuring inflation using core PCE (which excludes food and energy), there was no spike in inflation (on the contrary, there was a temporary drop). As Figure 3 shows, during the Covid-19 pandemic, core PCE inflation surged as well, revealing that higher inflation is more generalized this time.

FIGURE 3
PCE ANNUAL INFLATION

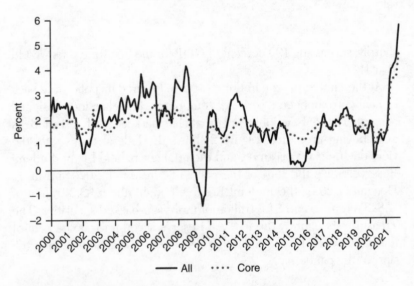

SOURCES: Bureau of Economic Analysis and author's calculations.

Theories of Inflation

There are various views on what determines the price level or inflation, some more popular than others among central bankers.[4] Fiscal policy plays a meaningful role in some, but not all these theories.

A view adopted by the majority of central bankers around the world is that inflation is, in essence, a self-fulfilling prophecy—that is, it depends on *expected* inflation. This explains why they are concerned with anchoring inflation expectations around their target. This view applies mostly to the medium and long terms, as it is recognized that economic fluctuations can disturb inflation in the short run. To explain these disturbances, central bankers tend to favor some version of the Phillips curve, which states a negative relationship between inflation and unemployment or output. In recent times, however, the empirical relationship between inflation and these real variables has all but disappeared.

Monetarism relates the price level to some monetary aggregate (e.g., currency) and inflation to the growth rate of that monetary aggregate. In a modern economy, currency accounts for a small fraction of transactions, so economists look at "broader" monetary aggregates, such as M1 or M2. Prices increase when the supply of money outstrips its demand. This theory offers a mechanism for deficits to create inflation when the central bank accommodates to the fiscal reality, that is, when it prints money to help finance the deficit. It has proved particularly successful in explaining high-inflation episodes (e.g., the Latin American experience in the 1980s). However, the theory struggles empirically when applied to modern developed economies with low inflation, for the most part, because the demand for money is not sufficiently stable or easy to predict.[5]

Finally, a body of related theories, collectively known as the "fiscal theory of the price level," links prices or inflation to the level of government debt and expected future fiscal surpluses. Though their mechanisms vary, they all predict higher prices as debt rises and

---

[4]Castillo-Martinez and Reis (2019) offer a good primer on these theories.

[5]For measures of the demand for money over a long-term horizons, its stability and implications in monetary models, see Lucas (2000) and Lucas and Nicolini (2015).

higher inflation as the debt growth rises. As with monetarism, these theories provide a direct link between deficits and inflation, essentially shifting the core element determining prices from monetary aggregates to government debt. And just like monetarism, the fiscal theory assumes a stable demand for government liabilities in order to make its predictions. The recent experience, with a strong foreign demand for U.S. dollar-denominated assets, particularly those issued by the U.S. government, makes it hard to evaluate the validity of the theory.

Fiscal Dominance

As mentioned above, the monetarist approach and the fiscal theory of the price level offer mechanisms that link fiscal policy to monetary policy and inflation.[6] For example, the use of seigniorage helps finance the deficit directly while inflation by itself reduces the real value of accumulated nominal liabilities. Furthermore, a low policy rate helps alleviate the fiscal burden of debt by reducing the interest paid to service it. The question is then whether the central bank will assist an expansionary fiscal policy. Fiscal dominance occurs when the fiscal authority forces the central bank to accommodate monetary policy to suit its preferred policy outcomes.[7]

Avoiding fiscal dominance involves designing a central bank that is protected from political pressures and seeks low inflation as one of its main goals. This sounds simple in theory but is hard to implement in practice, for several reasons. I will list three that are particularly relevant in the present context.

First, politicians appoint and, perhaps more importantly, reappoint central bank authorities, so central bankers are not completely isolated from political considerations. Second, central banks, like the Federal Reserve, may have mandates extending beyond inflation, which means they have to trade off inflation with other economic goals (e.g., employment) better aligned with the objectives of fiscal and political authorities. Third, central banks may be reluctant to act preemptively, deterring fiscal expansion, unless strong inflationary pressures materialize.

[6]Other theories, in the Keynesian tradition, link fiscal policy to inflation through the effects of the former on aggregate demand.

[7]Much of our understanding on this topic stems from the seminal ideas in Sargent and Wallace (1981), further articulated by Leeper (1991) and Sims (1994). For more recent treatments, see Martin (2015, 2021).

Inflation Risks Due to Fiscal Policy

There are currently several factors that point toward high inflation in the near future. First, short-term inflation expectations, both survey and market based, have been on the rise, catching up to actual inflation.[8] Second, supply chain disruptions and increased demand for certain products have also contributed to the increase in prices. In this section, I will assess the contribution of fiscal factors to current and future inflation.

Figure 4 provides an overview of the U.S. fiscal situation, including the most recent projections by the Congressional Budget Office (CBO), published in July 2021. All variables are in fiscal years and expressed as a percentage of GDP. Overall, though revenue has fluctuated around a constant as a fraction of GDP, since tax cuts are typically reversed,[9] outlays have trended up, as a fraction of GDP, with big spikes during the Great Recession and the Covid-19 pandemic. The upward trend and spikes in spending are mainly driven by transfers. As a result, the primary deficit has remained positive and large since 2008—it averaged zero between 1955 and 2007—while debt as a percentage of GDP increased to levels not seen since World War II.

Fiscal policy responded similarly during the two most recent crises, financing large economic assistance packages with deficits. And in both cases, the Federal Reserve accommodated the fiscal expansion with low interest rates and asset-buying programs. Yet inflation behaved very differently in these two episodes. As shown above, core PCE inflation actually went down during the global financial crisis while it has gone up significantly during the Covid-19 pandemic. Here, data and theory might offer some guidance to understand this difference.

Figure 5 shows the federal debt in the hands of the public, by type of holder. The global financial crisis prompted a big flight to

---

[8]For example, the median one-year ahead expected inflation rate from the New York Fed Survey of Consumer Expectations was 6.0 percent annually in November 2021. As a reference, this figure averaged 2.6 percent in 2019. Similarly, the five-year breakeven inflation rate, that is, the difference in the annual yields of five-year Treasury notes and five-year Treasury inflation-protected securities (TIPS), has been above 2 percent annually throughout 2021 and averaged 2.7 percent in December.

[9]See Romer and Romer (2009).

FIGURE 4
Fiscal Outlook in Terms of GDP

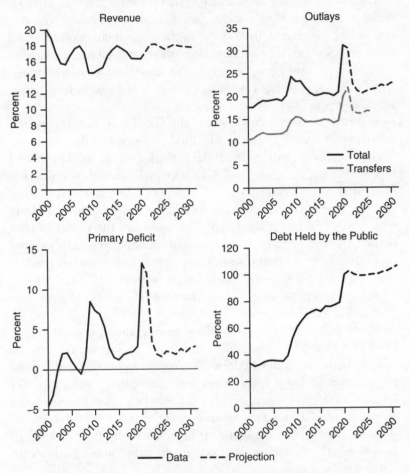

SOURCES: Congressional Budget Office, Office of Management and Budget, and author's calculations.

safety in global markets. As a consequence, most of the debt issued by the government over this period and in the years immediately thereafter was bought and held by foreign nationals. This increase in the global demand for U.S. government liabilities may explain the absence of inflation despite a large fiscal expansion.[10] In contrast,

[10]For example, see Andolfatto (2021).

FIGURE 5
FEDERAL DEBT BY TYPE OF HOLDER
(TRILLIONS OF DOLLARS)

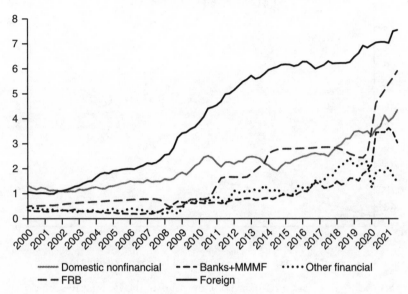

SOURCES: U.S. Treasury, Board of Governors of the Federal Reserve System, and author's calculations.

during the Covid-19 pandemic, most of the debt has been absorbed by the Federal Reserve, banks, and money market mutual funds. Though interest rates on government debt remain low, the chart suggests that the federal government may no longer rely on foreign demand to absob future deficits, at least to the extent it did in the past. In addition, the Federal Reserve will taper down its asset purchases over the next several months. Hence, most new debt issuances will likely have to be absorbed by domestic private agents. The risk posed by the current fiscal expansions being proposed and debated is that they will not meet a suffciently high demand for Treasuries, which may put pressures on both inflation and the cost of servicing the debt.

Figure 6 further inspects the effects of the deficit during the Covid-19 pandemic. The figure tracks the monetary aggregate M2 on the left axis and accumulated deficits by the federal government starting in October 2015 (which was the beginning of fiscal year

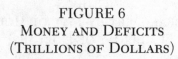

FIGURE 6
MONEY AND DEFICITS
(TRILLIONS OF DOLLARS)

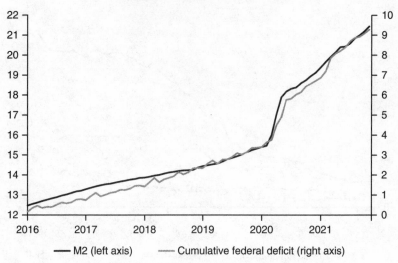

SOURCES: U.S. Treasury, Board of Governors of the Federal Reserve System, and author's calculations.

2016) on the right axis. Both series track each other well, suggesting that the recent expansion of money in the economy has a fiscal origin. Between 2016 and 2019, M2 grew at a rate of 5.6 percent annually. Between February and May 2020, it grew by 15.6 percent, reflecting the large transfers made to households and businesses during the initial phases of the pandemic.

This increase in the quantity of money pressures prices to rise (a one-time increase) but does not affect long-run inflation rates. In June 2020, M2 resumed growing at a steady pace but much faster than before the pandemic: 12.8 percent annually. If this pace persists, it would pressure the inflation rate upward. For this to be the case, future deficits need to be persistently larger than in the past. The CBO is currently projecting a deficit as a percentage of GDP of 4.7 percent in fiscal year 2022 and of 4.1 percent on average for the next 10 fiscal years. Legislation passed and proposed since these projections were published are expected to raise these figures.[11] As a reference, the deficit in the five years leading up to the pandemic (2015–2019) averaged 3.5 percent of GDP.

Fed Credibility and the New Monetary Policy Framework

In the various inflation theories sketched above, the central bank's desired or targeted inflation rate plays an important role. How much of a role depends on the central bank's commitment or credibility toward its objective. The risk of letting inflation rise measurably above target is that economic agents may start questioning it. For example, if the central bank announces a 2 percent inflation target, but allows inflation to rise to 4 percent before it acts, agents will rationally start to expect the actual target to be above 2 percent. In extreme situations, this makes the announced target meaningless.[12] More generally, it determines inflation as a function of the expected rather than the announced target.

In August 2020, the Federal Reserve adopted a new framework that seeks to achieve inflation that averages 2 percent over time.[13] Since inflation had been running below 2 percent annually in the recent past, higher temporary inflation is consistent with the Federal Reserve's objective. However, the new framework does not specify how much current inflation the Federal Reserve is willing to tolerate as it catches up with missing past inflation. Nor does it specify over which time horizon it will attempt to achieve 2 percent on average. These are not minor details but critical elements feeding the expectations of households and market participants. In time, the

---

[11]The Infrastructure Investment and Jobs Act was passed after the CBO projections were published. The CBO estimates this law will add $256 billion to the deficit over the 2022–2031 period. The Build Back Better Act passed by the House of Representatives and currently being discussed in the Senate would add $365 billion to the deficit over the next 10 years. However, if certain policies are made permanent rather than temporary (mostly, the child tax credit, child care, and preschool provisions), the law would add a total of $3 trillion to the deficit over 10 years, about 1 percentage point of GDP per year on average. See Congressional Budget Office (2021).

[12]It could be argued that this was the case with Argentina's failed inflation-targeting experience in 2016–2018, when the target was inconsistent with the fiscal reality and the expected accommodative stance of the central bank.

[13]See Board of Governors (2020).

boundaries of the new framework will be determined by the Federal Reserve's actions. At present, the risk is that the Federal Reserve will act too late and then have to work hard to reanchor expectations around its desired policy reaction function.

Another risk to the Federal Reserve's credibility is the addition or expansion of goals. By law, the Federal Reserve is mandated to "promote effectively the goals of maximum employment, stable prices, and moderate long-term interest rates" (Board of Governors 2000). It also has an implicit financial stability mandate. Though these goals are loosely defined, the Federal Reserve has, over the years through its actions, communicated to the public how it interprets them and how it conducts monetary policy in order to achieve them. For example, since January 2012, the Federal Reserve has explicitly interpreted its price stability mandate as meaning 2 percent annual inflation, thus matching stated policy with previous performance. There was still some uncertainty about the tolerance bounds around the target (though they were generally deemed as narrow) and whether, in practice, the Federal Reserve was implementing a ceiling rather than a target.

The push for the Federal Reserve to address other issues or broaden the scope of its mandates introduces uncertainty on the weight it places on its inflation target and the actions it is willing to take in order to achieve it. The new monetary policy framework states that "The maximum level of employment is a broad-based and inclusive goal that is not directly measurable and changes over time owing largely to nonmonetary factors that affect the structure and dynamics of the labor market" (Board of Governors 2020). Thus, the Federal Reserve has now added a vague employment objective to a loosely defined inflation target. The new framework may be the Federal Reserve's own worst enemy in maintaining the credibility of its inflation target.

References

Andolfatto, D. (2021) "Is It Time for Some Unpleasant Monetarist Arithmetic?" *Federal Reserve Bank of St Louis Review* 103 (3): 315–32.

Board of Governors of the Federal Reserve System (2000) "Section 2A. Monetary Policy Objectives." 12 USC 225a. 114 Stat. 3028 (December 27).

_____ (2020) "2020 Statement on Longer-Run Goals and Monetary Policy Strategy." Press Release (August 27).

Castillo-Martinez, L., and Reis, R. (2019) "How Do Central Banks Control Inflation? A Guide for the Perplexed." Available at https://personal.lse.ac.uk/reisr/papers/99-perplexed.pdf.

Congressional Budget Office (2021) "Budgetary Effects of Making Specified Policies in the Build Back Better Act Permanent." Report.

Federal Reserve Bank of New York (2021) "Survey of Consumer Expectations." Federal Reserve Bank of New York Center for Microeconomic Data.

Leeper, E. M. (1991) "Equilibria under Active and Passive Monetary and Fiscal Policies." *Journal of Monetary Economics* 27: 129–47.

Lucas, R. E. (2000) "Inflation and Welfare." *Econometrica* 68 (2): 247–74.

Lucas, R. E., and Nicolini, J. P. (2015) "On the Stability of Money Demand." *Journal of Monetary Economics* 73: 48–65.

Martin, F. M. (2015) "Debt, Inflation and Central Bank Independence." *European Economic Review* 79 (October): 129–50.

_____ (2021) "Fiscal Dominance." Federal Reserve Bank of St. Louis Working Paper No. 2020-040B (September).

Powell, J. H. (2021) "Monetary Policy in the Time of COVID." Speech at the Federal Reserve Bank of Kansas City's Economic Policy Symposium, Macroeconomic Policy in an Uneven Economy, Jackson Hole, Wyoming.

Romer, C. D., and Romer, D. H. (2009) "Do Tax Cuts Starve the Beast? The Effects of Tax Changes on Government Spending." *Brookings Papers on Economic Activity* (Spring): 139–200.

Sargent, T. J., and Wallace, N. (1981) "Some Unpleasant Monetarist Arithmetic." *Minneapolis Federal Reserve Bank Quarterly Review* 5 (3): 1–17.

Sims, C. A. (1994) "A Simple Model for Study of the Determination of the Price Level and the Interaction of Monetary and Fiscal Policy." *Economic Theory* 4 (3): 381–99.

10

FISCAL DOMINANCE AND THE RISK OF FINANCIAL REPRESSION

Mark Sobel

The United States is fully able to finance federal debts on the current order of magnitude and significantly higher debt with ease, especially amid quantitative easing (QE) and low interest rates. The United States has far more fiscal space than economists would have thought a decade ago. It should use it wisely to finance infrastructure and fight climate change. At the same time, our political system appears hamstrung in its ability to use fiscal policy as an effective policy tool. While Congress has appropriately taken advantage of America's copious fiscal space to provide support during crises, it seems incapable of putting the United States on a gradual consolidation path in normal times, while addressing such challenges as social needs, climate, and intergenerational equity.

Fiscal and monetary policies are clearly interlinked. But the buildup in debt, especially if tackling it could seriously constrain growth, might ultimately, years from now, generate unfortunate political pressures on the Fed to support financial repression, keeping real interest rates negative and tolerating higher than desired inflation.

Mark Sobel is U.S. Chairman of the Official Monetary and Financial Institutions Forum. He served at the U.S. Department of the Treasury for nearly four decades, including as the Deputy Assistant Secretary for International Monetary and Financial Policy from 2000 to early 2015. From 2015 through early 2018, he was the U.S. representative at the IMF.

The Question of Fed Independence

An assessment of fiscal dominance and the potential for a return of inflation must start with an analysis of Fed independence and its institutional setup. The term "Fed independence" is universally tossed about. I view independence as a misnomer (Sobel 2020). The Federal Reserve operates in an accountability framework. That framework has evolved considerably since the Fed's founding in 1913. Congress has legislated a dual mandate for the Fed. Its Board members are proposed by the executive, and Congress must approve them. The Fed chair is required to testify twice annually on the state of the economy and monetary policy. In recent years, the vice chair for supervision has also testified twice annually. The Fed now prepares financial stability reports two times per year. These are but the tip of the iceberg of the Fed's interactions with the Hill.

In essence, the Fed can be seen in critical ways as a creature of Congress. It also obviously interacts heavily with the executive branch: in its role as fiscal agent to the Treasury; its responsibilities for financial markets; and its broader duties in promoting the health, safety, and soundness of the U.S. economy and financial system. Consequently, the Fed can be subjected to a wide array of pressures.

As documented by Binder and Spindel (2017) in *The Myth of Independence*, the Fed's role in American society has evolved considerably over time, often with Congress scapegoating the Fed and forcing change in response to shocks to the economy. The Fed's role in helping finance WWII and the subsequent developments that led to the Fed-Treasury Accord in 1951 are a classic case. In the mid-1970s, Congress set the Fed's dual mandate of maximum employment and price stability. More recently, the Dodd-Frank Act critically altered the parameters for the Fed's bank supervision, but at the expense of the Fed's flexibility in providing 13 (3) support to the American financial system and economy in the face of financial crisis. In the meantime, the Fed faced significant pressures to be audited, a euphemism for the Fed being second-guessed by the GAO, and there were proposals to subject monetary policy to a rule.

The Fed can be subjected to executive branch pressure. According to most historians, President Nixon forced or cajoled Fed Chairman Arthur Burns to run a far more expansionary monetary policy than he wished, facilitating the "Great Inflation."[1] Presidents Clinton, Bush, and Obama took a hands-off approach to the Fed—a practice the Biden administration appears to be following. But President Trump sharply criticized the Fed for not lowering rates faster, according Chairman Powell the ultimate Trumpian compliment in labeling him as an "enemy" at least as great as Chinese President Xi Jinping!

So, why is the Fed normally regarded as independent and why do we speak of central bank independence? What is called "independence" should really be called "instrument independence," as distinct from "goal independence" (Debelle and Fischer 1994; Meyer 2000). Instrument independence means the Fed can alone choose how it deploys its own tools—interest rate and balance sheet policies—to secure its congressionally mandated goals.

In reality, the Fed isn't independent. Even instrument independence has evolved only over the past decades, aided by the success in keeping inflation low under the post-Volcker Great Moderation. But given the lessons of the Fed and U.S. history, one cannot necessarily presume that instrument independence is guaranteed or secure for the future.

The role of Congress and the executive branch, plus broader economic thinking, will be decisive. This discussion also begs the question about whether and how Congress might respond to the pandemic and the current bout of inflation. Could Congress blame the Fed for the current bout of inflation and scapegoat it? Is this a possibility that might be heightened as the Fed inevitably contends with climate change and inequality—despite the heroic and successful efforts made by a talented Federal Reserve in March and April of 2020 to avert economic catastrophe at home and abroad?

Should We Care if the Fed Has Instrument Independence?

A key question is whether we should care about the Fed retaining its instrument independence. After all, the intersection of fiscal and monetary policy is central to achieving stabilization objectives. Why should the Fed have such independence from the executive branch and Congress?

[1] See, e.g., www.federalreservehistory.org/people/arthur-f-burns.

The standard political economy answer is that, if the Fed alone can decide how to achieve its dual mandate, it will take decisions benefiting America's long-term interests, free from short-term political pressures. In many other countries lacking central bank independence, preelection spending, at times, has resulted in currency crashes and high inflation. Politically motivated monetary policy could increase uncertainty, lead to worse economic outcomes, and destabilize the economy and financial system.

According to some economists, a central bank, even if not independent, could operate according to a rule, limiting excessive discretion. But rules are often too rigid for achieving stabilization objectives, particularly as the underlying structure of an economy changes or shocks are faced. Critically, had the Fed recently been subjected to a rules-based monetary policy, its excellent and technically oriented staff and leaders could not have responded so quickly and creatively during the Global Financial Crisis and the pandemic, risking possible disaster for the U.S. and global economy. Hence, in response to the question of whether the Fed should have instrument independence, my answer is unequivocally, yes!

Fiscal Dominance and the Fed: Is It Possible in America?

The United States is fully justified in having adopted an activist fiscal posture to deal with the pandemic under the Trump and Biden administrations. But could U.S. fiscal debt and deficits become sufficiently large or impactful on financial markets, and thus end up constraining the Fed's pursuit of its dual mandate of price stability and maximum employment?

It is difficult to foresee that happening in the current environment. The United States has the deepest and most liquid capital markets in the world. The dollar is the world's financial and reserve currency. Nominal interest rates are extremely low and real rates are even lower. Historically, U.S. interest rates have been lower than nominal GDP growth. Despite the sharp rise in debt held by the public, from long under 40 percent of GDP to 100 percent now, debt service costs have plummeted to about 1 percent of GDP versus a historical average of around 2 percent. The Fed is expected to commence tapering and end QE in 2022, but concomitantly, fiscal deficits should be declining sharply. Given current negative real interest rates and low natural real rates, there is little reason to worry about America's ability to sustain current debt loads—however one assesses their wisdom.

One could further argue that Japan has current (gross) debt well over 250 percent of GDP and the Bank of Japan holds roughly half of the JGBs. ECB holdings are over three-fourths of eurozone GDP. Yet, Japan and the ECB have been unable to generate inflation for over a decade. The Fed's balance sheet, paltry by comparison, holds bonds equal to only little more than one-third of GDP. Hence, why should the United States fret about fiscal dominance?

Nevertheless, vigilance for the future will be required. The United States shouldn't be complacent. Earlier U.S. experiences are not comforting, such as price increases in the period prior to the Treasury-Fed Accord or the Great Inflation era. Of course, the history of the rest of the world, especially for emerging markets, is punctuated with episodes of fiscal dominance triggering financial crises. There's a reason for the saying that the IMF stands for "It's Mostly Fiscal." Fiscal space is a useful concept. Advanced economies appear to have much more fiscal space than would have been thought a decade or two ago. They should continue using such space prudently, for example, to modernize infrastructure and combat global warming. But no one knows the limits of fiscal space, let alone what the impact on rates will be when QE is no longer accommodating Treasury issuance.

While interest rates are low today, that does not mean they will be tomorrow. If debt service costs go significantly higher, that will mean fewer resources to back programs or upward pressures on the deficit. CBO projects that the ratio of U.S. debt to GDP could rise sharply in the 2030s and '40s, reaching 200 percent by 2050 under current policies. Entitlement programs are poised to grow rapidly, especially in light of aging. Given vested interests among older Americans, it may be difficult to curb this growth. There is little appetite to cut defense spending, especially amid growing tensions with China. Interest costs must be serviced, notwithstanding the perennial stupidity of debt ceiling dramas. America faces pressing infrastructure, climate, and social safety net needs.

The U.S. political system appears unable to find a consensus in addressing fiscal policy, either in terms of stabilization policy or the allocation of scare resources. Congress has approved fiscal support—whether sufficient or properly targeted is another question—during crises. But in normal times, Congress and the executive branch haven't been able to chart a responsible path forward. One side refuses to back tax hikes and instead focuses on cutting taxes, despite little apparent overall economic benefit and the impact in ballooning the deficit. This side calls for reducing spending, but in reality is not prepared to identify concrete spending cuts, except perhaps for social programs for lower-income Americans. The other side wishes to boost social spending but also is skittish about compensating spending cuts or raising revenues when the rubber meets the road if that will impact other than the top 1 or 2 percent.

Hence, given polarization, the instinct of the U.S. political system is to ignore arithmetic and treat deficits as a residual, allowing them to rise. A further political impulse is to posit rosy scenarios that fast growth will hold the ratio of debt to GDP in check, notwithstanding the secular trend of slowing and low U.S. potential growth; or to sunset spending on paper to fit budgetary parameters when it is well known that such spending will be extended at a later date.

Interestingly, Econ 101 taught us that government debt and deficits crowd out the private sector and lead to economic inefficiency and lower productivity. There is clearly a role for fiscal policy to provide public demand to offset shortfalls in private demand. But the concept of "crowding out" is scarcely heard any longer, even from the staunchest free-enterprise proponents.

Fiscal and Monetary Policy Blurring

Further complicating the picture, while economic literature often points to distinct roles for fiscal and monetary policies, the Global Financial Crisis and the pandemic have blurred the lines between the two, as well as the roles of treasuries and central banks (see Bartsch et al. 2020).

Monetary policy can create fiscal space. Quantitative easing has had the effect of financing increased Treasury issuance. Major central bank asset purchases have allowed a surge in their government bond holdings as a share of GDP. So have some of the regulatory moves that upped the demand for safe assets.

There is now much more discussion about outright coordination of fiscal and monetary policy. Providing intellectual backing for this discussion, economists observe that monetary policy loses its impact around the zero or effective lower bound, whereas fiscal policy is far more potent. The Fed's alphabet soup of crisis facilities in the Global

Financial Crisis and pandemic entailed the Fed taking on fiscal responsibilities, though the Treasury did repeatedly take first-loss positions. Many analysts observe that central bank purchases of Treasuries can boost demand and avert higher rates.

Fed monetary policy, in playing its role in the exercise of its responsibilities for overall financial stability and conditions, has been increasingly seen as offering a "put" for financial markets, limiting sharp stock and bond price declines.

Major advanced economy governments also increasingly rely on central bank seignorage as a means of financing, further allowing Congress and the executive branch to limit their responsibility.

The United States may have plenty of fiscal space, and even if the Japanese situation suggests there is little to be concerned about in terms of deficit financing without massive market disruptions, one cannot be complacent. Hence, more scenario analysis should be dedicated to how, in the case of further blurring, Fed instrument independence could be preserved.

Inflation or Financial Repression?

The concern over fiscal dominance may not be one of fearing that an outbreak of inflationary pressures will occur on a persistent basis. After all, the Fed, ECB, and BOJ failed to hit their inflation targets, undershooting them for well over a decade before the pandemic. Rather, the issue may have more to do with financial repression and pressures on the Fed to provide for a continuing favorable environment for large-scale government financing. Somewhat higher inflation might also play a part.

Central banks are intensifying efforts to push inflation higher and actually meet inflation targets. That is the upshot of the Fed and ECB strategic reviews. Japan has seemingly given up. Flexible average inflation targeting allows explicitly for overshooting the 2 percent Fed target to make up for past undershoots and to avoid prematurely choking off activity. But FOMC participants have been clear that sharply rising inflation and large ongoing overshoots will not be tolerated.

There would be good reasons for central banks to aim at slightly higher inflation in any case. There is little evidence that the difference between inflation of 2 percent, versus 3 or 4 percent, would disrupt economic agents and investment. Critically, slightly higher inflation in such circumstances could help erode the real value of government debt, which could be attractive politically. It could also help grease the wheels for relative price adjustments as well as compensate for the fact that many studies have found that quality adjustments could mean that CPI measures overstate underlying inflation by up to a percentage point.

Lately, academic discussions have increasingly focused on the underlying dynamics of debt sustainability, especially on the difference between interest rates and economic growth, or $r - g$ (Mauro and Zhou 2020; Blanchard 2019). Studies have pointed out that it is a common occurrence for $r - g$ to be less than zero, especially in the United States as well as for advanced economies since the crises. Indeed, $r - g < 0$ does suggest that authorities have greater scope to reduce debt-to-GDP ratios over time. But there is a risk that the $r - g < 0$ debate may be abused by politicians to avoid addressing underlying fiscal challenges and will obscure the reality that deficits and debt can still be rising without broader fiscal efforts.

Also, central banks have recently discussed yield curve control (YCC). The BOJ has been practicing YCC for several years. But under YCC, if the interest rate is set too low, the central bank could be compelled to purchase large amounts of government paper that markets would not stand ready to absorb.

Conclusion

My bottom line is not that fiscal dominance will lead to an inflationary rout. Nor am I concerned about current U.S. debt-to-GDP levels challenging Fed instrument independence. Rather, my concern stems from the inability of the American political system to implement appropriate policies for fiscal moderation in noncrisis periods. It is seemingly difficult to foresee that America's political parties will be able to achieve a consensus or truce on the stabilization, allocative, and distributive roles for fiscal policy anytime in the near future—and by not acting in the period ahead, critical problems may emerge down the road. The Fed could make an easy future scapegoat in such circumstances.

Meanwhile, there is little incentive for the executive and legislative branches to develop a consensus on a path for fiscal stabilization—for example, by agreeing on a primary balance and long-run debt-to-GDP objective on the basis of agreed technical assumptions about potential growth and interest rates. It's easier to avoid taking tough decisions and just run large deficits, provided they don't cause surging inflation or interest rates.

One never knows when, or if, America's fiscal space could approach a tipping point. Although we appear to be far from that juncture, Americans should be concerned that, given higher debt loads, sharp consolidation in the future could restrain growth. Moreover, the lack of incentives for appropriate political restraint could lead Congress and the executive branch to lean on the Fed to run more accommodative monetary policies than desired and to delay interest rate increases.

The past penchant for Congress to debate and act upon the Fed's roles and responsibilities in the wake of economic shocks, whether justified or not, may be heightened in the postpandemic environment, and especially given the current bout of inflation. In short, financial repression could become a perceived necessity for financing debt in the future, which could lead to pressures to compromise the Fed's instrument independence.

One would hope that America could run sound fiscal policies, taking the burden off of monetary policy and reducing the focus on the Fed as the only game in town. But alas, the days of the 1990 Budget Summit when leaders came together on a bipartisan basis to forge a fiscal path have since riven American politics and seem like an anachronistic anomaly.

The Fed has done a good job in using its tools to deliver on its mandate in the past decades since inflation was vanquished in the early 1980s. It has an outstanding staff and a sharply honed apolitical focus. This has redounded to the benefit of the United States. Given our fiscal policy inadequacies, the United States shouldn't subject the Fed and monetary policy to the risk of a similar fate.

References

Bartsch, E.; Bénassy-Quéré, A.; Corsetti, G.; and Debrun, X. (2020) "Stronger Together? The Policy Mix Strikes Back" (December 15). Available at https://voxeu.org/article/stronger-together-policy-mix -strikes-back.

Binder, S., and Spindel, M. (2017) *The Myth of Independence: How Congress Governs the Federal Reserve*. Princeton, N.J.: Princeton University Press.

Blanchard, O. (2019) "Public Debt and Low Interest Rates." *American Economic Review* 109 (4): 1197–229.

Debelle, G., and Fischer, S. (1994) "How Independent Should a Central Bank Be?" *Conference Series [Proceedings] Federal Reserve Bank of Boston* 38: 195–225..

Mauro, P., and Zhou, J. (2020) "$r - g < 0$: Can We Sleep More Soundly?" IMF Working Paper No. 20/52

Meyer, L. H. (2000) "The Politics of Monetary Policy: Balancing Independence and Accountability." Available at www.federal reserve.gov/boarddocs/speeches/2000/20001024.htm.

Sobel, M. (2020) "The Misnomer of Central Bank Independence." Available at www.omfif.org/2020/04/the-misnomer-of-central-bank -independence.

11

THE PROSPECT OF FISCAL DOMINANCE IN THE UNITED STATES: A NEW QUANTITY THEORY PERSPECTIVE

David Beckworth

The past two decades have seen a rapid expansion of the U.S. national debt. This growth can be traced to a spate of developments—the early 2000 tax cuts, the budget strains caused by the 2007–2009 recession, the 2017 tax cuts, and the 2020 pandemic relief packages—that have kept the U.S. primary balance in deficit since the early 2000s.[1] As a result of these persistent primary deficits, the federal debt as a percent of GDP has grown from 35 percent to almost 100 percent over this period.

This surge in public debt and the expected persistence of primary deficits moving forward, as seen in Figure 1, have some commentators wondering whether macroeconomic policy is headed toward a regime of fiscal dominance (Dorn 2021). As first noted by Sargent and Wallace (1981), fiscal dominance occurs when monetary policy is forced to accommodate fiscal policy by creating the seigniorage revenue needed to keep the government solvent. In this environment, monetary policy becomes passive to the whims of fiscal policy

---

David Beckworth is a Senior Research Fellow with the Program on Monetary Policy at the Mercatus Center at George Mason University, and an Adjunct Scholar at the Cato Institute's Center for Monetary and Financial Alternatives.

---

[1] The primary deficit refers to the difference between noninterest spending and receipts.

FIGURE 1A
UNITED STATES PUBLICLY HELD TREASURIES
(PERCENTAGE OF GDP)

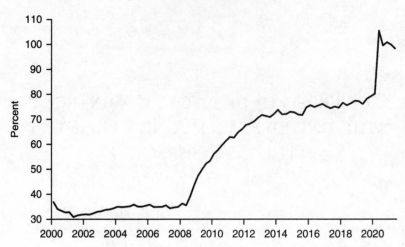

FIGURE 1B
UNITED STATES PRIMARY DEFICIT
(PERCENTAGE OF GDP)

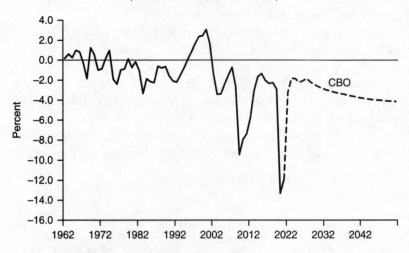

SOURCES: FRED and CBO data.

and loses its ability to control inflation. Fiscal dominance, then, typically leads to inflation becoming unanchored.

Historically, most cases of fiscal dominance have emerged during wartime when financially stressed governments have leaned heavily on seigniorage revenue. In a few cases, however, fiscal dominance has arisen during peacetimes (Bordo and Levy 2020). It is reasonable, then, to wonder whether the current U.S. fiscal position has planted the seeds for the next peacetime regime of fiscal dominance.

Most observers, to be clear, believe the Federal Reserve is still operating in a regime of monetary dominance. Here, monetary authorities actively stabilize inflation and fiscal policy passively responds to these efforts in a manner that keeps government solvent. Fiscal policy, in other words, accommodates monetary policy in this regime by absorbing the fiscal consequences of the central bank's actions (Leeper 2010).[2] This is the conventional view and, unsurprisingly, is held by U.S. monetary authorities (see, e.g., Waller 2021).[3]

One indication that monetary dominance in the United States is giving way to a regime of fiscal dominance would be sustained increases in the inflation rate. This would be a sign that the growth in national debt over the past two decades has compromised the fiscal authority's ability to passively absorb the costs of monetary policy.

Inflation has picked up in 2021, but the increase is largely tied to supply-side problems caused by the pandemic as well as the related federal relief programs (Rees and Rungcharoenkitkul, 2021). Both are likely to fade over the next year and make the current inflation rate a poor signal about the prospects of fiscal dominance. A better way to assess what is happening is to look at inflation forecasts at longer horizons where the influence of supply shocks has faded. Such forecasts provide a better sense of the expected trend inflation rate and, therefore, provide a superior way to gauge the prospects of fiscal dominance.

---

[2]Many observers, however, miss the point that, even in a monetary dominance regime, there is still a tight link between monetary policy and fiscal policy. Leeper (2010: 373) calls this the "dirty little secret" and reminds readers that "for monetary policy to successfully control inflation, fiscal policy must behave in a particular, circumscribed manner."

[3]The monetary dominance view is also implicit in the Federal Reserve's "Statement of Longer-Run Goals and Monetary Policy" that states: "The inflation rate over the longer run is primarily determined by monetary policy" (FOMC 2020).

Figure 2 provides two charts with long-run forecasts of PCE inflation, the inflation rate targeted by the Fed. Figure 2a, using data from the Survey of Professional Forecasters, shows the term structure of forecasted inflation for each year out to 2030 and does so for the four quarters of 2021. This graph reveals that inflation forecasts for 2021 rose each quarter as the actual inflation rate in 2021 surged. However, the chart also shows that at the medium- to long-run horizons the inflation forecast remain well anchored at the Fed's 2 percent target. Forecasters, therefore, do not see any threat of fiscal dominance.

Figure 2b adds in two market measures of expected inflation and looks at the five-year, five-year forward horizon. The market measures are the implied expected inflation from Treasury securities—the TIPS breakevens—as well as the average of three model-adjusted versions of the data.[4] The market measures provide a crosscheck on the findings from the consensus forecasts. The five-year, five-year forward horizon is useful here since it is looking at the average expected inflation rate over a five-year period, five years into the future. This is a forecast of trend inflation that sees beyond the near term where supply shocks affect inflation. Trend inflation this far out should largely reflect the stance of macroeconomic policy and therefore reveal whether fiscal dominance is emerging.

Figure 2b shows that, across all measures, trend PCE inflation remains well anchored near 2 percent. Both forecasters and markets are seeing through the current surge in inflation and believe the Fed will still be able to hit its inflation target over the next decade. A similar story emerges from long-term Treasury yields, which continue to remain low. They show no sign of fiscal dominance on the horizon. Accordingly, the Fed will comfortably remain in a regime of monetary dominance.

Now, the forecasters and markets may be wrong, but the fact they still believe in monetary dominance despite the projected path of the

---

[4]The models adjust the raw TIPS breakevens for issues like liquidity premiums and also make use of survey data. The DKW model is from D'Amico, Kim, and Wei (2018); the Aruoba model is from Aruoba (2016); and the HPR model is from Haubrich, Pennacchi, and Ritchken (2011). The TIPS breakevens and the model-adjusted versions of it are based on CPI inflation. To put these on a PCE basis, the spread between the CPI and PCE forecast in the Survey of Professional Forecasters was used to adjust these measures.

FIGURE 2A
Term Structure of PCE Inflation Expectations
(Survey of Professional Forecasters)

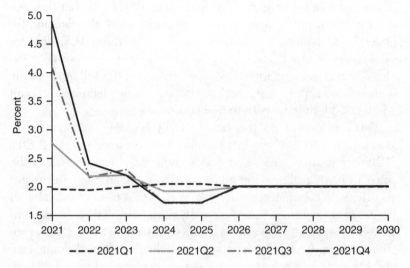

FIGURE 2B
5-Year Average Expected PCE Inflation Rate
Starting 5 Years in the Future

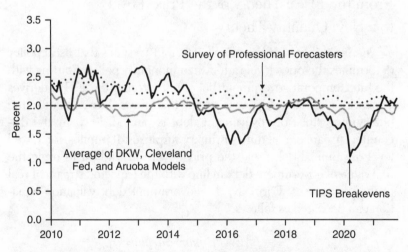

Note: Original CPI forecasts from models and TIPS adjusted to a PCE basis using spread between CPI and PCE forecasts in Survey of Professional Forecasters.

Sources: Federal Reserve Board, Cleveland Fed, Philadelphia Fed, FRED data.

national debt should give us pause. What are they seeing that makes them more optimistic about U.S. public finances than those commentators worried about fiscal dominance?

One possibility suggested by Andolfatto (2021a) is that they see the run-up in public debt as much or more about the demand for government liabilities than their supply. The rising U.S. debt-to-GDP ratio, in other words, may be an endogenous response to the elevated real demand for Treasury securities. In this telling, both the demand and supply of the national debt must be taken into account when considering the path to fiscal dominance.

This article explores this possibility by building on the work of Berenstein and Waller (2018) and Brunnermeier et al. (2020a, 2020b), who show a more general version of the fiscal theory of the price level that allows for nonpecuniary demand for government securities. What emerges from this work is that the market value of government securities can persistently deviate from their fundamental value if they are also valued for the transaction services they provide. This understanding changes the calculus of fiscal dominance and gives rise to a new quantity theoretic understanding of inflation. This idea is considered next.

From the Fiscal Theory of the Price Level to a New Quantity Theory

The fiscal theory of the price level (FTPL) states that fiscal policy determines the price level rather than monetary policy. Starting with the intertemporal government budget constraint, the FTPL derives a government debt valuation equation that shows the real value of the outstanding stock of government debt is pinned down by the discounted stream of real future primary surpluses. It implies, for a fixed level of nominal debt, that the price level must adjust to bring the real value of government debt in line with the expected stream of real primary surpluses. Formally, the government debt valuation equation can be stated as follows:

$$(1) \qquad \frac{D_t}{P_t} = E_t[PV(Primary\ Surpluses)],$$

where D_t is the nominal stock of government debt and includes Treasury and Federal Reserve liabilities, P_t is the price level, and

$E_t[PV(\cdot)]$ is the expected present value of future real primary surpluses at time t. Equation (1) can be seen as an asset-pricing equation where the nominal government debt acts as a residual claim to primary surpluses. Here, just like a stock price adjusts to bring the value of shares in line with the present value of dividends, the price level adjusts to bring the real value of nominal government debt in line with the present value of primary surpluses (Cochrane 2021).[5]

This understanding provides a useful way to value the national debt, but recent attempts to do so with equation (1) find the market value of government securities exceeds their fundamental value (Jiang et al. 2021). The difference can be attributed to a bubble term that arises from the liquidity services offered by government securities given their safe asset status (Reis 2021). The bubble term interpretation is supported by a growing number of studies that find Treasury securities offer liquidity services or a "convenience yield" and therefore function as money for many investors (Krishnamurthy and Vissing-Jorgensen 2012, 2015; Greenwood et al. 2015; Nagel 2016; Du et al. 2018).

Berenstein and Waller (2018) formalize this understanding and show that if there is a liquidity premium on government securities the market value of government debt can fluctuate even if there are no changes to current or future taxes or spending. Put differently, they show that within the FTPL framework, price level dynamics can be driven solely by the liquidity premium on the government securities.[6] More generally, the market value of public debt can be shaped by expectations on future primary surpluses and by expectations on future transaction services provided by Treasury and Fed liabilities.

Brunnermeier et al. (2020a, 2020b) reach a similar conclusion and formally show that this understanding implies the standard FTPL equation in (1) becomes the following:

$$(2) \qquad \frac{D_t}{P_t} = E_t[PV(Primary\ Surpluses)] + E_t[PV(Transaction\ Service\ Flows)],$$

where the second $E_t[PV(\cdot)]$ on the right is the bubble term that arises from the expected path of real transaction service flows provided by

---

[5]See Christiano and Fitzgerald (2000) and Sims (2013) for an introductory overview of FTPL.

[6]They note that this implies the government asset valuation equation cannot be seen as a solvency condition as is often claimed in the FTPL literature.

government liabilities.[7] This understanding is consistent with the literature that shows fiat money derives its value from a bubble (see, e.g., Samuelson 1958; Wallace 1980; Kiyotaki and Wright 1989; and Dow and Gorton 1993). More generally, this wedge term reflects people's willingness to forgo real resources in order to hold government securities for their liquidity services. This part of the FTPL equation, then, can be viewed as the present value of expected real liquidity demand for government securities.

Equation (2) can be restated by noting that *primary surpluses* = − *primary deficits* and rearranging terms so that the following equation emerges:

$$
(3) \quad \underbrace{D_t + P_t E_t[PV(\textit{Primary Deficits})]}_{\text{Expected Future Supply of } D_t} = \underbrace{P_t E_t[PV(\textit{Transaction Services Flows})]}_{\substack{\text{Expected Future Liquidity} \\ \text{Demand for } D_t}}.
$$

The left-hand side of (3) is the expected future supply of government debt stated in nominal terms. The right-hand side is the expected future liquidity demand for government debt also stated in nominal terms. This equation can be rearranged to isolate the price level:

$$
(4) \quad P_t = \frac{D_t + P_t E_t[PV(\textit{Primary Deficits})]}{E_t[PV(\textit{Transaction Service Flows})]} = \frac{E_t(\textit{Future Nominal Supply of } D_t)}{E_t(\textit{Future Real Liquidity Demand for } D_t)}.
$$

The price level in equation (4) is equal to the ratio of the expected nominal supply of government debt to the real liquidity demand for it. This understanding is like the standard monetary view of the price level as being determined by the difference between the nominal supply of money and real money demand.

---

[7]Brunnermeier et al. (2020a, 2020b) see the bubble term arising, in part, from the insurance role provided by Treasury securities for idiosyncratic risk of households. They show that this feature gives rise to the transversality condition not eliminating the terminal value in the limit of an iterated government budget constraint. This is the bubble.

Now take first differences of the natural log of (4) to restate it in terms of inflation and denote the natural log variables in lower case letters:

$$(5) \quad \pi_t = \frac{\Delta E_t(\text{future nominal}}{\text{supply of } d_t)} - \frac{\Delta E_t(\text{future real liquidity}}{\text{demand for } d_t)}.$$

Equation (5) says the current inflation rate is the difference between changes in the expected supply of government securities minus the expected real liquidity demand for them. Stated differently, equation (5) reveals that a quantity-theoretic relationship determines inflation. It is a more expansive quantity-theoretic view than the standard one since it includes Treasury and Fed liabilities.

This new quantity theory can help us understand why the medium- to long-run inflation expectations shown in Figure 2 remain anchored. Specifically, equation (5) implies that even though the U.S. government is expected to run primary deficits over the next few decades, the expected real liquidity demand for government securities is expected to grow at a similar pace. This understanding may be why forecasters and markets still see no signs of fiscal dominance.

Evidence for the New Quantity Theory

The new quantity theory, as noted above, explains the well-anchored inflation forecasts seen in Figure 2 by pointing to an offsetting growth in real liquidity demand for government securities. While there is no Congressional Budget Office forecast for such demand, there is other evidence that lends support to this interpretation, including safe asset demand, enhanced elasticity of the global dollar financial system, and a lock-in effect.

Safe Asset Demand

As noted earlier, Treasury securities and Federal Reserve liabilities are viewed as safe assets. That means they are highly liquid debt instruments expected to preserve their nominal value in adverse systemic events. Starting in the 1990s, a global shortage of safe assets began to emerge and became visible in the secular decline of safe asset interest rates, including yields on Treasury securities (Caballero et al. 2017).

This safe asset shortage arose for reasons that still persist today. First, globalization spurred rapid economic growth in emerging markets but did not increase their ability to proportionally create safe stores of value. Consequently, these countries turned to advanced economies to supply safe assets (Gourinchas and Rey 2007; Mendoza et al. 2009). Second, many parts of the world are aging, which increases the saving rate (Auclert et al. 2021) and shifts portfolios away from risker assets to safer ones (Kopecky and Taylor 2020). Both increase the demand for safe assets. Third, growing income inequality may also increase safe asset demand since higher-income households typically have a higher saving rate (Mian et al. 2021). Fourth, financial crises starting with the emerging markets in the 1990s and continuing through the Great Recession of 2007–2009, the eurozone crisis of 2010–2014, the mini recession of 2015–2016, and the pandemic of 2020 have increased risk aversion and, thereby, further raise demand for safe assets (Malmendier and Nagel 2011; Kozlowski et al. 2019). Finally, a number of financial innovations have increased the demand for safe assets, especially treasury securities. They include new regulatory requirements coming out of the Dodd-Frank Act and Basel III, the emergence of a new class of money funds called "stablecoins," and the Fed's new standing and Foreign and International Monetary Authority (FIMA) repo facilities.

It might be tempting to conclude the rapid run-up in public debt during the pandemic solved the safe asset shortage. Safe asset yields, however, remain well below their prepandemic levels almost two years after the pandemic started. This is not what satiated safe asset demand looks like and suggests the shortage will continue to be a source of real demand for U.S. government securities. Evidence from the U.S. financial accounts suggest this is the case as foreign holdings of Treasury securities and other government-backed U.S. assets continued to grow in 2021.

Enhanced Elasticity of the Global Dollar Financial System

U.S. government securities are not the only dollar-denominated assets sought after by investors. Privately provided assets like bank deposits, money market funds, commercial paper, and stablecoins also are viewed, in varying degrees, as relatively safe dollar-denominated assets. Most of these assets are liabilities issued by U.S. firms, but some are from non-U.S. firms as well. Together they make up the global dollar financial system whose size reached $75.6 trillion in 2021Q2 according to the Bank for International Settlement estimates.

The ability of this global dollar financial system to respond to dollar-demand shocks depends on the elasticity of the global banking system to provide dollars during panics. They are the first line of defense for firms and households, but their ability to issue new dollar liabilities becomes impaired during panics. This is especially true for non-U.S. banks that may have currency mismatchs on their balance sheets. The second line of the defense is the Fed, which can provide unlimited dollars to the global banking system through its emergency liquidity facilities. The Fed's response in crises, then, ultimately determines the elasticity of the global banking system and, in turn, the global dollar financial system (Aldasoro et al. 2020).

The question, then, for investors holding dollar-denominated assets is how elastic will the Federal Reserve make the global dollar financial system. The more elastic the system, the safer are the dollar-denominated assets and, as a result, the greater the demand for them.

During the global financial crisis of 2007–2009 and the 2020 Covid-19 pandemic, the Fed demonstrated very clearly it was going to enhance the elasticity of the global dollar financial system. It did so by opening the money market fund, commercial paper, and primary dealer facilities as well as dollar swap lines to 14 countries. It also created the FIMA repo facility and started two new corporate bond facilities. These Fed interventions were very successful in stabilizing the global dollar financial system and preventing wider financial market contagion (Aldasoro et al. 2020; Bahaj and Reis, 2020a, 2020b). These interventions, then, created expectations of enhanced elasticity in the global dollar financial system and, as a result, increased demand for dollar-denominated assets including government securities.[8] Ironically, then, the Fed, in stabilizing global dollar

---

[8]Some observers, however, view these enhanced expectations of elasticity in a less favorable light. They see this development creating a moral hazard problem (Bevilacqua et al. (2021). Along these lines, the increased demand for dollar-denominated assets could lead to a version of Krishnamurthy and Lustig's (2019) "global dollar cycle," where the increased use of the dollar makes the global economy more susceptible to future swings in overnight dollar markets and more reliant on Fed interventions. As a result, the cycle continues and demand for dollar-denominated assets continues to grow.

funding markets, has inadvertently increased real demand for U.S. government liabilities.

The Dollar Lock-In Effect

A final source of ongoing demand for U.S. government securities is the rise of "dollar dominance," where the reach of the dollar in the invoicing of international trade, bank funding, corporate borrowing, money markets, and central bank reserve holdings far exceeds any other currency (Gopinath 2019). This development has created a lock-in effect among international investors, where they demand a relatively large amount of dollar-denominated assets since there are no other safe assets available on the same scale provided by the global dollar system.

He et al. (2016) show that in such a setting, a "nowhere else to go" equilibrium can emerge where investors coordinate on the largest provider of assets that is perceived to be relatively safe. This provides demand for the securities of the largest provider of debt and entrenches it as the main provider of safe assets. Gopinath and Stein (2021) similarly show that a single dominant currency equilibrium can emerge under certain circumstances, such as the first-mover advantage the dollar had over the euro. Both theoretical results point to a lock-in effect demand for dollar-denominated assets that is likely to grow over time and make it increasingly hard for another currency system to compete. This lock-in effect, in short, should provide future growth in real demand for U.S. government securities.

Figure 3 provides evidence consistent with lock-in demand for dollar-denominated assets. The top-left chart shows U.S. financial liabilities to the rest of the world. These are the claims the rest of the world has on the U.S. financial system and are largely comprised of liquid fixed-income securities, though corporate equities holdings have recently grown. Altogether, foreigners are holding $31.26 trillion of U.S.-issued, dollar-denominated assets as of 2021Q2. As seen in the top-right chart, this is almost double the size of the next largest provider of safe assets to the world, the eurozone.

This chasm is even greater for credit creation of dollar-denominated assets outside of the United States. The bottom-left chart shows that growth in bank loans and debt securities denominated in dollars and issued outside the United States has dramatically outpaced the

FIGURE 3

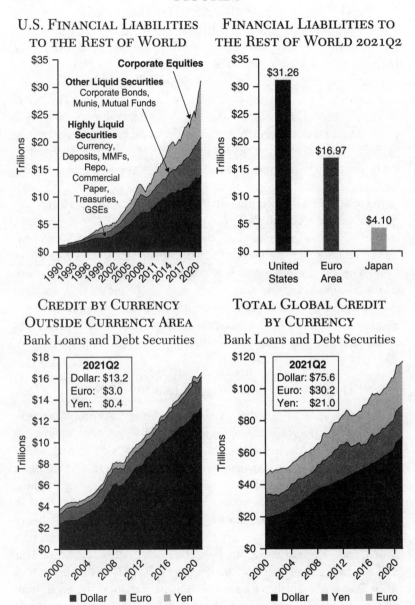

U.S. FINANCIAL LIABILITIES TO THE REST OF WORLD

Corporate Equities

Other Liquid Securities
Corporate Bonds, Munis, Mutual Funds

Highly Liquid Securities
Currency, Deposits, MMFs, Repo, Commercial Paper, Treasuries, GSEs

Trillions

FINANCIAL LIABILITIES TO THE REST OF WORLD 2021Q2

Trillions

$31.26 — United States
$16.97 — Euro Area
$4.10 — Japan

CREDIT BY CURRENCY OUTSIDE CURRENCY AREA
Bank Loans and Debt Securities

2021Q2
Dollar: $13.2
Euro: $3.0
Yen: $0.4

Trillions

TOTAL GLOBAL CREDIT BY CURRENCY
Bank Loans and Debt Securities

2021Q2
Dollar: $75.6
Euro: $30.2
Yen: $21.0

Trillions

■ Dollar ■ Euro ▨ Yen

■ Dollar ■ Yen ▨ Euro

SOURCES: U.S. Financial Accounts; Euro Area Statistics; Japan Ministry of Finance; Bank for International Settlements Global Liquidity Indicators; and author's calculations.

growth of euro-denominated credit outside the eurozone. Specifically, between 2000Q1 and 2021Q2, dollar credit outside the United States grew from $2.3 trillion to $13.2 trillion while euro credit outside the eurozone only grew from $0.9 to $3.0 trillion. So, both the rate of increase and the absolute level of credit creation by currency is being dominated by the global dollar system.

This pattern is further confirmed when looking at total global credit creation. The bottom-right chart shows total credit creation in bank loans and debt security in the world by currency. Here too, the global dollar system completely dominates the other currencies in both the rate of increase and the absolute level of credit creation. Dollar-denominated credit reached $75.6 trillion in 2021Q2 compared to $30.2 trillion for the euro-denominated credit and $21.0 trillion for yen-denominated credit.

Figure 3 reveals, then, that scale of the global dollar system far exceeds its closest rivals and the chasm between them is growing over time. This outcome is consistent with a dollar lock-in effect where investor demand for safe assets converges on the global dollar system and increasingly relies on it to supply safe assets. This indicates another source of strong real demand for U.S. government debt going forward.

Policy Implications of the New Quantity Theory

This new quantity theory, as outlined above, interprets the well-anchored inflation forecasts seen in Figure 2, as well as the ongoing low Treasury yields, being the result of strong growth in real liquidity demand for U.S. government securities offsetting the rapid increase in public debt. There are several important policy implications that follow from this understanding.

First, as noted by Andolfatto (2021b), the new quantity theory implies that had there been no run-up in public debt over the past two decades, inflation would have been dramatically lower. This understanding finds support in Beckworth (2021), who shows that since Treasury securities function as a form of money, the accommodating fiscal policy of the past two decades can be seen as providing an offset to a series of money demand shocks during this time that would have otherwise weakened aggregate demand growth and, in turn, dragged down real economic growth.

Second, the three sources of demand for U.S. government securities—safe asset demand, enhanced elasticity of the global dollar financial system, and the lock-in effect—are likely to persist for the foreseeable future and create disinflationary pressures on the other side of the pandemic. If so, it means a regime of monetary dominance will continue, but one where the Federal Reserve struggles to hit its inflation target as it did before the pandemic.

Third, the new quantity theory implies there is a new calculus for fiscal dominance. One cannot simply look at the stock of national debt and draw conclusions about the prospects for fiscal dominance. A high debt-to-GDP ratio alongside a stable inflation rate may reflect an elevated real demand for Treasury securities (Andolfatto 2021a). Caution, then, should be exercised in interpreting reduced-form measures of the national debt.

Finally, this ongoing real demand for U.S. government securities implies an ongoing stream of seigniorage revenue that needs to be managed wisely. So far, these seigniorage flows have allowed Congress to spend and cut taxes without worrying much about the consequences. This "exorbitant privilege" or transfer of real resources from the world to the United States may eventually fade, and it is difficult to predict when such a tipping point would be reached. It behooves the U.S. government, therefore, to start planning for this day. One policy response would be to set up a U.S. sovereign wealth fund to manage some portion of this exorbitant privilege. It would be similar in spirit to the Norwegian sovereign wealth fund that manages a portion of the country's petroleum revenues.

Conclusion

The U.S. national debt is now near 100 percent of GDP and is expected to double that by 2050, according to the Congressional Budget Office. This outlook has some observers worried that a regime of fiscal dominance may soon emerge, making monetary policy subservient to fiscal policy. This article has shown an alternative interpretation of these facts: the elevated debt-to-GDP alongside well-anchored inflation expectations reflects an elevated real demand for government securities. This understanding falls out of the fiscal theory of the price level with a bubble and is called the new quantity theory.

References

Aldasoro, I.; Ehlers, T.; McGuire, P.; and Peter, G. Von (2020) "Global Banks' Dollar Funding Needs and Central Bank Swap Lines." *BIS Bulletin* No 27.

Andolfatto, D. (2021a) "Is It Time for Some Unpleasant Monetarist Arithmetic?" *St. Louis Federal Reserve Bank Review* (Third Quarter): 315–32.

_____ (2021b) "EEA-ESEM Panel: Macroeconomic Consequences of the Pandemic." *Macro Mania blog* (September 29).

Aruoba, B. (2016) "Term Structures of Inflation Expectations and Real Interest Rates." Federal Reserve Bank of Philadelphia Working Paper No. 16-09/R.

Auclert, A.; Malmberg, H.; Martenet, F.; and Rognlie, M. (2021) "Demographics, Wealth, and Global Imbalances in the Twenty-First Century." NBER Working Paper No. 29161 (August).

Bahaj, S., and Reis, R. (2020a) "Central Bank Swap Lines during the Covid-19 Pandemic." *Covid Economics* 2 (April 8): 1–12.

_____ (2020b) "Central Bank Swap Lines: Evidence on the Effects of the Lender of Last Resort." Available at https://personal.lse.ac.uk/reisr/papers/99-cbswaps.pdf.

Beckworth, D. (2021) "The Safe Asset Shortage and the Low Inflation of 2010–2019: A Money Demand View." SSRN Working Paper.

Bevilacqua, M.; Brandl-Cheng, L.; Danielsson, J.; Ergun, L. M.; Uthemann, A.; and Zigrand, J. P. (2021) "The Calming of Short-Term Market Fears and Its Long-Term Consequences: The Central Banks' Dilemma." SSRN Working Paper.

Berenstein, A., and Waller, C. (2018) "Liquidity Premiums on Government Debt and the Fiscal Theory of the Price Level." *Journal of Economic Dynamics and Control* 89: 173–82.

Bordo, M. D., and Levy, M. (2020) "Do Enlarged Fiscal Deficits Cause Inflation: The Historical Record." Hoover Economics Working Paper No.20124.

Brunnermeier, M.; Merkel, S.; and Sannikov, Y. (2020a) "The Fiscal Theory of the Price Level with a Bubble." NBER Working Paper No. 27116.

_____ (2020b) "Debt as Safe Asset: Mining the Bubble." Princeton Department of Economics Working Paper.

Caballero, R.; Farhi, E.; and Gourinchas, P. O. (2017) "The Safe Assets Shortage Conundrum." *Journal of Economic Perspectives* 31 (3): 29–46.

Christiano, L., and Fitzgerald, T. (2000) "Understanding the Fiscal Theory of the Price Level." *Cleveland Federal Reserve Bank Economic Review* 36 (2): 1–38.

Cochrane, J. (2021) *The Fiscal Theory of the Price Level*. An online book at www.johnhcochrane.com/research-all/the-fiscal-theory -of-the-price-level-1.

D'Amico, S.; Kim, D.; and Wei, M. (2018) "Tips from TIPS: The Informational Content of Treasury Inflation-Protected Security Prices." *Journal of Financial and Quantitative Analysis* 53 (1): 395–436.

Dorn, J. A. (2021) "Fiscal Dominance and Fed Complacency." *Alt-M Blog* (April 8).

Dow, J., and Gorton, G. (1993) "Security Market Returns and the Social Discount Rate: A Note on Welfare in the Overlapping Generations Model." *Economic Letters* 44: 23–26.

Du, W. X.; Im, J.; and Schreger, J. (2018) "The U.S. Treasury Premium." *Journal of International Economics* 112: 167–81.

FOMC (2020) "Statement on Longer-Run Goals and Monetary Policy Strategy." Available at www.federalreserve.gov/monetarypolicy /review-of-monetary-policy-strategy-tools-and-communications -statement-on-longer-run-goals-monetary-policy-strategy.htm.

Gopinath, G. (2019) "Dollar Dominance in Trade and Finance." In J. Cochrane, J. Taylor, and K. Palermo (eds.), *Currencies, Capital, and Central Bank Balances*, 53–81. Stanford, Calif.: Hoover Institution Press.

Gopinath, G., and Stein, J. C. (2021) "Banking, Trade and the Making of a Dominant Currency." *Quarterly Journal of Economics* 136 (2): 783–830.

Gourinchas, P., and Rey, H. (2007) "From World Banker to World Venture Capitalist: U.S. External Adjustment and the Exorbitant Privilege." In R. Clarida (ed.), *G7 Current Account Imbalances: Sustainability and Adjustment*. Chicago: University of Chicago Press.

Greenwood, R.; Hanson, S.; and Stein, J. C. (2015) "A Comparative-Advantage Approach to Government Debt Maturity." *Journal of Finance* 70 (4): 1683–722.

Haubrich, J.; Pennacchi, G.; and Ritchken, P. (2011) "Inflation Expectations, Real Rates, and Risk Premia: Evidence from Inflation Swaps." Federal Reserve Bank of Cleveland, Working Paper.

He, Z.; Krishnamurthy, A.; and Milbradt, K. (2016) "What Makes U.S. Government Bonds Safe Assets?" *American Economic Review* 106 (5): 519–23.

Jiang, Z.; Lustig, H.; Van Nieuwerburgh, S.; and Xiaolan, M. (2021) "The U.S. Public Debt Valuation Puzzle." NBER Working Paper No. 26583.

Kiyotaki, N., and Wright, R. (1989) "On Money as a Medium of Exchange." *Journal of Political Economy* 84: 757–75.

Kopecky, J., and Taylor, A. (2020) "The Murder-Suicide of the Rentier: Population Aging and the Risk Premium." NBER Working Paper No. 26943.

Kozlowsk, J.; Veldkamp, L.; and Venkateswaran, V. (2019) "The Tail That Keeps the Riskless Rate Low." *NBER Macroeconomics Annual 2018*, 33: 253–83.

Krishnamurthy, A., and Lustig, H. (2019) "Mind the Gap in Sovereign Debt Markets: The U.S. Treasury Basis and the Dollar Risk Factor." Paper presented at the Kansas City Federal Reserve's Jackson Hole Symposium. Available at www.kansas cityfed.org/documents/6963/Krishnamurthy_JH2019.pdf.

Krishnamurthy, A., and Vissing-Jorgensen, A. (2012) "The Aggregate Demand for Treasury Debt." *Journal of Political Economy* 120 (2): 233–67.

_____ (2015) "The Impact of Treasury Supply on Financial Sector Lending and Stability." *Journal of Financial Economics* 118 (3): 571–600.

Leeper, E. M. (2010) "Monetary Science, Fiscal Alchemy." *Economic Policy Symposium Proceedings*, Jackson Hole, Federal Reserve Bank of Kansas City, 361–434. Available at https://ideas.repec.org/a/fip/fedkpr/y2010p361-434.html.

Malmendier, U., and Nagel, S. (2011) "Depression Babies: Do Macroeconomic Experiences Affect Risk Taking?" *Quarterly Journal of Economics* 126 (1): 373–416.

Mendoza, E.; Quadrini, V.; Rios-Rul, J. V. (2009) "Financial Integration, Financial Development, and Global Imbalances." *Journal of Political Economy* 117 (3): 371–416.

Mian, A.; Straub, L.; and Sufi, A. (2021) "What Explains the Decline in R°? Rising Inequality versus Demographic Shifts." Paper presented at the Kansas City Federal Reserve's Economic Symposium, Jackson Hole.

Nagel, S. (2016) "The Liquidity Premium of Near-Money Assets." *Quarterly Journal of Economics* 131 (4): 1927–71.

Rees, D., and Rungcharoenkitkul, P. (2021) "Bottlenecks: Causes and Macroeconomics Implications." *BIS Bulletin* No. 48.

Reis, R. (2021) "The Constraint on Public Debt When r < g But g < m." BIS Working Paper No. 939.

Samuelson, P. (1958) "An Exact Consumption-Loan Model of Interest with or without the Social Contrivance of Money." *Journal of Political Economy* 66: 467–82.

Sargent, T. J., and Wallace, N. (1981) "Some Unpleasant Monetarist Arithmetic." *Federal Reserve Bank of Minneapolis Quarterly Review* 5 (3): 1–15.

Sims, C. (2013) "Paper Money." *American Economic Review* 103 (2): 563–84.

Wallace, N. (1980) "The Overlapping Generations Model of Fiat Money." In J. Karken and N. Wallace (eds), 49–82. *Models of Monetary Economics*. Federal Reserve Bank of Minneapolis.

Waller, C. (2021) "Treasury–Federal Reserve Cooperation and the Importance of Central Bank Independence." Speech delivered to the Peterson Institute for International Economics (March 29).

PART 3

AN EXPANDED FED MANDATE?

12
CENTRAL BANKS:
INDEPENDENT OR ALMIGHTY?
Otmar Issing

Today most major central banks are endowed with the status of independence. Historically, this was anything but the norm. There are important reasons why central banks were not independent.

The Long Journey to Independence

First, and above all, the independence of the central bank seems to contradict core principles of democracy. A critic in Germany questioned: "All power within the state comes from the people—except that of the Deutsche Bundesbank?" (Hoffmann 1989: 53). Should competence for such an important task as setting interest rates for the whole economy be given to unelected technocrats? (Tucker 2018).

Second, for a long time most economists were not in favor of independence for the central bank (for the United States, see Johnson 1970). It is interesting to note that this position was taken by two camps that otherwise had little in common. On the one hand, there were economists like Tobin who argued that the most efficient coordination between monetary and fiscal policy could be achieved by having the central bank act as part of the government. On the other side of the spectrum was the group of liberal—in the European sense—economists like Milton Friedman and Karl Brunner.

Otmar Issing is President of the Center for Financial Studies at Goethe University, Frankfurt, and former Chief Economist at the European Central Bank.

They argued, in the tradition of Herbert Simons, that (discretionary) monetary policy decisions should not be handed over to central bankers who, in many cases, had demonstrated severe incompetence. Overall, for a long time central bank independence was not treated as a major issue: there was hardly any relevant international discussion.

Against this background, it seems surprising that around 1990, so many countries decided to endow their central banks with the status of independence (Masciandaro and Romelli 2015). Two reasons for this change of mind can be identified (Issing 2018). First, the "Great Inflation" in the United States in the 1970s triggered, after a significant time lag, a number of studies explaining the institutional background of this development. In the end, innumerable publications have delivered empirical evidence: there is a strong negative correlation between the degree of central bank independence and inflation.

Second, this consensus emerged at a time when Europeans were preparing the introduction of a common currency and discussing the statute of the future European central bank. Here the example of the Deutsche Bundesbank, as the only truly independent central bank in Europe, played an important if not decisive role. The D-Mark, alongside the Swiss franc, had been the most stable currency in the world and Germany had also escaped the "Great Inflation" (Issing 2005). It is no wonder that the German government insisted on the status of independence for the future European central bank. All other countries aiming to participate in the European Monetary Union had to accept this position—more or less reluctantly—at a time when their own national central banks were not independent.[1]

A German expert of constitutional law delivered the following argument for endowing—in this case the Bundesbank—with the status of independence: "The voluntary waiver of power by the political leadership in favour of monetary policy-makers is limited, authorized by the constitution and revocable at any time by the ordinary legislation" (Stern 1980).

---

[1] See Issing (2008: 59) for a statement reflecting the deep reservation against central bank independence from then-French President Francois Mitterand shortly after he signed the Maastricht Treaty, in which independence for the future European central bank is enshrined.

In the case that independence is grounded in the constitution, such a change is more difficult to achieve (Tucker 2018). The European Central Bank's independence is even enshrined in an international treaty that can only be changed by a unanimous decision by all member states.

The United Kingdom was a latecomer in this respect, waiting until May 1997 to give its central bank the status of (somewhat limited) independence. Chancellor Gordon Brown's statement encapsulates the change of mind of politicians in many countries:

> The previous arrangements for monetary policy were too short-termist, encouraging short but unstable booms and higher inflation, followed inevitably by recession. This is why we promised in our election manifesto to . . . reform the Bank of England to ensure that decisionmaking on monetary policy is more effective, open, accountable and free from short-term political manipulation [Brown 1997].

The consensus that had emerged can be summarized as follows: central bank independence in a democracy can be constitutionally legalized; it is a prerequisite for a stable currency; and it has to be restricted to a clear and limited mandate.

The Process of Overburdening

In the decade following the "victory" of independence, the world enjoyed the period of the Great Moderation. Inflation came down from rather high levels and remained stable.

Growth and employment were at least satisfactory, while variability of output substantially declined. Was this "Goldilocks economy" just the result of luck, due to a decline in exogenous shocks, or did it stem from improved macro policies, especially monetary policy? The jury is still out. In any case, this period considerably enhanced the reputation of central banks and their leaders (Issing 2017a). It was almost unavoidable that, as a consequence, expectations regarding the ability of central banks to control the economy reached an unprecedented and unsustainable peak. This prestige was further heightened during the financial crisis, when central banks were perceived as having saved the world from a repeat of the Great Depression of the 1930s.

The *Annual Report* of the Bank for International Settlements (BIS 2016: 22) presents a concise assessment:

> [T]he extraordinary burden placed on central banking since the crisis is generating growing strains. During the Great Moderation, markets and the public at large came to see central banks as all-powerful. Post-crisis, they have come to expect the central bank to manage the economy, restore full employment, ensure strong growth, preserve price stability, and foolproof the financial system. But in fact, this is a tall order on which the central bank alone cannot deliver. The extraordinary measures taken to stimulate the global economy have sometimes tested the boundaries of the institution. As a consequence, risks to its reputation, perceived legitimacy and independence have been rising.

Disappointment with "politics" in general and a loss of trust in politicians have also contributed to heightened public expectations of central banks.

Central banks were not known for warning against such elevated expectations. Indeed, central bankers seemed to rather enjoy this high status. On top of this already fragile position came new obligations. Central banks have been made responsible for macro- and microprudential policies. However, there can be situations in which a conflict may arise with the primary objective of maintaining price stability (and, in case of a dual mandate, high employment).

The main challenge for central banks stems from the responsibility for financial stability. The financial crisis triggered an intense discussion over the extent to which central banks should be made directly responsible for financial stability and how they should deliver on this goal. A consensus has emerged that preserving price stability is not enough. The Great Moderation demonstrated that huge risks to financial stability can develop during times of low inflation. Following Minsky, a stable environment might even foster the build-up of financial fragilities that might end in a collapse of the whole system.

Is there a tradeoff between price stability and financial stability? (Issing 2003). This is the key question provoked by the above consensus. While a short-term conflict may arise, there is no reason to sacrifice price stability over the medium to long term to preserve financial stability. However, a central bank will lose its reputation if it is perceived to have underestimated or even neglected the threat of financial instability. This is true almost regardless of whether or not the central bank has an official or legal mandate for financial stability.

Would it not be appropriate to explicitly include financial stability in the mandate of the central bank? Before addressing this problem, one should ask what monetary policy can achieve to preserve financial stability. One observation is obvious: the inflation targeting approach is unable to meet this challenge.

According to one approach, macroprudential policy should be the main tool for preserving financial stability, and financial stability should become an "explicit objective of monetary policy to be used when macroprudential policies fail as an instrument of last resort" (Smets 2013: 151–52).

However, this approach could blur the ranking of the central bank's objectives. And relying on macroprudential policies in the first place might bring monetary policy into an untenable position. If and when macroprudential policies fail in a boom phase, it might be too late for an appropriate reaction by monetary policy. The challenge might be close to "pricking the bubble," which would cause turmoil in financial markets, cause major economic costs, and have a negative impact on the reputation of the central bank (Issing 2017b).

The ECB's monetary policy strategy presents a much more promising approach. Concerns about financial stability are an endogenous element of the ECB's monetary policy aimed at maintaining price stability.

Further Self-Imposed Overburdening

As if overburdening from the sources explained above and the ensuing risk for their reputation were not enough, central banks continue to assume further responsibilities. This will be shown for the Fed and the ECB.

Unavoidably, monetary policy has an impact on the distribution of income and wealth. These implicit consequences are a clear departure from a concept in which a central bank takes decisions targeted at specific sectors or groups in society—for example, by giving credit at special conditions to students, specific sectors, or companies. Such preferential actions are a highly political act that must be reserved to policymakers who are ultimately responsible to their voters.

In its communication on the new strategy, the Fed announced that it will conduct its monetary policy in a way that will have important distributional effects. In his speech at the annual Jackson Hole symposium in 2020, Fed Chairman Jerome Powell emphasized that, as America's long prepandemic economic expansion—and, one might add, expansionary Fed policy—continued, "The gains began to be shared more widely across society. The Black and Hispanic unemployment rates reached record lows, and the differentials between these rates and the white unemployment rate narrowed to their lowest levels on record" (Powell 2020).

To assume such a responsibility raises a number of issues:

- Can the process of the economy running hot always be stopped before inflation gets out of control?
- How should a conflict with the goal of price stability be resolved?
- And above all: once the Fed has to tighten monetary policy, those groups mentioned will be the first to lose their jobs. This was an unavoidable effect in the past when monetary policy in the end triggered a recession.

However, the explicit acceptance of responsibility for distribution will place an additional pressure on the central bank. In any case, it will be exposed to a political debate that will go beyond what we have experienced up to now—and the central bank's independence will come under strong attack.

In the summer of 2021, the European Central Bank published the result of its strategy review. A major change is the inclusion of challenges stemming from climate change (Issing 2021):

> Within its mandate, the Governing Council is committed to ensuring that the Eurosystem fully takes into account, in line with the European Union's climate goals and objectives, the implications of climate change and the carbon transition for monetary policy and central banking [ECB 2021].

Accordingly, the council has published an ambitious action plan to deliver on this commitment. The reference to the mandate is quasi-obligatory and specified by the profound implications of climate change for price stability.

Climate change, and corresponding government policies in response to it, can have powerful effects on economic development. These consequences are reflected in all kinds of variables—e.g., growth, inflation, and employment—that will in turn affect forecasts, and in this way influence monetary policy decisions. Identifying the impact of climate change brings a major challenge in terms of adopting existing models and developing new ones. Research in this field and the intention to develop relevant statistical data and indicators to assess factors such as the carbon footprint of financial institutions, alongside the work on modeling, will require huge efforts. Even at a central bank, resources are not unlimited, and existing competences are probably far away from the scientific fields, which are at the core of projecting and addressing climate change, and of assessing complete carbon footprints of individual private or public actors.

Including aspects of climate change in the economic as well as monetary and financial analyses—plus creating an integrated approach—is a complex task, and it remains open to what extent this might affect monetary policy decisions. By contrast, indirect implications of climate change's direct consequences follow from the adaption of the design of its monetary policy operational framework in relation to disclosures, risk assessment, corporate sector asset purchases, and the collateral framework.

Here is not the place to go into details. The basic underlying idea is to form an in-house judgment on the value of assets that incorporates climate risks and regulatory requirements (disclosure). The "climate-policy-adjusted" price (or risk) will then be the basis for actions by the ECB, from eligibility as collateral to corporate-sector asset purchases.

To call this a tremendous challenge is still a euphemism. Financial markets will price in problems for companies stemming from factors such as the foreseeable end of burning coal—at least in some countries or regions. How should the central bank know better than markets? This is just a very simple example. Assessing climate risks implied in complex production processes in the chemical or other industries (with value chains across the world, including many countries with no or almost no transparency) and finding the correct price for corresponding assets must also take into account potential reactions to government policies. And what about the risk that the central bank might overstate this risk and create a kind of "green bubble"?

On the other hand, there is hardly any likelihood of preventing companies from "cheating" by collecting cheap(er) money through the issue of bonds with the label "green" and redirecting these funds to the production of "brown" products. The ECB will also have to explain how such a policy will be compatible with the principle of market neutrality, which is set out in the Maastricht Treaty.

Climate change is probably the biggest challenge of our time. Central banks cannot ignore this and must not be seen as being blind to these risks. At the same time, confronting climate change is above all the responsibility of governments that are accountable to their parliaments and ultimately to their voters. Central banks are not made independent so that they can go beyond their mandate or actively correct decisions by parliaments. And with their climate-oriented actions, they should not deliver arguments that stronger measures by governments are unnecessary. If they raise expectations beyond their capabilities in this field, they will undermine their reputation and lose support for their independence, which in the end is indispensable for maintaining price stability.

Besides analytical problems, the ECB justifies its self-declared role in this field with the argument that climate change can have implications for price stability. However, does this imply the ECB, assuming inflation is at target, would argue against significant gradual future increases of carbon taxes that would push trend inflation above 2 percent? According to the new strategy, the ECB would have to tighten monetary policy in response to such improved climate policies. It is stunning that the ECB did not address this core question, including whether welfare-improving carbon taxes should be excluded from the price index it is targeting. This lack of clarity and transparency does not bode well. It allows for a lot of discretion that risks increasing uncertainty and interference of unelected central bankers in democratic decisions by parliaments.

The biggest threat to the ECB's independence comes from its self-imposed role as the guarantor of the euro area in its composition. Criticism that the ECB has transgressed its mandate began immediately after its capital markets intervention of 2010, in the course of which it purchased government bonds of countries that otherwise would have experienced substantial increases in long-term interest rates. This role was taken to the extreme by the famous "whatever it takes" announcement of ECB President Mario Draghi. ECB monetary policy decisions—above all, massive purchases of bonds in the QE program—that particularly benefited countries with a high level of debt further underline this view. The decision to support member countries is, however, a clear responsibility of governments of the euro area and not the task of the central bank.

Conclusion

Not least due to their success during the Great Moderation and in helping to prevent a depression after the collapse of financial markets in 2007–2008, central banks were already exposed to elevated expectations. What followed was an overburdening with additional competences in micro- and macroprudential supervision. In the meantime, central banks have assumed additional new responsibilities.

However, central banks are not almighty. Central bankers should instead show a sense of humility. They must clarify and announce what monetary policy can achieve—and even more importantly—what it cannot deliver. Merely de facto accepting excessive expectations or even contributing themselves to this development implies a major threat to their reputation, because disappointment over failures to meet these expectations must follow.

Even when central banks are successful in affecting issues that are not within their core mandate, polities over time will not accept that an independent central bank extends its actions into the domain that must be reserved for politicians who are accountable to parliament and ultimately the voters.

The spread of central bank independence was based on the idea of a clear and limited mandate. To turn the argument around: Who could convincingly argue that independence should be given to a central bank that invades deeply into a sphere that must be reserved for the democratic process? "Unelected power" must be limited and continuously justified by appropriate policy.

References

Bank for International Settlements (2016) *Annual Report*. Basel: BIS.

Brown, G. (1997) Speech before the House of Commons (May 20). Available at https://publications.parliament.uk/pa/cm199798/cmhansrd/vo970520/debtext/70520-06.htm.

European Central Bank (2021) "The ECB's Monetary Policy Strategy Statement." Available at https://www.ecb.europa.eu /home/search/review/html/ecb.strategyreview_monpol_strategy _statement.en.html.

Hoffmann, D. (1989) "Zur Unabhängigkeit der Deutschen Bundesbank." In E. Stein and H. Faber (eds.), *Auf einem Dritten Weg, Festschrift für H. Ridder zum siebzigsten Geburtstag.* Neuwied.

Issing, O. (2003) "Monetary and Financial Stability: Is There a Trade-off?" Bank for International Settlements (March).

_____ (2005) "Why Did the Great Inflation Not Happen in Germany?" *Federal Reserve Bank of St. Louis Review* (March/April, Part 2): 329–35.

_____ (2008) *The Birth of the Euro.* New York: Cambridge University Press.

_____ (2017a) "Central Banks: Are Their Reputation and Independence under Threat from Overburdening?" *International Finance* 20 (1): 92–99.

_____ (2017b) "Financial Stability and the ECB's Monetary Policy Strategy." ECB Legal Conference, European Central Bank, Frankfurt.

_____ (2018) "The Uncertain Future of Central Bank Independence." In S. Eijffinger and D. Masciandaro (eds.), *Hawks and Doves: Deeds and Words—Economics and Politics of Monetary Policymaking.* London: CEPR.

_____ (2021) "An Assessment of the ECB's Strategy Review." *Central Banking* (August 10).

Johnson, H. G. (1970) "Recent Developments in Monetary Theory: A Commentary." In D. R, Croome and H. G. Johnson (eds.), *Money in Britain: 1959–1969.* London: Oxford University Press.

Masciandaro, D., and Romelli, D. (2015) "Ups and Downs of Central Bank Independence from the Great Inflation to the Great Recession: Theory, Institutions and Empirics." *Financial History Review* 22 (3): 259–89.

Powell, J. H. (2020) "New Economic Challenges and the Fed's Monetary Policy Review." Speech at the Jackson Hole Conference (August 27).

Smets, F. (2013) "Financial Stability and Monetary Policy: How Closely Interlinked?" *Sveriges Riksbank Economic Review* 3: 121–60.

Stern, K. (1980) *Das Staatsrecht der Bundesrepublik Deutschland*, Band II, München.

Tucker, P. (2018) *Unelected Power*. Princeton, N.J.: Princeton University Press.

13
A CENTRAL BANK MANDATE FOR OUR TIME: THE FED'S DE FACTO FISCAL ROLE AND ITS ANTI-EQUALITY IMPACT

Karen Petrou

Even extrastimulative fiscal policy will do little to reduce near-term economic inequality given the force of countervailing Fed de facto fiscal intervention. The Fed consistently describes its dual mandate in purely monetary policy terms, but the manner in which it executed policy since 2008 has direct fiscal impact by virtue of market valuation, credit allocation, debt monetization, and even new money creation effects. There is in fact no pure monetary policy mandate for the U.S. central bank. Its express mandate demands not just maximum employment and price stability, but also moderate long-term interest rates. This express mandate comes in concert with an over-arching one governing the federal government and the Fed focused on general welfare, full employment, real income, and similar objectives. The Fed should honor its full mandate as now dictated in law and quickly reduce its anti-equality fiscal footprint. Should it fail to do so, an increasingly populist Congress will turn to confiscatory fiscal policy and an expressly political central bank.

When I finished my book, *Engine of Inequality: The Fed and the Future of Wealth in America* (June 2020), I was only able to touch on the Fed's burst of accommodative policy and market support and the parallel fiscal boost embodied in the CARES Act (March 2020).

Karen Petrou is Managing Partner at Federal Financial Analytics, Inc.

However, I did show in broad terms how monetary and fiscal policy were likely to fight each other to, at best, a standstill. Since then, this has sadly proved the case. The Fed has stayed a course that, while essential at the outset of a crisis, now prolongs U.S. economic inequality despite the trillions Congress threw to combat it. The net result is a nation that avoided macroeconomic and financial cataclysm but is now even more unequal than its record-breaking numbers demonstrated in late 2019 (Federal Reserve Board 2021a), along with slow growth and frightening financial markets. This is perhaps the most critical conundrum of our time: How could all these good intentions backed by so many trillions have had such a perverse result on the inequality that frustrates growth (Cingano 2014), increases the odds of renewed financial crisis (Paul 2020), impoverishes so many Americans, and makes the nation ever more ungovernable?

This chapter builds on my earlier discussion of the inequality bottlenecks to monetary policy transmission (Petrou 2021: chap. 6), to demonstrate how post-2008 policy has given the Federal Reserve enormous fiscal sway. This comes partially from the new money created by sovereign obligations as a result of ultralow rates and quantitative easing (QE). It also comes from how those policies combine with post-2008 bank regulation and all the recent market interventions also to give the Fed the final word on credit allocation and market valuations. QE's monetization of U.S. debt also has a direct fiscal impact as does the simple power of the Fed's market footprint to frustrate fiscal policy.

One might say that debt monetization and credit allocation are inevitable features of QE, but they are instead affirmative Fed choices with a direct fiscal impact. This is particularly problematic given the destructive social-welfare, macroeconomic, and systemic implications of persistent downward mobility. This chapter thus concludes with a discussion of how to not only understand but frame the Fed's mandate in light of its significant de facto fiscal impact.

Importantly, recognizing that monetary policy not only has a fiscal impact but often trumps fiscal efforts is not saying that a central bank should attempt directly to exercise fiscal influence in areas such as credit allocation or investment choice. Instead, it is an acknowledgment forced upon us by what the Fed and many other central banks have done in the name of their mandates and the far-reaching impact this has on output, financial-market valuation, and income and wealth distribution.

The Fed's Fiscal Footprint

My book lays out how post-2008 U.S. monetary and regulatory policy directly and significantly reduced economic equality. In response, I've often heard that monetary policy must proceed on an independent course guided by objective economic insights in fulfillment of a mandate not only described as "dual," despite the law's triple injunctions, but all too often read far too narrowly with regard to what Congress means by full employment and price stability (Petrou 2021: chap. 7).

Federal Reserve Board chairs since Ben Bernanke have all clung to this version of an above-it-all mandate, going on to say that, if their actions have adverse distributional impact, then it is up to fiscal policy to tidy up the mess. Chairman Powell has been considerably more vocal about the need for specific policies than his forebears, but he is at least as resolute that monetary policy has no income or wealth inequality impact that isn't for the better (House Financial Services Committee 2021b). However, fiscal policy cannot overcome a sharp, downward equality drag from monetary policy when monetary policy exercises so much control over interest rates, the economy, and financial markets.

There are three main reasons why anti-equality financial policy cannot be corrected by even the ultrastimulative fiscal policy seen after the great financial crisis and again after the 2020 Covid crash.

The Fed's Giant Footprint

Although the Fed has begun to taper its huge portfolio, its holdings now stand at nearly $9 trillion (about 36 percent of GDP) compared to about $800 billion prior to the 2008 crisis. It will take a very long time for the Fed to reduce the size of its giant footprint in financial markets, and when rates start to normalize, asset prices could take a sharp downturn. Interestingly, when asked on November 3, 2021, about the impact of all this QE, Chairman Powell admitted that, while theory suggests a huge portfolio allows for interest-rate control near the zero lower bound, its macroeconomic benefits remain unknown (Federal Reserve Board 2021b).

The composition of the Fed's portfolio exacerbates QE's overall market impact by targeting specific sectors. It consists of Treasury obligations and agency housing bonds. The Fed's huge holdings of Treasury obligations (more than $5 trillion) have helped lower yields and reduced taxpayer costs. However, the more the Fed monetizes federal debt via its asset purchases, the easier it is for Congress to ascribe to modern monetary theory (Kelton 2020) and grow the deficit. The Fed's Treasury holdings do not dictate how Congress chooses to spend the largesse borne of the Fed's portfolio, but fiscal policy is nonetheless directly driven by it.[1]

The Fed's more than $2 trillion of housing bonds similarly drive up demand for these obligations and thus reduce the cost of mortgage lending. This is fiscal policy because credit is allocated to a preferred sector based not on a market's dynamics, but on what the Fed chooses to do as the most important player in it.

Another example of central banks acting as agents of fiscal policy is a program initiated by the Bank for International Settlements (BIS 2021) encouraging green-bond portfolio investments. One might think such a program is outside the Fed's statutory mandate, but recall the $750 billion backstop it created in 2020 for a preferred segment of the corporate bond market for a demonstration of the Fed's now explicit fiscal role in action (Federal Reserve Board 2020).

The Fed's 2020 entry into the corporate bond market was also an expansive reading of the Fed's charter. As recently as 2016, Janet Yellen, then Fed chair, suggested the U.S. central bank hold corporate obligations, but she later indicated that doing so was outside its statutory mandate (Harrison 2016). More than five years on, the Fed dual mandate is no impediment to direct market intervention even though the central bank continues to cling to public protestations about how limited its mandate is when it comes to anything it decides not to do. A case in point: the Fed set up a huge backstop even for junk corporate exchange-traded funds at the same time it refused to support state and local government debt without direct congressional direction and, even when it got that, the Fed backed that sector in far smaller amounts than many members of Congress believed they had required (House Financial Services Committee 2021a).

---

[1]See, for example, Davidson and Weaver (2021) for many recent statements from the administration and Congress that huge deficits are unlikely to have adverse inflationary or growth impact because low rates make it affordable.

The Nature of Money

As a new BIS study convincingly demonstrates, rates at or near zero in inflation-adjusted terms also blur the distinction between what we used to think of as the money supplied by a central bank—bank reserves—with the money now minted by finance ministers such as the U.S. Treasury Department through the bonds floated to fund federal operations (Hofmann et al. 2021). When government-issued bonds are used as money by global markets—and Treasury bonds are now money in every sense of the word—the difference between central banking and sovereign obligations ceases to be a question for public debate; it's a fact of life.

Fiscal Policy's Smaller Footprint

The third reason monetary policy must be held accountable for inequality instead of expecting fiscal policy to offset its impact is that any fiscal policy taxpayers are likely to endorse will surely be insufficient in the face of all the market forces dictated by the changing nature of money, Fed's own holdings, ultralow rates, and continuing interventions and even bailouts.

In simple terms, the two most important forces determining economic equality are the extent to which low- and moderate-income households see appreciable wage gains or government transfer payments and whether wealth grows from accumulated savings and home ownership or from financial market investment. Fiscal policy in part determines take-home pay, transfer payments, and direct federal subsidies for housing and other income or wealth generators and thus has a significant role firing up U.S. output. However, other than the direct impact of near-term changes to tax law, fiscal policy takes time to take hold. In contrast, the Fed now overwhelms fiscal policy's long-term impact by driving much, if not all, of what the private sector does every day with every dollar. The Fed's hand is now not only the heaviest in the market but also the one with the greatest power over the short-term decisions that lay the foundation of the longer-term investment and growth fiscal policy may seek to foster.

In the manufacturing-based economy that once defined the United States, the Fed did not need to directly support financial markets. That is because financial markets supported long-term capital formation, which operated in concert with monetary policy delivered through traditional bank channels via positive real interest rates. Today, in the U.S. financialized and service economy, wealth comes from private equity, venture capital, and speculative investments (e.g., bitcoin) focused on short-term or even instantaneous return. The long-term, stable, low-risk investments on which conservative investors counted have evaporated as Fed-driven rates plummet and investors go for the quick buck because there isn't a long-term one to better it.

One of the most important insights in Thomas Piketty's paradigm-busting book, *Capital in the Twenty-First Century*, demonstrates that inequality is cumulative: the richer you are, the richer you get, and the poorer you are, the poorer you get—unless or until something breaks the cycle (Piketty 2014: 704). Sometimes the engine-buster is someone who breaks loose via an invention, a lottery, or a similar fluke and sometimes it's a catastrophic event such as war or devastating financial crisis. Mostly, though, the engine of inequality either reverses or revs up due to policy intervention.

Recent U.S. history demonstrates the negative feedback loop between fiscal and monetary policy, although the net impact of the two depend on applicable distributional and policy factors. In the 1930s, a notorious Fed policy mistake short-circuited the New Deal (Shlaes 2007). It occurred again after the 2007–2009 great financial crisis. The Obama administration enacted then-unprecedented fiscal stimulus, but the Fed kept its ultra-accommodative policies and financial-market bulwarks in place long after the crisis, leading to the weakest economic recovery since the Second World War (Morath 2016) and a stunning spike in both income and wealth inequality (Petrou 2021: 30).

While U.S. fiscal policy since the pandemic has been awesomely accommodative, it did not reverse the inequality engine, only slowed it down a bit thanks to short-term household economic assistance and small-business lending. Fixing many causes of American inequalities such as pre-K education are critical, but the economy these children enter in 20 or more years will be still more unequal and they will have still less of a chance unless the anti-equality policies driving financial markets every day are quickly reversed. Because these policies are principally of the Fed's making, only the Fed can undo them to give lower-income households a fighting chance at intergenerational economic advancement.

The Federal Reserve Mandate As It Is

Questioned often about inequality by members of Congress and the public, Fed leadership says that the central bank's hands are tied by law from doing more than hoping for the best (see, for example, Powell 2020). Its congressional mandate permits, so the Fed says, only limited efforts to ensure maximum employment and price stability. However, the Fed has fallen short on its mandate as it understands it as well and even more importantly on the actual mandate as articulated in federal law.

Analyses from the Federal Reserve Banks of Richmond, St. Louis, and Kansas City provide useful historical context for the statutory requirements that define what the Fed must do (Steelman 2011; Thornton 2012; Kahn and Taylor 2014). Importantly, and as these analyses make clear, and as stated in the 1977 Federal Reserve Reform Act, the mandate is not just maximum employment and price stability, but also moderate long-term interest rates. Moreover, the Fed's mandate should be considered in concert with the broader economic policy mandate Congress has set for the federal government in general and the Fed in particular.

Dating back to 1946, Congress declared that:

> [I]t is the continuing policy and responsibility of the federal government to use all practicable means consistent with its needs and obligations and other essential considerations of national policy with the assistance and cooperation of industry, agriculture, labor, and state and local governments, to coordinate and utilize all its plans, functions, and resources for the purpose of creating and maintaining, in a manner calculated to foster and promote free competitive enterprise and the general welfare, conditions under which there will be afforded useful employment, for those able, willing, and seeking work, and to promote maximum employment, production, and purchasing power [Employment Act of 1946].

The 1977 Federal Reserve Act does not obliterate the overarching mandate of the Federal Reserve as a part of the federal government also to achieve Congress's express statutory mandate for the federal government as a whole.

Indeed, the Full Employment and Balanced Growth Act—better known as the Humphrey-Hawkins Act of 1978—expressly adds the Federal Reserve as a party responsible for achieving the broad, government-wide mandate by adding it to the entities cited in 1946 required to coordinate with U.S. fiscal authorities to achieve an array of policy objectives that continue to prioritize the "general welfare," which now incorporates an array of additional objectives in areas such as trade, agriculture, and manufacturing. The 1978 act also revised U.S. employment goals to include "genuine full employment" and "real income," while deleting "purchasing power" in favor of price stability.

Unsurprisingly given the Fed's focus on markets, the employment focus of the 1977 and 1978 mandates was only expressly reflected in regular Federal Open Market Committee (FOMC) statements after September of 2010. Each of the Reserve Bank studies noted above ponders the question of why the Fed waited so long to add maximum employment to its longstanding public prioritization of fighting inflation, but it may well have been due to the depth of the 2008 crisis, not to mention the acute political pressure on the central bank then to show that it was doing more than propping up big banks.

Although maximum employment and price stability are now a Fed mantra, moderate interest rates—another and equally binding statutory injunction—are still missing. In 2007, a Fed governor explained the complete disregard of this third mandate on grounds that neither maximum employment nor price stability is possible without moderate long-term interest rates (Mishkin 2007). That might well have been true before 2008, but it is now clearly incorrect as evidenced by the nexus of ultralow rates, slow growth, and spiraling inflation.

Even judged by only its three statutory mandates, the Fed failed on every count from 2008 to 2020. Up to the Covid-19 crisis, employment was anything but maximum as the Fed belatedly acknowledged early last year (Powell 2021). Then as now, wages for low-, moderate-, and middle-class households were insufficient to make ends meet, many people worked part-time or several jobs, many families needed multiple wage earners, and more than a few Americans simply dropped out of the work force in total frustration. After 2010, the Fed failed consistently to meet the 2 percent inflation threshold it considers price stability, flunking this criterion so decisively that even the Fed acknowledged that its postcrisis policy needed redesign (Federal Reserve Board 2018). Now, inflation has risen sharply despite the Fed's assertions until late October that it was only "transitory" (Smialek and Phillips 2021). And, of course, interest rates hovering at the zero lower bound or below it after taking even a small amount of inflation into account aren't "moderate."

Acute economic inequality and general macroeconomic malaise make it clear also that the Federal Reserve Board has failed to support the "general welfare." Of course, the Fed alone cannot be blamed for this failure or the failure of fiscal policy. Nevertheless, U.S. law expressly requires more of the Fed in terms not solely of an abstract dual mandate, but of policies advancing shared prosperity that work in concert with statutory fiscal goals, not against them, to achieve increasingly theoretical monetary policy results.

Conclusion: A Meaningful Monetary Policy Mandate

This chapter has shown that the distinctions Fed officials seek to draw between monetary policy purity and fiscal policy intervention are not only anachronistic but also misleading. The sheer scale of monetary policy intervention since the great financial crisis and the pandemic not only endow monetary policy with direct and indirect fiscal impact, but also outgunned fiscal policy in several key respects.

Some have suggested that, given the Fed's unmatched powers to throw trillions of dollars as it sees fit, Congress should control this authority and stipulate that certain public welfare objectives (e.g., climate-risk mitigation) be directly advanced by central bank operations and asset purchases. To do so without subsequent political accountability is to give a central bank undue authority. To do so with accountability exposes the full scope of central bank operations and activities to political control sure to seek not only to direct public welfare investments, but also to set interest rates or other policies to enhance individual political prospects.

To recognize the Fed as it has become, and to forestall a politically driven mandate, the Federal Reserve should honor its current, triple mandate and the overall context in which Congress has placed it in the federal economic mandate, abandoning its long, unsuccessful wait for the wealth effect somehow to work growth, resilience, and inflation wonders.

A full discussion of how equality-focused monetary policy should proceed is outside the scope of this chapter.[2] However, Congress's full mandate for the Fed expressly and directly orders it to recognize American economic inequality and, armed by better data and a clear sense of its mission, realign its employment, price stability, and interest rate goals to generate a "prosperity effect"—that is, growth that starts at the bottom of the income and wealth distributions to generate shared prosperity, stable growth, and market stability.

References

Bank for International Settlements (2021) "BIS Plans Asian Green Bond Fund for Central Banks" (October 21). Available at www.bis.org/press/p211021.htm.

CARES Act (2020) Coronavirus Aid, Relief, and Economic Security Act, Pub. L. No. 116–136, 134 Stat. 281 (March 27).

Cingano, F. (2014) "Trends in Income Inequality and its Impact on Economic Growth." OECD Social, Employment and Migration Working Paper No. 163 (December).

Davidson, K., and Weaver, A. E. (2021) "Morning Money: Manchin's Debt Worries Belie Brighter Budget Picture." *Politico* (October 26).

Employment Act of 1946. Available at www.legisworks.org/congress /79/publaw-304.pdf.

Federal Reserve Board (2018) "Federal Reserve to Review Strategies, Tools, and Communication Practices It Uses to Pursue Its Mandate of Maximum Employment and Price Stability" (November 15). Available at www.federalreserve.gov/newsevents /pressreleases/monetary20181115a.htm.

_____ (2020) "Federal Reserve Announces Extensive New Measures to Support the Economy" (March 23). Available at www.federalreserve.gov/newsevents/pressreleases/monetary 20200323b.htm.

_____ (2021a) "Distribution of Household Wealth in the U.S. since 1989." *DFA: Distributional Financial Accounts* (2019:Q4), accessed October 22, 2021. Available at www.federalreserve.gov /releases/z1/dataviz/dfa/distribute/table.

---

[2]For a fuller discussion, see Petrou (2021: chap. 11).

_____ (2021b) "Transcript of Chair Powell's Press Conference" (November 3). Available at www.federalreserve.gov/mediacenter /files/FOMCpresconf20211103.pdf.

Federal Reserve Reform Act of 1977. Available at www.govinfo .gov/content/pkg/USCODE-2019-title12/pdf/USCODE-2019 -title12-chap3-subchapI.pdf.

Full Employment and Balanced Growth Act of 1978. Available at www.gpo.gov/fdsys/pkg/STATUTE-92/pdf/STATUTE-92 -Pg1887.pdf.

Harrison, D. (2016) "Janet Yellen Sees Benefits to Central Bank Stock Purchases." *Wall Street Journal* (September 29).

Hofmann, B,; Lombardi, M. J.; Mojon, B.; and Orphanides, A. (2021) "Fiscal and Monetary Policy Interactions in a Low Interest Rate World." BIS Working Paper No. 954 (July).

House Financial Services Committee (2021a) "Virtual Hearing: Examining the Role of Municipal Bond Markets in Advancing— and Undermining—Economic, Racial and Social Justice" (April 28). Available at https://financialservices.house.gov/calendar /eventsingle.aspx?EventID=407537.

_____ (2021b) "Hearing on Monetary Policy and the State of the Economy" (July 14). Available at https://financialservices .house.gov/calendar/eventsingle.aspx?EventID=408105.

Kahn, G. A., and Taylor, L. (2014) "Evolving Market Perceptions of Federal Reserve Policy Options." *Federal Reserve Bank of Kansas City Economic Review* 99 (1).

Kelton, S. (2020) *The Deficit Myth: Modern Monetary Theory and the Birth of the People's Economy*. New York: Public Affairs.

Mishkin, F. S. (2007) "Monetary Policy and the Dual Mandate." Speech at Bridgewater, Va., (April 10). Available at www.federal reserve.gov/newsevents/speech/mishkin20070410a.htm.

Morath, E. (2016) "Seven Years Later, Recovery Remains the Weakest of the Post-World War II Era." *Wall Street Journal*, (July 29).

Paul, P. (2020) "Historical Patterns of Inequality and Productivity around Financial Crises." Federal Reserve Bank of San Francisco, Working Paper 2017-23 (March).

Petrou, K. (2021) *Engine of Inequality: The Fed and the Future of Wealth in America*. Hoboken, N.J.: John Wiley.

Piketty, T. (2014) *Capital in the Twenty-First Century*. Cambridge, Mass.: Harvard University Press.

Powell, J. (2020) "Monetary Policy and the Economy." *CSPAN* (February 20). Available at www.c-span.org/video/?469082-1 /monetary-policy-economy.

_____ (2021) "Getting Back to a Strong Labor Market." Speech at the Economic Club of New York (February 10). Available at www.federalreserve.gov/newsevents/speech /powell20210210a.htm.

Shlaes, A. (2007) *The Forgotten Man: A New History of the Great Depression.* New York: HarperCollins.

Smialek, J., and Phillips, M. (2021) "The Fed Chair Strikes a Wary Tone on Inflation, but Says This Isn't the Time to Raise Interest Rates." *New York Times* (October 22).

Steelman, A. (2011) "The Federal Reserve's 'Dual Mandate': The Evolution of an Idea." *Federal Reserve Bank of Richmond Economic Brief* (December).

Thornton, D. L. (2012) "The Dual Mandate: Has the Fed Changed Its Objective?" *Federal Reserve Bank of St. Louis Review* 94 (2).

14

THE FED'S MANDATE IN A
LOW INTEREST RATE WORLD

Scott Sumner

This chapter looks at the Federal Reserve's mandate in light of issues raised by the new environment of ultralow nominal interest rates. I focus on three questions. (1) How should we interpret ambiguous language in the Fed's current mandate? (2) How can Congress further clarify the mandate? (3) Should the Fed's mandate be expanded beyond its current scope?

I begin by examing the somewhat vague wording of the mandate and how that wording might or might not be consistent with various alternative monetary policy regimes. In particular, I focus on the mandate to achieve moderate long-term interest rates.

Next, I consider some areas where the law is incomplete. I argue that policy would improve if Congress would clarify the scope of the Fed's role in macroeconomic stabilization. Does Congress want the Fed to essentially *steer* the level of aggregate demand, or does Congress prefer the Fed merely engage in occasional *gestures* that tend to increase or decrease aggregate demand? What tools does Congress want the Fed to use, and how aggressively should it use those tools?

Finally, I examine proposals to add one or more policy goals to the Fed's mandate. These include recent suggestions that the Fed use monetary policy to address financial stability, economic inequality, and even the environment. I argue that it would be a mistake to add

---

Scott Sumner is the Ralph G. Hawtrey Chair of Monetary Policy at George Mason University's Mercatus Center.

to the Fed's mandate, and that the current mandate is appropriate. Any changes should focus on clarification, not addition.

Interpreting the Mandate

Because the Fed's actions are constrained by legislation, it does not have a completely free hand in setting policy. In 1977, Congress gave the Federal Reserve the following mandate:

> The Board of Governors of the Federal Reserve System and the Federal Open Market Committee shall maintain long run growth of the monetary and credit aggregates commensurate with the economy's long run potential to increase production, so as to promote effectively the goals of maximum employment, stable prices, and moderate long-term interest rates [Federal Reserve Reform Act of 1977; Zhu 2013].

It is not at all obvious how this mandate should be interpreted. Fed officials frequently refer to their "dual mandate" of stable prices and high employment. The prevailing view is that the third part of the mandate, "moderate long-term interest rates" is most effectively achieved via a policy of stable prices. This view is based on the assumption that the Fed has relatively little control over long-term real interest rates.

Even the goals of stable prices and high employment are subject to interpretation. Beginning in the early 1990s, the Fed has aimed for roughly 2 percent inflation. In 2012, it adopted an official inflation target of 2 percent inflation for the personal consumption expenditures (PCE) price index, with some allowance for temporary deviations from the 2 percent target to address the goal of maximum employment. In 2020, the Fed adopted a "flexible average inflation target" (FAIT), under which the Federal Open Market Committee (FOMC) would aim for an average of 2 percent PCE inflation over the medium to long run, again with an equal weight given to their employment mandate.

It cannot be emphasized strongly enough that this mandate is not intelligible without a macroeconomic model of the economy. The Fed does not target inflation and employment independently; it influences aggregate demand, which then impacts inflation and employment. There is no way to know which policy best meets the congressional mandate without knowing how aggregate demand impacts inflation and employment and also what weight should be placed on each variable if achieving one goal comes at the expense of the other.

For instance, consider a policy that was able to keep the price level precisely constant over time. At first glance, that might seem consistent with the "stable prices" part of the mandate. But that policy might not be consistent with the dual mandate if stable prices led to less than full employment. And it is not even clear that Congress intended the Fed to aim for a constant price level. If that were the goal, why not say so explicitly? Why use vague language like "stable prices"? Which prices should be stable? It seems clear that the mandate was written in such a way as to give the Fed some room for interpretation.

The widespread use of the term "dual mandate" suggests that most people don't pay much attention to the mandate for moderate long-term interest rates. In the past, it has generally been assumed that this goal can best be achieved by keeping prices relatively stable. In that case, it is enough to focus on price stability and high employment. Today, however, that view is very much in doubt.

Many developed countries have experienced substantial periods of negative interest rates. In the United States, elected officials have often been critical of ultralow interest rates, arguing that a zero interest rate hurts savers. While the term "moderate" is not defined in the legislation, surely interest rates of negative 1 percent do not qualify. In my view, the language was probably a compromise between elected officials that favored somewhat low interest rates to help borrowers and those that favored somewhat higher interest rates to help savers.

There is another problem with ultralow interest rates—they lead to a greatly increased demand for base money. In countries such as Japan and Switzerland, the demand for base money has soared to more than 100 percent of GDP. This results in bloated central bank balance sheets, in some cases leading to the purchase of unconventional assets such as equities.

In my view, the most plausible interpretation of moderate interest rates is nominal rates in the single digits. That is, nominal interest rates at a level that is lower than during the late 1970s and early 1980s but higher than the zero or negative rates now seen in many developed countries. Keeping nominal rates positive would make it easier for the Fed to avoid being forced to buy large quantities of non-Treasury assets to meet the high demand for base money (cash and bank reserves) at zero rates.

While higher nominal interest rates might allow for a smaller balance sheet, it would be dangerous to arbitrarily raise nominal interest rates above zero at a time when the *equilibrium interest rate* was negative. Positive nominal interest rates are best achieved by setting an inflation or nominal GDP (NGDP) growth target at a high enough rate to keep equilibrium nominal rates above zero, at least most of the time.

In my view, the target trend rate of NGDP growth should be no lower than 4 percent regardless of how low the trend rate of real GDP growth falls. Indeed, given the dramatic fall in the equilibrium real interest rate in recent decades, even higher NGDP growth rates might be necessary in the future to keep nominal interest rates above zero. A *level targeting* approach that makes up for demand shortfalls during recessions would also help to keep the equilibrium interest rate above zero. This might involve a level target for the price level or NGDP.

Because the equilibrium real interest rate is positively correlated with the trend rate of growth in real GDP, the nominal interest rate is positively correlated with the trend rate of growth in NGDP. Thus the Fed cannot permanently raise nominal interest rates with a tight money policy (which would actually slow NGDP growth); the only truly effective way of ensuring that nominal interest rates remain moderate is to ensure that monetary policy is expansionary enough for at least 4 percent trend growth in NGDP.

This doesn't necessarily mean the Fed must target NGDP growth. A Taylor Rule-type policy approach that targets inflation at a high enough rate to ensure at least 4 percent long-run NGDP growth, while also minimizing output gaps, is equally consistent with the Fed's dual mandate, as are many other policy options. The point is that to achieve moderate long-term interest rates and to avoid a bloated Fed balance sheet, any Fed policy regime should result in substantial growth in NGDP over time.

In Japan, there has been almost no growth in NGDP over the past 25 years, a recipe for zero interest rates and an extremely large central bank balance sheet. In contrast, Australia stayed above the zero lower bound during the Global Financial Crisis of 2008–2009 due to their more rapid trend rate of growth in prices and NGDP. Kirchner (2021) showed, however, that more recently, the Reserve Bank of Australia erred in allowing inflation to fall persistently below the Reserve Bank of Australia's 2–3 percent target range, due to mistaken concerns about financial stability. This pushed Australian interest rates down to the zero lower bound and made it more difficult for monetary policy to address the Covid downturn in Australia. Monetary policy is most effective when long-term interest rates are moderate, which means high enough to largely avoid the zero lower bound.

When Congress called for moderate long-term interest rates, they may have been confused about the distinction between real and nominal rates. Nonetheless, we now find ourselves in a world where there are two very real benefits to maintaining moderate interest rates, at least on average. First, they allow the Fed to avoid being forced to adopt an overly large balance sheet, which in other countries has been associated with central banks engaging in credit allocation. Second, moderate nominal interest rates allow the central bank to continue using conventional monetary policy tools when necessary to prevent high unemployment. These arguments are likely to have some appeal to elected officials on both the left and the right and seem broadly consistent with the Fed's congressional mandate.

Clarifying the Mandate

In addition to being somewhat vague, the mandate that the Fed received from Congress is also *incomplete*. More specifically, Congress has not indicated how aggressively the Fed should pursue its mandate. Should the Fed do "whatever it takes" to ensure stable prices and high employment, or should the Fed make occasional gestures in that direction, while allowing Congress to also play a role in determining the path of aggregate demand?

I wish that Congress had specifically instructed the Fed to do whatever it takes to achieve its mandate, but that doesn't seem to be the case—certainly the Fed does not interpret its mandate that way. In late 2008, for example, the Fed did far too little stimulus to achieve its dual mandate. More importantly, they knew they were doing too little and therefore called for assistance from fiscal policymakers. At the time, there were few complaints from Congress that the Fed was doing too little; indeed, during the Great Recession, the overwhelming majority of complaints coming from politicians were that the Fed was doing too much.

There are several areas where the Fed's mandate could be clarified and strengthened:

- Congress could indicate whether the Fed is allowed to pay negative interest rates on bank reserves—something that is already done by the Swiss National Bank, the Bank of Japan (BOJ), and the European Central Bank, among others.
- Congress could be more specific about what sort of assets the Fed is authorized to purchase. This clarification might involve two scenarios. First, Congress should describe which assets the Fed should purchase during normal times, that is, when nominal interest rates are above zero. Second, policymakers should clarify which assets the Fed is allowed to purchase if necessary to achieve its mandate during a period where the economy is at the zero lower bound.

Central banks are more effective and less politicized when they have a relatively small balance sheet. To achieve that goal, Congress could instruct the Fed to confine their asset purchases to Treasury securities during normal times—that is, when nominal interest rates for T-bills are positive. This would ensure that the Fed doesn't cross the line from macroeconomic stabilization to credit allocation and is how the Fed operated before 2008. That goal can be achieved more effectively if the Fed refrains from paying interest on reserves (IOR).

In the case where *nominal* interest rates have fallen to zero or below, the Fed could be given permission to pay negative IOR and to buy as many non-Treasury securities as necessary to achieve the dual mandate. This is why the "moderate long-term interest rate" part of the Fed's mandate is so important. If the equilibrium interest rate falls below zero, achieving the mandate might require exceptionally large asset purchases. It is better to avoid that problem by setting a nominal target path (prices or NGDP) that is high enough to mostly avoid the zero lower bound.

Some economists argue that fiscal policy should pick up the slack when nominal interest rates fall to zero. In my view, that would be a serious error. While there are costs from the Fed buying unconventional assets, those costs are trivial compared to the costs of fiscal stimulus, which imposes massive future tax liabilities on the economy, slowing long-run economic growth. In contrast, while the BOJ's purchases of equities were certainly not ideal, they were far less costly than the extremely wasteful (and ineffective) fiscal stimulus done by the Japanese government during the 1990s and 2000s.

To summarize, monetary policy is most effective when the central bank commits to do whatever it takes to achieve its dual mandate. This means that if the Fed has a 4 percent NGDP target, then each and every day, the policy instrument should be set in a position where expected NGDP growth equals 4 percent. This outcome can be achieved most effectively if the following conditions are met:

1. The Fed sets the target growth rate for its target variable (inflation or NGDP growth) at a high enough rate to keep nominal interest rates above zero. This *strategy* is important because it ensures the Fed can hit its target without the sort of bloated balance sheet that would force the Fed to make decisions about credit allocation, decisions better left to elected officials.
2. The Fed should have the option of paying negative IOR and the option of buying as many assets as necessary in order to achieve its congressional mandate. I call this *tactic* the "whatever it takes" approach.

The implications of this second point are widely misunderstood. Eggertsson and Proulx (2016) showed that when monetary stimulus is not credible, the central bank might have to make truly enormous asset purchases to achieve its inflation target, perhaps several hundred percent of GDP. But the implication of this study is not that quantitative easing (QE) doesn't work, rather that any QE program needs to be combined with a credible policy to do whatever it takes to achieve on-target inflation (or NGDP growth.) And that credible policy must, at a minimum, involve a "whatever it takes" approach to asset purchases when at the zero lower bound.

Because this distinction is so poorly understood, it may be helpful to illustrate the point with a numerical example. The Japanese monetary base is currently over 140 percent of GDP, while inflation has been averaging slightly above zero in recent years. If that sort of massive balance sheet has produced less than 1 percent inflation, how much more QE would be required to achieve a 10 percent inflation target in Japan? Surprisingly, the answer is "much less than zero."

For example, suppose the BOJ announced that, henceforth, it would depreciate the yen at 8 percent per year against the U.S. dollar. If the U.S. inflation rate were 2 percent, then this policy would be expected to lead to an average Japanese inflation rate of roughly 10 percent in the very long run (due to purchasing power parity). So how much QE would be needed to achieve that much inflation in Japan?

Here it helps to think about what the final equilibrium would look like, and then work backward to estimate the demand for base money in that long-run equilibrium. If Japan began experiencing 10 percent inflation per year, then Japanese nominal interest rates would rise sharply. Indeed, the interest parity condition implies that a policy of depreciating the yen at 8 percent per year would push Japanese interest rates to 8 percent above the level of U.S. interest rates. And, in virtually all developed countries with relatively high nominal interest rates, the demand for base money is quite modest—certainly less than 10 percent of GDP (assuming no payment of IOR.) So if the BOJ were to actually adopt a credible "whatever it takes" approach to targeting inflation at 10 percent, then they would almost certainly be forced to reduce the Japanese monetary base from 140 percent of GDP to less than 10 percent of GDP.

A policy of 10 percent inflation, of course, is not optimal. The point of this exercise is to show that there is no consistent relationship between the changes in the size of the central bank balance sheet and the amount of inflation. In some cases, particularly countries suffering hyperinflation, large exogenous increases in the base cause high inflation. In other cases (such as Japan and Switzerland), large increases in the monetary base are endogenous responses to the strong demand for base money at zero or negative interest rates. And those ultralow equilibrium interest rates are ultimately caused by very low trend rates of inflation (and low NGDP growth).

Changing the Mandate

In recent years, there has been a great deal of discussion about whether the Fed should pursue goals other than price stability and high employment. The most commonly cited additional mandates for monetary policy include financial stability, economic inequality, and climate change.

Because economic inequality and climate change are long-run problems, and because monetary policy is roughly neutral in the long run, it seems unlikely that any foreseeable change in monetary policy would significantly impact those areas of concern. Borio (2021) argues that monetary policy can best address economic instability by focusing on its primary goal of providing macroeconomic stability. Skinner (2021) argued that a politicized Fed would be less able to achieve its core functions.[1]

At a superficial level, financial stability seems a more promising area for monetary policy to address. It is widely believed that low interest rates can fuel speculative excess in the financial markets, which might later lead to a financial crisis and recession. Indeed, many have argued that this sort of boom-and-bust cycle occurred during the 1920s and then again during the 2000s.

In practice, however, it is unlikely that monetary policy can play a useful role in providing financial stability, *beyond that which is achieved by stabilizing the growth path of nominal spending*. While a highly unstable monetary policy can be disruptive for the financial markets, it is not clear that focusing on financial stability would offer any benefits beyond those achieved by stabilizing aggregate demand.

In the previous sections, we saw how the recent move toward ultralow interest rates had raised challenges for how the Fed could most effectively achieve its mandate. Low rates also have confused the issue of how monetary policy relates to financial stability. More specifically, the 40-year downtrend in both real and nominal interest rates has had two side effects that have led many pundits to wrongly conclude that monetary policy was generating asset price bubbles:

1. The decline in long-term equilibrium real interest rates has dramatically increased the price-earnings ratio in the equity market, and also has increased the price-rent ratio in the real estate market. As a result, many asset classes now look wildly overvalued when using 20th century benchmarks.
2. The decline in interest rates over the past 40 years has caused economists to repeatedly misjudge the stance of monetary policy. Thus, in 2008, falling interest rates led many economists to

---

[1] It is possible that the Fed might be able to do something on the regulatory front (although I'm skeptical of even that claim), but here I'll confine my analysis to the Fed's role in determining monetary policy.

assume that the Fed had adopted an expansionary monetary policy, whereas policy was actually quite contractionary. The equilibrium interest rate was falling even faster than the Fed's target rate (see Cúrdia 2015).

Those who saw asset markets as overvalued during a period of very low interest rates were inclined to blame the overvaluation on excessively expansionary monetary policy. In fact, the high valuation ratios were a rational market response to a new normal of much lower *equilibrium* long-term interest rates.

From the perspective of 2021, the seemingly high level of the tech stock heavy NASDAQ index back in 2000 no longer looks excessive. Nor does the high level of house prices in 2006. In both cases, however, prices fell from their peak values during the subsequent recession, which was initially seen as confirming the view that the previous asset price levels had represented an irrational "bubble."

The misdiagnosis of asset price bubbles has been compounded by a misdiagnosis of the stance of monetary policy, which in recent decades has generally reacted too slowly to declines in the equilibrium rate of interest. After the asset price booms ended in 2000 and 2006, Fed officials assumed that the policy stance was expansionary due to declining levels of interest rates, but policy was in fact becoming more contractionary as the equilibrium interest rate fell faster than the policy rate. This led to recessions in 2001 and 2008, which were (wrongly) seen as confirming the view that financial excess was destabilizing to the economy.

During the 1920s, New York Fed President Benjamin Strong was under pressure to use monetary policy to restrain an overheated stock market. He resisted the pressure, arguing:

> Must we accept parenthood for every economic development in the country? That is a hard thing for us to do. We would have a large family of children. Every time one of them misbehaved, we might have to spank them all.[2]

After Strong died in mid-1928, the new leadership at the Fed took the opportunity to sharply tighten monetary policy in the hope of popping the stock market bubble—that is, "spanking" stock speculators.

[2]This passage is from a letter from Strong to New York Fed economist Carl Snyder, May 21, 1925, quoted in Ahamed (2009: 277).

At first, the rate increases failed to slow the boom in stock prices. By late 1929, however, real interest rates were raised to roughly 6 percent, high enough to sharply slow the economy. The Fed succeeded in ending the stock market boom, but at the cost of "spanking" the broader economy. Monetary policy cannot independently aim for macroeconomic stabilization and the smoothing of asset prices. It must choose one or the other.

Conclusion

The new environment of persistently low equilibrium interest rates creates new challenges for monetary policymakers. While the Fed has traditionally interpreted its mandate as being stable prices and high employment, policy would benefit from taking the third leg of the mandate more seriously—moderate long-term interest rates. To achieve that goal, an inflation or NGDP growth rate target must be set high enough to keep nominal interest rates above zero, at least most of the time.

It would be helpful for Congress to clarify the Fed's responsibility for demand management. Does Congress prefer that the Fed do "whatever it takes" to achieve their mandate? Should that include the option of negative interest on bank reserves? Which assets should the Fed be allowed to purchase? In my view, it is better to give monetary policymakers the tools to achieve their mandate, rather than rely on costly fiscal stimulus, which imposes a burden on future generations.

The Fed should resist calls to extend its mandate beyond the current remit. Monetary policy is not an effective tool for addressing long-run real problems such as economic inequality and climate change. Calls to use monetary policy to address financial instability often are based on a confused understanding of the role of interest rates in the financial markets. A low interest rate policy does not necessarily mean that policy is expansionary, and high interest rates are not an effective tool for popping asset price bubbles.

References

Ahamed, L. (2009) *Lords of Finance: The Bankers Who Broke the World*. New York: Penguin Press.

Borio, C. (2021) "The Distributional Footprint of Monetary Policy." Speech given at the Bank for International Settlements (June 29). Available at www.bis.org/speeches/sp210629a.pdf.

Cúrdia, V. (2015) "Why So Slow? A Gradual Return for Interest Rates." *Federal Reserve Bank of San Francisco Economic Letter* 2015-32 (October 12).

Eggertsson, G. B., and Proulx, K. (2016) "Bernanke's No-Arbitrage Argument Revisited: Can Open Market Operations in Real Assets Eliminate the Liquidity Trap?" NBER Working Paper No. 22243 (May).

Kirchner, S. (2021) "Reforming Australian Monetary Policy: How Nominal Income Targeting Can Help Get the Reserve Bank Back on Track." Mercatus Working Paper (January).

Skinner, C. P. (2021) "Central Bank Activism." *Duke Law Journal* 71 (2): 247–328.

Zhu, J. (2013) "Federal Reserve Reform Act of 1977." Available at www.federalreservehistory.org/essays/fed-reform-act-of-1977.

15

THE FED'S RISKY EXPERIMENT

Charles Plosser

In August of 2020, Fed Chairman Jerome Powell unveiled the revised "Statement on Longer-run Goals and Monetary Policy Strategy" (Powell 2020). The revision made several significant changes to the original statement first announced in January 2012.[1] Importantly, it changed the Fed's interpretation of its inflation and employment mandates. The breadth and lack of clarity expressed in the new interpretations led Levy and Plosser (2020) to conclude that going forward, the Fed laid the foundation for a less transparent, more discretionary regime that will likely result in a more uncertain or unpredictable path for monetary policy.

As discussed by Levy and Plosser (2020), the new interpretations elevated and broadened the employment mandate to mean maximum "inclusive" employment shifting away from the previous interpretation where the Fed focused on something akin to the "natural rate" of unemployment. This new interpretation stresses the level of employment and adds a vague and unprecedented distributional element to the Fed's objectives. In the absence of more quantitative guidance, it offers the Fed enormous flexibility to interpret and justify its actions and makes it more difficult for the public to judge its

Charles Plosser is a Visiting Fellow at the Hoover Institution, Stanford University; former President and CEO of the Federal Reserve Bank of Philadelphia; and a member of the Shadow Open Market Committee. He thanks Peter Ireland, Andrew Levin, and Mickey Levy for comments.

[1]See Lacker (2020) for an interesting discussion of how the original statement came about.

success and hold it accountable. It also risks introducing dangerous political undercurrents to its decisionmaking process.

On the inflation side of the mandate, the Fed replaced its inflation targeting (IT) regime with an average inflation target (AIT). Vice Chairman Clarida (2020a) referred to this new target as an "aspiration," not meant to be construed as an arithmetic average but a "flexible" concept. In addition, the Fed articulated an asymmetric element to its strategy by intentionally overshooting its aspirational inflation objective to make up for any shortfalls in inflation while emphasizing that it does not intend to similarly seek to offset overshoots, thus reinforcing the idea that the "average" target is in no sense an average of expected outcomes. The Fed has not offered any quantitative guidance as to how this strategy will be implemented. Here again, the lack of clarity allows for a wide range of discretionary policy actions by the Fed, increasing policy uncertainty.

There is little doubt that the economic experience of the post-global financial crisis of 2007–2009 had a strong influence on the new strategic approach adopted by the Fed, and it is reflected in its implementation of the new strategy. The Fed's new strategy to monetary policy is reflected in three guiding principles.

- The Fed seeks to conduct monetary policy to achieve a "flexible" average inflation rate of 2 percent. When inflation has run below the target for a period of time, the Fed will seek an above-target inflation rate for some time to make up for the shortfall. This make-up strategy will not be applied to periods of above-target inflation.
- The Fed's view of inflation dynamics is fundamentally changed. Much less emphasis is now placed on the sensitivity of inflation to variations in economic "slack"—that is, the Phillips curve is presumed to be flat. Hence, employment can increase and unemployment can fall without undesirable consequences for inflation. As employment or unemployment is no longer a useful guide to inflation determination, the Fed will rely predominantly on anchoring inflation expectations to control the path of inflation.
- The Fed's new views regarding inflation allow it to use its primary interest rate instrument to aggressively pursue its new inclusive employment goals. Specifically, it will not increase its

federal funds rate target until its employment objective is achieved. Subsequent policy moves will be outcome based with respect to inflation, not based on forecasts. Thus, the Fed will no longer act preemptively with respect to inflation as it has in the past.

The key questions are: (1) Did the Fed take away the right lessons from its postcrisis review? (2) Are the solutions it adopted transparent, credible, effective, and robust? (3) What are the risks if the Fed fails to execute the strategy as planned or it does not deliver the desired outcomes? In what follows I will review the background and rationale for the Fed's new strategies and highlight the challenges and risks they pose, particularly in the current environment.

Background and Rationale for the New Strategy

Chairman Powell (2020) stressed four developments that shaped the Fed's new approach to monetary policy. First, he argues that the longer-run growth rate of the U.S. economy has fallen. The reasons for the decline are not well understood but likely involve a combination of factors including productivity growth and demographics that mostly lie beyond the scope of monetary policy. Nevertheless, the Fed sees this environment as being a feature of the economy for the foreseeable future and so justifying a "new" approach to monetary policy. The second development, an implication of the first, is that the general level of *real* interest rates (i.e., nominal rates less expected inflation) has declined. These factors have led to an environment in which the "normal" level of the funds rate is lower.[2] As a result, the Fed is concerned that it will confront the effective lower bound (ELB) on nominal interest rates more frequently, thus limiting its ability to reduce its nominal funds rate target in response to shocks. The Fed is also concerned that the inability to provide more stimulus at the ELB risks a decline in inflation expectations that may limit its ability to achieve its inflation objective. The ELB has been a fixation of the Fed for well over a decade and it continues to loom large in its approach to policy.

---

[2]In Fed terminology, r^* has declined.

The third element cited by Powell is the benefits for employment and the labor market more generally, of the more than decade-long expansion, an outcome not surprising or unusual for long expansions. Fourth, Powell notes that the steady strengthening of the labor market following the global financial crisis did not lead to a significant rise in inflation, even though interest rates were kept quite low throughout the period and the Fed's balance sheet rose more than five-fold.

The message the Fed took from its analysis seems to be that the character of recessions and recoveries has changed in a fundamental way and that going forward, its approach to monetary policy should also change. That is, the future recoveries will look similar to the recovery from the 2007–2009 financial crisis, with low interest rates, slow growth, low inflation, and a reliance on balance sheet expansion and forward guidance as the important tools of monetary policy. The changes in the Fed's strategy and its implementation of monetary policy reflect this revised view of how the economy and the monetary system work.

Implementing the New Strategy

The Fed's reshaping of monetary policy focuses on three elements. The first addresses the perceived limitations caused by the ELB. As mentioned, the Fed adopted what it calls a "flexible" average inflation targeting (FAIT) regime while seeking to anchor longer-term inflation expectations at 2 percent. If the Fed had stopped at that, then one might think that the Fed was adopting a version of price-level targeting (PLT), something that many economists have considered desirable.[3] As its name implies, FAIT requires that outcomes below the desired target would be offset or made up by allowing or achieving outcomes above the average target and, likewise, outcomes exceeding the desired target would be offset with outcomes below the target, hence achieving the desired target on average. Thus, when the average inflation goal is 2 percent, then the price

[3]Eggertsson and Woodford (2003) present a theoretical discussion of monetary policy at the ELB. They note that price-level-targeting, though unlikely to be optimal, can improve performance relative to rules that are not history dependent. See Plosser (2019) for a brief discussion of the pros and cons of implementing price-level targeting.

level would be expected to grow along a 2 percent trend consistent with longer-term inflation expectations. This would have been simple and easily understood by markets and the public. But the Fed added a complication. It chose an asymmetric target.

Specifically, the Fed intends to allow, or engineer, inflation to offset persistent *shortfalls* from its 2 percent target but will intentionally not seek to offset overruns. The Fed realizes that such an asymmetric approach cannot yield the average inflation it has specified. So it has explicitly acknowledged that its concept of "average" is a "flexible" one, as the average inflation will likely be above 2 percent if the approach is successful. The Fed seems to think it can anchor inflation expectations and achieve its 2 percent target without an operating strategy that can deliver such an outcome.

Some Fed critics interpreted the Fed's previous inflation targeting regime as implicitly managed as if the 2 percent target was a ceiling. This interpretation was wrong, but one might not be far off base in characterizing the new asymmetric regime as one where 2 percent inflation is treated as the inflation floor. This new operating regime embeds an inflationary bias into the conduct of monetary policy that is inconsistent with its stated goal of anchoring inflation and inflation expectations at 2 percent.

The magnitude of this inflation bias is hard to judge as the Fed has not offered much in the way of quantitative guidance as to how the strategy will be implemented. How much and for how long must inflation run below target before the deliberate overshooting strategy kicks in? What is the magnitude and degree of overshooting expected before the policy changes to reestablish the long-run 2 percent goal? The benefits of the asymmetry are far from apparent and it complicates the communication and the effective execution of the strategy. As pointed out, it is not even clear how such a strategy could achieve an average inflation rate of, say, 2 percent under the best of circumstances if only shortfalls are offset. Thus, this new approach may find it hard to anchor longer-term inflation expectations at 2 percent. Such basic concerns are hardly comforting or a transparent form of communication or commitment.

Of course, much of the complexity in the Fed's new approach to inflation stems from its emphasis on the ELB. The Fed's approach to the ELB seems to adopt a strategy suggested by Reifschneider and Williams (2000) and others that is commonly referred to as "lower for longer."[4] The theory is that by promising to hold rates lower for longer, the Fed seeks to raise inflation expectations over the short to medium term, thus helping to lower real rates and boost current economic activity even though the Fed cannot lower the nominal short-term rate. While such an approach is valid in some theoretical models, to be effective, it requires the central bank to be highly credible in its promises to deliver on the temporary higher inflation in the future without undermining the public's longer-term expectations of inflation. If the Fed is unable to manipulate public expectations in this manner, the strategy fails to deliver the desired stimulus and undermines the Fed's inflation objective. There is no substantive evidence that this works in practice.

Clarida (2020b) offered his own interpretation of the new inflation strategy. Interestingly, his view is not really the asymmetric FAIT regime, as described by Powell (2020) or Clarida (2020a). Rather, it is a regime-switching approach like that suggested in Bernanke (2017) and Bernanke, Kiley, and Roberts (2019). Clarida (2020b) envisions a temporary price-level targeting (TPLT) framework where monetary policy continues to use IT in normal times but, when the ELB becomes binding, it switches to a PLT or AIT-like framework. Unlike the Fed's new strategy, the TPLT regime is only initiated when and if the policy rate reaches the ELB, although the quantitative metrics regarding implementation remain unspecified. The view expressed by Clarida, in the regime-switching framework, also differs from the new language of the Fed in that it envisions returning to an IT regime in normal times.

Nevertheless, a simple AIT or PLT strategy, if credible, could be useful in addressing the ELB problem, without the additional complexity of asymmetry or a regime-switching framework. The alternative strategies proposed by the Fed and Clarida are much more difficult to communicate, execute, and less transparent.

---

[4]To deal with the ELB, some central banks have attempted to use negative policy rates, although the success has been mixed at best. Bordo and Levin (2017) explore central bank digital currency and its possible implications for delivering negative rates at the ELB. Other central banks, including the Fed, have chosen to use large-scale asset purchases, or quantitative easing (QE), to provide more accommodation at the ELB. Here, too, the effectiveness has been questioned and its unintended consequences for financial stability and central bank independence can be worrisome. See Plosser (2009, 2016, 2018, 2020) for discussions related to unconventional monetary policies and Fed independence.

The second element of the Fed's implementation involves its view of the dynamics of inflation, which seem to have changed dramatically. For decades, the Fed's operated under the premise that low inflation was caused by an economy characterized by high rates of unemployment or other measures of "slack," and that high inflation was driven by low rates of unemployment or tightness in the labor market. Despite the warnings from Milton Friedman (1968) and Edmund Phelps (1967), the simple logic of this Phillips curve perspective has been that the Fed could raise or lower the nominal interest rate to restrain or stimulate the real economy, thus raise or lower the unemployment rate, which would control the inflation rate. Of course, this view was significantly undermined in the 1960s and 1970s when inflation soared to double digits while the unemployment rate rose, giving rise to what became known as "stagflation." This generated serious doubts about the robustness of the Phillips curve. Moreover, the five years prior to the recession beginning in February 2020, with its extremely low interest rates, low unemployment, and low inflation, cast further doubt regarding the reliability of the Phillips curve as a model for the inflation rate. Since the 1970s, much research was devoted to reviving the Phillips curve with alterations and refinements. Nevertheless, the empirical relationship between inflation and unemployment continues to be elusive.[5] Attempts to forecast inflation based on unemployment rates have not been particularly successful and the Fed has finally acknowledged the problem.[6]

The conclusion reached by the Fed is that the below-target inflation of the late 2010s was a consequence of the ELB and its impact on inflation expectations and the flattening of the Phillips curve, so that inflation became unresponsive to the decline in unemployment, or other measures of "slack," and the low interest rate policy.[7] The Fed seems to have abandoned the Phillips curve, not such a bad thing, but what is the Fed's new theory of inflation? It appears that the Fed has adopted the view that to control inflation, it simply has

---

[5]See Stock and Watson (2009) and Atkeson and Ohanian (2001), for example.

[6]One thing economists have concluded is that inflation expectations are important in understanding the dynamics of inflation. This view has motivated many central banks, including the Fed, to adopt inflation targets to provide a measure of commitment and an anchor to help achieve inflation goals.

[7]See Powell (2020) and Clarida (2020a).

to manipulate expectations to achieve its desired outcome. Tell the public and the market that it should expect inflation to exceed its 2 percent target for some period of time, after episodes of sustained low inflation, then to expect it to lower inflation back to its long-term goal. So, what is the cause of inflation? What policy tools does the Fed have to move inflation up or down and how do they work? These questions were not addressed in the Fed's new monetary framework. It is difficult to believe that the Fed can make its promises credible, thereby anchoring expectations, without linking its promises to its tools and actions. While the Fed has professed its desire to achieve its inflation target, its apparent reliance on verbal pronouncements of its intentions to control it opens the door to a highly discretionary use of its traditional tools to achieve other objectives.

As mentioned, the recovery following the global financial crisis certainly exhibited some unique empirical characteristics that did not fit easily within the Fed's traditional framework. The Fed's new strategy reveals its view that the problems stemmed from external factors, specifically, declining real growth that caused the confrontation with the ELB and the structural changes in the Phillips curve, which, of course, was never a reliable basis for understanding inflation dynamics.

Yet, there were many other changes to the postcrisis environment. Financial regulations and the way the Fed chose to conduct policy likely impacted the transmission of monetary policy, but seemed to be ignored or deemed irrelevant by the Fed in adopting its new strategy. For example, the Fed began paying interest on reserves (IOR), thus changing the way banks responded to a change in the quantity of reserves or the interest rate paid on reserve balances, which was often above other short-term rates. The Fed's QE policy flooded the banking system with reserves, eviscerating the federal funds market and blowing up the Fed's balance sheet. In addition, the Fed adopted a new operating regime in the form of a floor system that changed the role of the Fed's balance sheet. Finally, new regulations significantly changed the way bank capital requirements were calculated and imposed new liquidity constraints on banks. In the Fed's view, none of these changes in its own approach to the conduct of policy framework, or in the regulatory environment, played any role in understanding the inflation outcomes following the financial crisis.

The implicit decoupling of inflation outcomes from the Fed's standard policy tools and its actions, such as low interest rates, and having long since discarded money growth as a useful tool or indicator, frees the Fed to implement the third element of its new strategy—namely, using its monetary policy tools to focus primarily on its newly interpreted maximum inclusive employment objective. Specifically, the Fed issued explicit guidance that it would not raise interest rates until its employment goals are achieved.

This strategy acts to delay the timing of when the Fed is likely to shift its policy stance to control inflation. The Fed has reinforced this by declaring that it will not act preemptively to avoid inflation, but will only do so in response to inflation outcomes once its employment goal is met. This is a particularly risky approach to policy. As Levy and Plosser (2020) noted, such promises, or forward guidance, could leave the Fed in a very awkward position if inflation increased notably *before* the Fed reached its goal of maximum inclusive employment, which has now happened. This is the scenario that the Fed ruled out in its new framework. While it has thrown out its prior approach to inflation dynamics, it has not offered an alternative, except to say that it can anchor expectations of inflation at 2 percent without an explanation of how it will use its tools to achieve such an outcome. Moreover, the Fed's new emphasis on the distributional aspects of maximum employment is likely to further mire the Fed in political controversies threatening its independence and lead to delay in implementing a less accommodative policy.

A Progress Report: Is This Time Different?

It is about a year into the Fed's new approach to monetary policy, but it is worth looking at how that policy is playing out.

The pandemic recession began in February 2020, but it has evolved quite differently from the last recession, which was distinguished by a financial crisis. This time, financial institutions were healthy entering the recession and have largely remained so. There was no housing crisis and the market for homes remained robust. The economic fallout was largely the result of the government-imposed economic shutdowns in response to Covid-19, rather than economic imbalances or other internal economic weaknesses.

The recession also proved very brief, beginning in February 2020 and ending in April 2020. Nonetheless, the contraction was very

FIGURE 1
REAL GROSS DOMESTIC PRODUCT

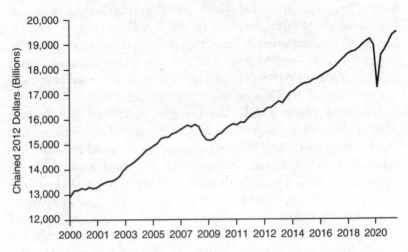

SOURCE: St. Louis Fed, FRED.

sharp and deep. Just as remarkable was the robust rebound. By 2021 Q2, real GDP had returned to its prerecession peak. Figure 1 gives a snapshot of the remarkable difference in the global financial crisis and the episode caused by the pandemic- and policy-related shutdowns. The Fed's new framework imagined that the recovery following the 2007–2009 financial crisis would be the prototype of the future: relatively slow growth, policy constrained by the ELB, and persistent low inflation insensitive to monetary policy accommodation or resource slack. Unfortunately, the 2020 recession and recovery evolved very differently from what was anticipated. Perhaps it is worth considering whether the Fed's new framework—drawn up based on the global financial crisis and its aftermath—is robust or an appropriate strategy for monetary policy over the longer run.

Beyond the behavior of GDP, other dimensions of the 2020 recession and recovery proved quite different as well. Fiscal policy was extremely aggressive. Federal spending expanded sharply relative to the global financial crisis and, as a share of GDP, is expected to remain elevated. The deficit as a percent of GDP surpassed its previous peak reached in WWII of 119 percent and is likely to exceed 130 percent in 2021. Fiscal policy continues to be on an unsustainable path, likely putting political pressure on the Fed to continue monetizing a significant portion of the government debt. Over 55 percent of the expansion in the federal debt was purchased by the Fed between February 2020 and October 2021, compared to less than 10 percent in the 12 years from December 2007 to December 2019. These figures so do not include agency debt or holdings of agency mortgage-backed securities (MBS), which are not part of the public debt.[8]

Goodhart and Pradan (2020) argue that government spending growth in many countries is unsustainable. Moreover, governments are likely to find citizens unwilling to support the required tax increases, or the reduction in government subsidies, especially those related to income, health, and welfare, much of which is driven by demographics and the aging of populations. The political difficulty of raising taxes or cutting spending means the only alternative to managing the growth in public debt will be to inflate it away. Thus, the return of inflation over the longer term is highly likely in their view.

Monetary growth was significant following the onset of the pandemic. It began in March 2020 with the Fed's intervention to stabilize the Treasury market. From the end of February 2020 to the end of May 2020, the Fed purchased nearly $1.7 trillion of Treasury securities. During that same period, the money stock, as measured by M2, increased by about $2.4 trillion. As can be seen in Table 1 and Figure 2, rapid money growth continues. Compared to the global financial crisis, this episode is extraordinarily different. Since the beginning of the pandemic (end of February 2020) to the end of October 2021 (20 months), M2 grew at an annual rate of 20.8 percent. During the last 12 months, beginning in October 2020, growth was over 13 percent and the three-month growth rate is 12.4 percent. It is instructive to note that this is still twice the 6.1 percent growth rate of the 10-year period, December 2009 to December 2019.

For some, the modest growth in money after the financial crisis might be part of the story why inflation remained low during the following decade, although this consideration did not seem relevant to the Fed. For those who wonder about the effect of money growth on inflation, the Fed has embarked on a bold and risky experiment. The

---

[8]Bordo and Levy (2020) discuss the broad historical linkages of fiscal deficits to inflation.

TABLE 1
Money Stock: M2
(Percentage Change at Annual Rate)

10 yr. 12/09–12/19	3 mos. 7/21–10/21	6 mos. 4/21–10/21	12 mos. 10/20–10/21	20 mos. 2/20–10/21
6.1	12.4	10.7	13.1	20.8

Fed has mostly dismissed the role of money as a useful tool of monetary policy and particularly as a guide to inflation. If that view proves unwise or mistaken, and a change in policy is not forthcoming, the financial markets and the economy may be in for a very bumpy ride over the next several years.

But the Fed's efforts at accommodation extended beyond its low interest policy and money growth. It doubled down on its asset purchases program, acquiring about $4.4 trillion in securities (including $3.1 trillion in Treasuries and $1.2 trillion in agency MBS) from

FIGURE 2
Money Stock M2

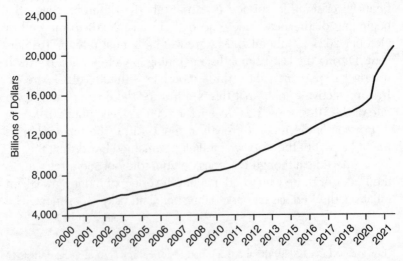

Source: St. Louis Fed, FRED.

February 2020 through October 2021. This policy continued over a year into the recovery when consumer spending was strong, investment healthy, and GDP had surpassed its prior peak. During the last recession, it took the Fed over six years to add $4 trillion to its balance sheet. Thus, by its own criteria, the Fed is pursuing an accommodation of historic proportions.

Inflation accelerated appreciably beginning in May 2020 following steep declines in March and April (see Figure 3). Table 2 shows the year-over-year PCE inflation stands at 5.6 percent as of October 2021. For reference, the average inflation over the 10-year pre-Covid interval was 1.5 percent. Interestingly, the admittedly volatile, 1-month rate of PCE inflation has been above an annualized rate of 3 percent in 14 of the last 18 months. The price level returned to its January 2020 prepandemic peak in June 2020 and has continued its steady rise. The two-year PCE inflation rate (through October 2021) is now 3.1 percent and above the prepandemic trend of 1.5 percent. In fact, the three-, four- and five-year average inflation rates are all between 2.3 and 2.5 percent. So, there is no shortfall of inflation from

FIGURE 3
PCE Chain Price Index
(SA, 2012 = 100)

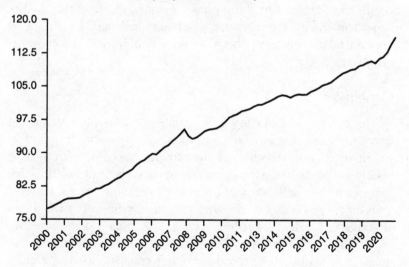

Source: St. Louis Fed, FRED.

TABLE 2
PCE INFLATION
(PERCENTAGE CHANGE AT ANNUAL RATE)

10 yr. 12/09–12/19	3 mos. 7/21–10/21	6 mos. 4/21–10/21	12 mos. 10/20–10/21	20 mos. 2/20–10/21
1.5	5.8	5.9	5.1	3.4

target over at any look-back horizon up to five years. Even a 10-year look-back (or from the date the Fed's inflation target announcement in January 2012) shows average inflation of 1.8 percent.

A natural question is to ask the Fed to put its FAIT approach in context. The make-up of the shortfall in the price level of the last two to five years has been accomplished, and the average inflation rate exceeds its target. With current inflation running above 5 percent, how much longer does the Fed want inflation to run "hot?" At what point will it become uncomfortable? Monetary policy remains highly accommodative. Inflation expectations have increased, and the Fed must guard against those expectations rising further and becoming entrenched above 2 percent. These are the sort of quantitative metrics that the Fed has not communicated to the public. Unless the Fed begins to take steps to bring inflation down, the long-run goal of 2 percent inflation could face a serious challenge. Uncertain or unpredictable monetary policy does not contribute to a stable or sustainable recovery.

Conclusion

The Fed's new monetary policy strategy represents a significant departure from past practices and a remarkable restructuring of its priorities. Its new "flexible" asymmetric average inflation targeting plan is a complicated approach to the management of inflation that requires moving inflation and inflation expectations up and down in a specific, yet credible, way that presumably improves the Fed's attempts to conduct short-term stabilization policy at the effective lower bound. Yet it offers almost no quantitative guidance that informs the public how the desired movements and time frames should be judged, much less information about how the Fed will use its tools to accomplish these unquantified goals. Thus, the framework lacks transparency and credibility.

The new strategy says that the Fed remains committed to a long-run goal of 2 percent inflation. But, without greater clarity and transparency, the added complexity comes with greater risks. The approach involves a more active, discretionary, and perhaps, volatile path of monetary policy. For example, higher inflation rates intended to make up for shortfalls could last longer or go higher than anticipated and lead to a loss of credibility and the absence of an anchor for inflation expectations. This may jeopardize longer-term inflation goals and economic stability as the Fed seeks to regain control and restore credibility. Inflation and inflation expectations are not like a faucet that the Fed can turn off and on as it pleases.

The second remarkable change in the Fed's new monetary strategy is the elevation of a revised maximum *inclusive* employment goal as its foremost objective. This change is reflected in its extraordinary new guidance that it will not raise its federal funds rate target until its employment objective is achieved. This guidance was thought to be justified based on experience following the financial crisis of 2007–2009, when low interest rates and low unemployment (or "slack") failed to increase inflation. The Fed seems to have concluded that, in its new world, there has been a decoupling of its policy tools from the inflation process. It seems to have not contemplated that inflation could rise before maximum employment is reached. While far from specific, the earlier versions of the Fed's strategy statement said that, in circumstances when its two goals—price stability and employment—appeared to be in conflict, it would follow a "balanced approach" to its conduct of policy. The Fed's new strategy statement removed that phrase. What is the public to think the Fed will do?

Of course, what the Fed did not believe would happen when it adopted its new strategy is now a reality. Inflation is up sharply while many Fed speakers say the economy remains a long way from its inclusive employment goals. The Fed is stressing the temporary nature of current inflation, emphasizing supply-side issues such as "bottlenecks" in product and labor markets. Stressing the temporary supply-side induced inflation allows the Fed to maintain current policies and avoid the inherent conflict between its guidance to continue aggressive ease to promote employment and its commitment to maintain its inflation goal.

This policy reflects the inflation bias that is an inherent feature of the new strategy. But the degree to which the current price increases will lead to more persistent or sustained inflation will depend on the degree to which the current policy mix of aggressive monetary and fiscal policies is maintained. Failing to adjust the current stance of policy could ensure that the current inflation becomes more persistent, much as the Fed did in the 1970s when excessive attention on employment turned what might have been a temporary inflation episode into a more than a decade-long economic disaster.

The Fed is facing a dilemma of its own making. If it chooses to move more decisively to deal with inflation, its credibility may be undermined for abandoning its employment guidance, likely leading to political pushback, and if it remains firm to its employment commitment and fails to contain inflation or inflation expectations, it loses credibility as well for failing to follow through on its inflation commitment. The Fed is walking a fine line. It did not need to find itself in this predicament. Will the new framework prove to be a strategic one or one of blunder that harms the Fed's credibility and must be abandoned or repeatedly revised? A framework that is simple and more systematic rather than one that is complex and discretionary would be preferable.

References

Atkeson, A., and Ohanian, L. E. (2001) "Are Phillips Curves Useful for Forecasting Inflation?" *Federal Reserve Bank of Minneapolis Quarterly Review* 25 (1): 2–11.

Bernanke, B. S. (2017) "Temporary Price-Level Targeting: An Alternative Framework for Monetary Policy." *Ben Bernanke's Blog* at Brookings (October 12).

Bernanke, B. S.; Kiley, M. T.; and Roberts, J. M. (2019) "Monetary Policy Strategies for a Low-Rate Environment." *AEA Papers and Proceedings* 109 (May): 421–26.

Bordo, M. D., and Levin, A. T. (2017) "Central Bank Digital Currency and the Future of Monetary Policy." NBER Working Paper No. 23711 (August).

Bordo, M. D., and Levy, M. D. (2020) "Do Enlarged Fiscal Deficits Cause Inflation: The Historical Record." NBER Working Paper No. 28195 (December).

Clarida, R. H. (2020a) "The Federal Reserve's New Monetary Policy Framework: A Robust Evolution." Speech delivered at the Peterson Institute for International Economics (August 31).

_____ (2020b) "Federal Reserve's New Framework: Context and Consequences." Speech delivered at the Brookings Institution, Washington, D.C. (November 16).

Eggertsson, G. B., and Woodford, M. (2003) "The Zero Bound on Interest Rates and Optimal Monetary Policy." *Brookings Papers on Economic Activity 2003*, No. 1: 139–211.

Friedman, M. (1968) "The Role of Monetary Policy." *American Economic Review* 58 (1): 1–17.

Goodhart, C., and Pradan, M. (2020) *The Great Demographic Reversal*. London: Palgrave Macmillan.

Lacker, J. M. (2020) "A Look Back at the Consensus Statement." *Cato Journal* 40 (2): 285–319.

Levy, M. D., and Plosser, C. (2020) "The Murky Future of Monetary Policy." Prepared for the Hoover Institution's Monetary Policy Conference (October 1).

Phelps, E. S. (1967) "Phillips Curves, Expectations of Inflation and Optimal Unemployment over Time." *Economica* 34 (135): 254–81.

Plosser, C. (2009) "Ensuring Sound Monetary Policy in the Aftermath of Crisis." Speech delivered at the U.S. Monetary Policy Forum, New York (February 27).

_____ (2016) "Balancing Central Bank Independence and Accountability." In J. H. Cochrane and J. B. Taylor (eds.), *Central Bank Governance and Oversight Reform*. Stanford, Calif.: Hoover Institution Press.

_____ (2018) "The Risks of a Fed Balance Sheet Unconstrained by Monetary Policy." In M. D, Bordo, J. H. Cochrane, and A. Seru (eds.), *The Structural Foundations of Monetary Policy*. Stanford, Calif.: Hoover Institution Press.

_____ (2019) "A Cautionary Note on Price-Level Targeting." *Defining Ideas*. A Hoover Institution Journal (May 1).

_____ (2020) "Operating Regimes and Fed Independence." *Cato Journal* 40 (2): 361–71.

Powell, J. H. (2020) "New Economic Challenges and the Fed's Monetary Policy." Speech delivered at the Federal Reserve Bank of Kansas City Economic Symposium, Jackson Hole, Wyoming (August 27).

Reifschneider, D., and Williams, J. C. (2000) "Three Lessons for Monetary Policy in a Low Inflation Era." *Journal of Money, Credit and Banking* 32 (4): 936–66.

Stock, J. H., and Watson, M. W. (2009) "Phillips Curve Inflation Forecasts." In Fuhrer, J.; Kodrzycki, Y.; Little, J.; and Olivei, G. (eds.), *Understanding Inflation and the Implications for Monetary Policy: A Phillips Curve Retrospective*. Cambridge, Mass.: MIT Press.

PART 4

HELICOPTER MONEY AND FISCAL QE

16

HELICOPTER MONEY, FISCAL QE, THE MAGIC ASSET, AND COLLATERALIZING THE CURRENCY

William Nelson

George Selgin diligently reminds us that one of the major problems with the Federal Reserve's "floor system" for conducting monetary policy is that it weakens the ability of the Fed to resist political pressure to use its balance sheet for fiscal purposes, which he calls "fiscal QE" (Selgin 2018, 2020). Under that system, the Fed oversupplies reserve balances, pushing the federal funds rate down to the interest rate the Fed pays on reserve balances, known as "interest on reserves." As a result, in a floor system, the Fed can expand its balance sheet essentially without bound without losing control of interest rates. There could be pressure to expand the Fed's liabilities, in particular, by creating helicopter money, or to expand the Fed's assets by purchasing assets or making loans. In contrast, under a "corridor system," which the Fed used before 2008, the central bank's assets could not exceed the public's demand for currency by much or the Fed would create reserve balances that exceeded banks' demand, and the federal funds rate would fall to zero. This chapter examines helicopter money and fiscal QE (quantitative easing), as well as the so-called magic asset and collateralizing the currency. In particular, it points to the risk the Fed faces by funding long-term investments with short-term liabilities—namely,

William Nelson is Executive Vice President and Chief Economist at the Bank Policy Institute and an Adjunct Professor at Georgetown University.

if interest rates go up quickly, and by a lot, the Fed can lose money. And, if it loses enough money, the Fed risks either losing control of monetary policy or breaking the law.

Helicopter Money

Ben Bernanke (2016) explains that the Fed could use helicopter money to stimulate the economy by crediting the Treasury's account at the Fed with funds that the Treasury would then use to finance a tax cut without raising the federal debt. He describes such an action as a step the Fed could take to stimulate the economy if it were unable to do so by lowering interest rates.

An Exigent Use for Helicopter Money

While such a coordinated action between the Fed and Congress to stimulate the economy seems unlikely given the other monetary policy tools the Fed has and the consensus on the importance of central bank independence, it is less hard to imagine the Fed using exactly the same action to avoid an imminent catastrophe. In particular, if Congress fails to lift the debt ceiling, and the country is on the brink of default, the Fed could use helicopter money to provide the government the money it needed to avoid default, assuming the Bernanke version of helicopter money is legal. The Fed would credit the Treasury's general account (exactly the same action that Bernanke envisions) with whatever amount was seen as necessary, say $500 billion. The plan would get around the debt limit because even though Fed liabilities minus Treasuries is clearly net borrowing by the federal government, the amount is not included in federal debt.

Of course, this is a horrible idea. If the Fed used this approach once to avoid a federal default, Congress would realize that the Fed could do it again and do it perpetually. It is difficult to see why Congress would ever take the difficult action of raising the debt ceiling again. But if the alternative to the helicopter drop is to default on the debt, something that could cause a U.S. and global recession and destroy the dollar's hegemony, the action is not inconceivable.

Transcripts from two emergency meetings of the Federal Open Market Committee (FOMC 2011, 2013), which the Fed held to discuss what it could do in reaction to a federal default, already describe some extraordinary actions. The plans included a range of options including accepting defaulted Treasuries as collateral at the discount window up through purchasing defaulted securities in the open market (at market value). Although none of these options were as extreme as simply providing the Treasury with the necessary funds, they certainly indicate a willingness on the part of the Fed to think creatively.

Because the Fed is not legally allowed to lend money to the Treasury, the legality of such a helicopter drop onto the Treasury hinges on whether the action would be a loan. In the Bernanke example, there is no expectation that the helicopter drop would be repaid (at least not directly). So to stay on the right side of the law in the debt ceiling case, the Fed would need to give the Treasury the money necessary to avoid default without any expectation to be repaid.

The legality therefore hinges on what constitutes an expectation to be repaid, and that, in turn, could depend on the asset that would be created on the Fed's balance sheet that corresponds to the helicopter drop amount, which would be a liability. Bernanke has described the helicopter drop as representing the present value of future seigniorage. In that spirit, the asset could be similar to mortgage servicing rights, a bank asset equal to the value of the future fees a bank will collect on a mortgage that it has securitized but is still servicing. If the Fed were to create for itself an asset equal to the present value of interest it will earn on assets financed by currency, its equity would jump.[1] The Fed is required by law to remit any amounts that would raise its equity above a de minimis level to the Treasury, so the added equity would be immediately dropped into the Treasury general account (TGA).

The Magic Asset

If that sounds preposterous to you, it shouldn't. The Fed already plans to book an asset—officially called the "deferred asset" but commonly called "the magic asset"—if it made losses so that it's capital would not go negative. The magic asset reflects future

---

[1]An equivalent way to get to the same outcome would be to record currency at fair value. Because currency pays no interest, its fair value as a liability is zero. If booked at zero, the Fed's equity would go up by the amount of currency.

profits that will be retained rather than remitted to the Treasury to make up for current losses. The Fed's audited 2019 financial statement states:

> If earnings during the year are not sufficient to provide for the costs of operations, payment of dividends, and maintaining surplus at an amount equal to a Reserve Bank's allocated portion of the aggregate surplus limitation, remittances to the Treasury are suspended. This decrease in earnings remittances to the Treasury results in a deferred asset that represents the amount of net earnings a Reserve Bank will need to realize before remittances to the Treasury resume [Board of Governors 2020: 15, n. 3].

While the Fed envisions that the magic asset would just equal accumulated losses, I don't see why it can't be as big as the Fed would like it to be. In this case, as big as is necessary to finance the government until the debt ceiling is raised. (I'll return to the magic asset in the discussion of potential Fed losses.)

Helicopter Money for Individuals

It is impossible to write a paper these days about central banking without mentioning central bank digital currency (CBDC). Although the technical details vary, CBDC almost always involves individuals essentially having accounts at the Fed. Such an arrangement would facilitate having helicopter money for individuals, not just for Treasury. For example, Saule Omarova (2021) argues that the Fed could use credits and debits to the CBDC accounts of individuals and businesses to stimulate and restrain the economy. The credits would be skewed toward the underprivileged and socially beneficial industries. The debits would be skewed toward the wealthy and large corporations.

Fiscal QE

By unlinking monetary policy from the size of the balance sheet, the Fed could engage in fiscal policy with its assets as well as with its liabilities. As Omarova (2021: 1268) observes: "In effect, the Fed would be able to conduct monetary policy by managing the liability side of its own ledger. That, however, immediately raises an important question: What needs to happen on the asset side of the Fed's balance sheet in order to accommodate this shift?"

She is creative with her answer. The Fed should extend discount window loans to "qualified lending institutions," which would, in turn, lend to "productive enterprises" and not "socially suboptimal speculative activities." The Fed would also buy the debt of a National Investment Authority that would finance "large-scale, transformative public infrastructure projects," such as high-speed rail lines and a green energy network.

Omarova is far from alone in suggesting that the Fed could use its balance sheet to invest in assets seen as socially beneficial. For example, several years ago, the proponents of the Green New Deal indicated that it could be financed by the Fed: "As the checks go out, the government's bank—the Federal Reserve—clears the payments by crediting the seller's bank account with digital dollars. In other words, Congress can pass any budget it chooses, and our government already pays for everything by creating new money" (Kelton et al. 2018).

More recently, Yanis Varoufakis of Project Syndicate calls on central banks to use QE to support worthy causes:

> Instead of ending QE, the money it produces should be diverted away from commercial banks and their corporate clients (which have spent most of the money on share buy-backs). This money should fund a basic income and the green transition (via public investment banks like the World Bank and the European Investment Bank). And this form of QE will not prove inflationary if the basic income of the upper middle class and above is taxed more heavily, and if green investment begins to produce the green energy and goods that humanity needs [Varoufakis 2021: 12].

Actually, in the case of Varoufakis, it isn't clear whether he has assets or liabilities in mind. QE doesn't create funding for commercial banks; it creates assets that the banking industry has to hold (i.e., reserve balances). For QE to "fund a basic income and the green transition," the Fed would lend money directly to (or buy the debt of) whoever was conducting those programs.

A bit more circumspectly, in March 2021, the Network for Greening the Financial System (NGFS) issued "Adapting Central

Bank Operations to a Hotter World: Reviewing Some Options." At this point, the NGFS suggests that central banks could modify their existing operations to help fight climate change:

> A few options may be more impactful from a climate related perspective than others. These include measures aimed at (i) adjusting the pricing of targeted credit operations to a climate-related lending benchmark; (ii) positively screening collateral; (iii) aligning collateral pools; and (iv) tilting asset purchases. These measures would typically leverage and foster market mechanisms. They typically consist of modifying existing tools without fully overhauling their design (e.g., leveraging pricing schemes for targeted credit operations) in order to encourage lenders to originate or invest more in low-carbon and transition assets. Seen from this perspective, they could be consistent with the smooth implementation of monetary policy, although still technically challenging to operationalize [NGFS 2021: 19–20].

However, the natural next step would be for central banks to initiate QE programs to fight climate change. Indeed, with the balance sheet unbounded, once such programs are seen as desirable, why not?

It is illuminating to contrast the suggestion that the Fed buy green assets and shun brown assets to the Fed's own principals for its balance sheet policy. In 2002, the Fed (and everyone else) projected that the federal debt would be entirely repaid relatively soon and so launched a major study to consider alternative assets the Fed could purchase (Federal Reserve 2002) The study starts by articulating four "principles for managing the Federal Reserve's portfolio." The first principle is "achieve good monetary control." The second is that the Fed should "structure its portfolio and undertake its activities so as to minimize their effect on relative asset values and credit allocation within the private sector" (Federal Reserve 2002: 1)

Similarly, the second "broad point of agreement" in the March 2009 Fed-Treasury agreement on the Fed's role in a financial crisis states that the Fed should not "allocate credit to narrowly defined sectors or classes of borrowers. Government decisions to influence the allocation of credit are the province of the fiscal authorities" (Board of Governors (2009: 6).

In the immediate term, the Fed may need to address one of the consequences of its massive purchases of Treasury securities and agency MBS (mortgage-backed securities) over the past 20 months: It may lose a tremendous amount of money.

Risk of Losses and Collateralizing the Currency

By investing in long-term securities funded with short-term liabilities in amounts that overwhelm the funding advantage from currency (a zero-interest liability), the Fed is taking on significant interest rate risk. Indeed, with plausible if somewhat extreme assumptions and a reckless amount of simplification, I demonstrate that the Fed could be faced with a choice of losing control of monetary policy or violating the legal requirement that it maintain sufficient assets to collateralize the currency.

Background

Section 16 of the Federal Reserve Act spells out the legal requirement that the Fed collateralize the currency:

> Any Federal Reserve bank may make application to the local Federal Reserve agent for such amount of the Federal Reserve notes hereinbefore provided for as it may require. Such application shall be accompanied with a tender to the local Federal Reserve agent of collateral in amount equal to the sum of the Federal Reserve notes thus applied for and issued pursuant to such application. The collateral security thus offered shall be notes, drafts, bills of exchange, or acceptances acquired under section 10A, 10B, 13, or 13A of this Act, or bills of exchange endorsed by a member bank of any Federal Reserve district and purchased under the provisions of section 14 of this Act, or bankers' acceptances purchased under the provisions of said section 14, or gold certificates, or Special Drawing Right certificates, or any obligations which are direct obligations of, or are fully guaranteed as to principal and interest by, the United States or any agency thereof, or assets that Federal Reserve banks may purchase or hold under section 14 of this Act *or any other asset of a Federal reserve bank*. . . . The said Board of Governors of the Federal Reserve System may at any time call upon a Federal Reserve bank for additional security to protect the Federal Reserve notes issued to it [Board of Governors 2003; emphasis added].

The italicized words were added on October 28, 2003. Sweep accounts had resulted in historically low levels of reserve balances and, in the wake of the large discount window loans required after the 9/11 terrorist attacks, Congress expanded the set of eligible collateral to ensure that the Fed would still be able to collateralize the currency—even if it had to sterilize a large discount window loan by selling Treasury securities. Although "any other asset" seems unequivocal, a critical question is whether it applies to magical assets.

As described above, if the Fed were to make losses, rather than deduct those losses from capital, the Fed plans to create the "magic asset." Would the magic asset be eligible to collateralize currency? We don't know. It certainly qualifies as "any other asset." But if the currency can be collateralized by hypothesized future profits, including at a time when the Fed would be making losses and could reasonably be expected to keep doing so for a while, then the statute is effectively meaningless. The statute puts a limit on how negative the Fed's capital can go—no more negative than the amount of the Fed's noncurrency liabilities.[2] But if the Fed can create an asset specifically designed to keep capital from ever going negative, and that asset counts as collateral for currency, then the Fed can never violate the statutory requirement.

Even if the magic asset isn't eligible to collateralize the currency, the Fed can still guarantee that currency is sufficiently collateralized in two ways. First, the Fed can ensure that it is always profitable by funding most of its assets (which earn interest) by currency (which is interest free); that is, it has to keep its balance sheet small enough so that reserve balances are low. However, it officially decided in January 2019 that it would conduct policy with a high, not low, level of reserve balances. As I will describe below, getting back to scarce reserve balances may, in some circumstances, not be possible without running afoul of the currency collateralization requirement.

Second, the Fed can acquire assets in whatever amount is necessary to keep noncurrency liabilities greater than its accumulated losses. Essentially, since currency is exogenous, whenever the Fed buys an asset, noncurrency liabilities, in particular reserve balances, go up by the amount of the asset. But if the Fed is making losses in

---

[2] If (1) assets > currency and (2) capital = assets − (currency + noncurrency liabilities), then (3) noncurrency liabilities > −capital.

part because of the massive amount of reserve balances, this strategy is explosive.

An additional question is whether the statute refers to the par or fair value of the securities. The Fed has elected to conduct its accounting based on par values, but that is neither here nor there for determining congressional intent. The statute makes more sense if interpreted as referring to fair values. It is, after all, a collateral requirement, and the Federal Reserve Board is specifically allowed to "call upon a Federal Reserve bank for additional security to protect the Federal Reserve notes issued to it" (Board of Governors 2003).

Projection of Fed Balance Sheet and Income under Stress

In the simulation described below, the FOMC tapers its asset purchase in a manner consistent with its announcement at the November 2021 FOMC meeting. By the time tapering is done, underlying inflation has become entrenched at 4 percent. To reduce inflation, the FOMC allows the balance sheet to run off as securities mature and it raises the federal funds rate 50 basis points a meeting until it is 6 percent, concluding in December 2023.

A 6 percent target federal funds rate is high by the standards of recent decades, but it is not unreasonable to consider as a stress case. To reduce inflation, the Fed would need to raise the funds rate above the neutral rate sufficiently to reduce the pace of growth below trend and push the unemployment rate above the NAIRU. The pace of tightening over 2016–2018 during an extremely gradual expansion when inflation was below target is not a good guide for such a tightening.

As shown in Figure 1, Fed tightening in the mid-1990s and mid-2000s, on average, required a 4 percentage point increase in the real federal funds rate over 1.5 years. If inflation expectations increase 2 percentage points, then a 4 percentage point increase in the real federal funds rate would require a 6 percentage point increase in the nominal federal funds rate. Viewed another way, if the Fed needed to create 1 percentage point of monetary restraint, inflation expectations had risen to 4 percent, and r^* is 1 percent, then it would need a nominal federal funds rate of 6 percent.

Properly forecasting the Fed's income and balance sheet requires tracking all of the line items on the Fed's balance sheet and accounting for the maturities of each of the securities it holds and will acquire.

FIGURE 1
Real Federal Funds Rate

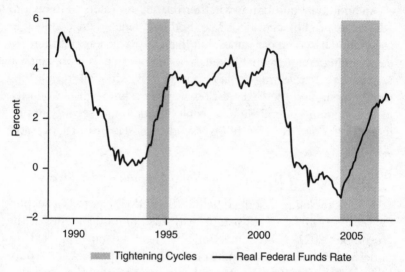

SOURCES: Bureau of Economic Analysis, PCE excluding food and energy;
Federal Reserve Bank of New York, effective federal funds rate.

It also requires assumptions about the paths for interest rates all along the maturity spectrum. Although it is important that some independent agency or institution conduct such scenario analysis, I will not do it. Instead, I will use a highly simplified Fed balance sheet and assumptions about just the path for overnight rates.[3]

Fed's Balance Sheet

The Fed's initial balance sheet, shown in Table 1, is based on the H.4.1 statistical release as of December 9, 2021 (Tables 2 and 5). The Fed held $1.1 trillion in Treasuries with less than 1 year maturity, $4.5 trillion in Treasuries with longer maturities, and $2.6 trillion in agency MBS. It also had $0.3 trillion in unamortized net premiums on those securities (the difference between the price at which they bought the security and the security's par value), which I apportion $0.2 trillion to Treasuries and $0.1 trillion to MBS. The remaining Fed assets are de minimus. Total assets are $8.5 trillion.

---

[3]Additional details on the forecast are available on request.

TABLE 1
Simplified Fed Balance Sheet
(December 8, 2021, $Trillions)

Assets		Liabilities and Capital	
T-Bills	1.1	Currency	2.2
Other Treasuries	4.7	TGA	0.1
MBS	2.7	Reserve Balances, RRPs, and Other Deposits	6.2
Total	8.5	Total	8.5
		Capital	0.0

Note: $0.3 trillion in net unamortized premiums is allocated between "Other Treasuries" ($0.2 trillion) and MBS ($0.1 trillion).
Source: Board of Governors (2021).

There was $2.2 trillion in currency outstanding and $0.1 trillion in the TGA at the Fed, the two largest liabilities on which the Fed does not pay interest. Reserve balances equaled $4.3 trillion, and reverse repurchase agreements equaled $1.8 trillion. "Other deposits," which include deposits of central counterparties (CCPs), government sponsored enterprises (GSEs), and foreign official institutions, equaled $0.2 trillion (I assume "other deposits" are mostly CCP deposits and so earn interest). In the projection, I define the sum of reserve balances, reverse repos, and other deposits as the residual between assets and noninterest-paying liabilities. Capital and remaining liabilities are de minimis.

I assume that the FOMC tapers its asset purchases as announced at the December 2021 FOMC meeting. Treasury purchases, $60 billion a month in December, are reduced $20 billion each month. MBS purchases, $30 billion a month in December, are reduced $10 billion a month. The final purchases are in March 2022. I assume further that currency grows at a 5 percent annual rate and that the TGA rises to $300 billion in January and to $500 billion in March 2022, where it stays.

Beginning at the end of March 2022, the FOMC allows its Treasury securities and agency MBS to mature without reinvestment. I assume the maturities of Treasury bills are distributed evenly between 0 and 1 year. The New York Fed's most recent Annual

Report on the SOMA indicates that the average maturity of its holdings of Treasury securities is 7.3 years. If the average maturity of the securities with less than one-year maturity is six months, then the average maturity of the remaining Treasury securities is 8.8 or approximately nine years. I assume that the maturities of Treasury securities other than bills are distributed evenly between 1 and 17 years. I also assume that 10 percent of MBS mature each year, which is approximately the percentage of mortgages typically repaid for reasons other than refinancing. Using these assumptions, the Fed's balance sheet in September 2023 (which, as discussed below, is when it is done raising interest rates) is shown in Table 2.

Fed income is the difference between the interest that the Fed earns on its assets and the interest it pays on its liabilities. In this simulation, Treasury bills earn the target federal funds rate (the bottom of the target range), Treasury notes earn 2 percent (roughly the amount they earned in 2020), and MBS earn 3 percent (also roughly the amount they earned in 2020). Reserve balances and reverse repurchase agreements both pay the target federal funds rate.

The FOMC increases its target for the federal funds rate by 50 basis points per meeting beginning in May 2022, the meeting after tapering ends and when the balance sheet begins to shrink. The IORB and RRP rates move up with the target funds rate. As shown in Figure 2, starting in March 2023, when the IORB rate has risen to 4 percent, the Fed begins to make losses. By September 2023, the Fed is losing $9 billion every FOMC period. According to plan, when

TABLE 2
Fed Balance Sheet after Tightening,
September 2023, $ trillions

Assets		Liabilities and Capital	
T-Bills	0	Currency	2.4
Other Treasuries	4.4	TGA	0.5
MBS	2.4	Reserves Balances, RRPs, and Other Deposits	3.9
Total	6.8	Total	6.8
		Capital	0.0

FIGURE 2
PROJECTION OF FEDERAL RESERVE PROFITS
FOMC TIGHTENS 50 BASIS POINTS PER
MEETING TO 6 PERCENT

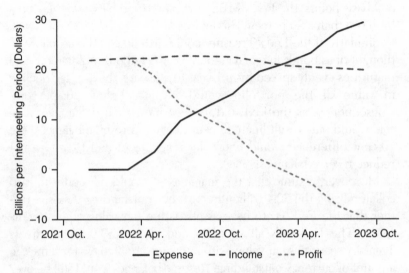

SOURCES: Author's calculations; statistical release H.4.1, Federal Reserve Bank of New York; system open market operations during 2020.

the Fed makes a loss that would otherwise reduce its capital below zero, it increases the magic asset. By September 2023, the magic asset equals $25 billion.

Sales

With the Fed losing money and expected to do so for a while, and those losses seemingly being caused by the Fed writing extremely large checks to big banks, suppose Congress took away the Fed's ability to pay interest on reserve balances or pay interest to nonbanks using the ON RRP facility. To conduct monetary policy, the Fed would need to rapidly shrink reserve balances down to the level demanded by banks consistent with maintaining the fed funds rate at 6 percent. With the 6-percentage-point opportunity cost of holding reserve balances, demand would fall sharply. Banks would switch to satisfying their liquidity requirements using Treasury securities to the fullest extent possible.

The Fed would have a problem, though. Its Treasury bills would be gone, so it would have to sell MBS and its portfolio of Treasury notes. Based on the current convexity and duration of a typical MBS portfolio and an assumption that the 10-year rate had increased 300 basis points, the Fed's MBS portfolio would have experienced a bit more than a 20 percent capital loss.[4]

Similarly, if the Fed's Treasury note portfolio could reasonably be thought of as bonds in equal amounts with coupons of 2 percent and maturities evenly spaced from 1 year to 16 years, the average decline in value of the portfolio would be just below 20 percent. Consequently, as the Fed sold its securities, each dollar par value sold would only result in an 80-cent decline in reserve balances; the 20-cent difference would boost the magic asset and therefore not reduce reserve balances.

Moreover, assume that the magic asset would not count toward collateralizing the $2.4 trillion in currency outstanding. Assume further that the Fed has to have assets with a fair value equal to currency. The Fed sells all its MBS and all but $3.0 trillion in its Treasury securities par value, with fair value equal to $2.4 trillion, the amount of currency outstanding. Reserve balances would still be over $0.5 trillion, which could be higher than what would be demanded by the banking system if it fully economized on its holdings. If reserve balances were more than banks demanded, and the Fed were no longer able to pay interest on reserve balances, interest rates would fall to zero. The Fed would have lost control of monetary policy.

Conclusion

This chapter describes three serious challenges the Fed faces because its balance sheet is unbounded. The first is that there is nothing stopping it from using helicopter money. It could do so to stimulate the economy, to increase social justice, or to avoid a financial and economic catastrophe. Second, the Fed could expand its asset holding by investing in worthy causes in coordination with the Treasury and Congress. Third, by expanding its portfolio far beyond the

[4]Change in price $= -$(Duration)*(Change in rate) $+$ (Convexity/2)*(Change in rate) 2; MBS duration is currently 4.49, and convexity is -1.54. The 10-year rate is 1.5 percent and would be 4.5 percent in the situation considered: $-(4.7)*(3) + (-1.7/2)*(3)$ 2 $= -21.75$.

amounts that can be funded with currency, which is interest free, and investing in longer-term assets, the Fed risks losing hundreds of billions of dollars and potentially control of monetary policy. None of these challenges arise if the Fed were to conduct policy as it did before the 2008 financial crisis using a scarce-reserve framework. As the FOMC has observed, both approaches (abundant reserves and scarce reserves) offer sufficient interest rate control to conduct monetary policy effectively.

References

Bernanke, B. S. (2016) "What Tools Does the Fed Have Left? Part 3: Helicopter Money." Brookings.edu blog (April 11).

Board of Governors (2003) "Federal Reserve Act, Section 16: Note Issues" (October 28).

_____ (2009) "The Role of the Federal Reserve in Preserving Financial and Monetary Stability: Joint Statement by the Department of the Treasury and the Federal Reserve" (March 23).

_____ (2020) "Federal Reserve Banks Combined Financial Statements" (2018–2019). Available at www.federalreserve.gov /aboutthefed/files/combinedfinstmt2019.pdf.

_____ (2021) "Factors Affecting Reserve Balances—H.4.1" (December 8).

Federal Reserve (2002) System Study Group on Alternative Instruments for System Operations. "Alternative Instruments for Open Market and Discount Window Operations" (December).

FOMC (2011) "Conference Call of the Federal Open Market Committee on August 1, 2011." Available at www.federalreserve .gov/monetarypolicy/files/FOMC20110801confcall.pdf.

_____ (2013) "Conference Call of the Federal Open Market Committee on October 16, 2013." Available at www.federal reserve.gov/monetarypolicy/files/FOMC20131016confcall.pdf.

Kelton, S.; Bernal, A.; and Carlock, G. (2018) "We Can Pay for a Green New Deal." Huffington Post (November 30).

Network for Greening the Financial System [NGFS] (2021) "Adapting Central Bank Operations to a Hotter World: Reviewing Some Options" (March): 4–54.

Omarova, S. T. (2021) "The People's Ledger: How to Democratize Money and Finance the Economy." Vanderbilt Law Review 74 (5):1231–300.

Selgin, G. (2018) *Floored! How a Misguided Fed Experiment Deepened and Prolonged the Great Recession.* Washington: Cato Institute.

_____ (2020) *The Menace of Fiscal QE.* Washington: Cato Institute.

Varoufakis, Y. (2021) "A Progressive Monetary Policy Is the Only Alternative." *Project Syndicate* (October 28).

17
HELICOPTER MONEY AND PEOPLE'S QE
Frances Coppola

In my book (Coppola 2019), I define helicopter drops as one-off distribution of money to households and businesses. Importantly, this money is created by the central bank, not raised from the market by issuing debt or from the population in the form of a tax. Fiscal authorities can, of course, do one-off handouts without central bank involvement, by borrowing from markets. But this simply redistributes money from investors to households and businesses. Therefore, I define helicopter drops as specifically financed by central banks whether directly or indirectly.

Fiscal and Political Consequences of Helicopter Money

At the present time, central banks cannot distribute helicopter money. They don't have access to household and business bank accounts, and they don't hold distribution information such as names and addresses. Helicopter money is therefore always and everywhere distributed by fiscal authorities. We could say that central banks create the helicopters' payload, but the fiscal authorities actually fly the helicopters. And for this reason, helicopter money at the moment is subject to political whims. It is not simply a monetary policy tool.

Were central banks to introduce digital currency, that could be used as a vehicle for distributing money directly to households and businesses, bypassing the fiscal authority. However, that does not

Frances Coppola is a columnist with CoinDesk. She is the author of the *Coppola Comment Finance & Economics* blog, which is a regular feature on the *Financial Times's Alphaville* blog.

mean that helicopter money would not be subject to political pressures. Consider a fiscal authority that, faced with high unemployment and a growing welfare bill, was determined to force people into work through cutting unemployment benefits. If an inflation-targeting central bank decided to stimulate demand with helicopter drops using central bank digital currency (CBDC), it would directly conflict with the fiscal authority's attempts to reduce unemployment. That is because it would effectively replenish the money withdrawn from the unemployed and reduce their incentive to work.

So, helicopter money has fiscal and political consequences. It needs to be used in cooperation with the fiscal authority, not independently of it. In the wake of the Covid-19 crisis, most countries have done fiscal handouts of one sort or another, some of which amount to helicopter drops. The most obvious example is U.S. stimulus checks. Another is the U.K.'s Self-Employment Income Support Scheme, a total of five one-off drops to self-employed people. Both of these helicopter drops were effectively financed by the central banks because of the scale of quantitative easing (QE).

Fiscal QE

I don't like the term "fiscal QE." I prefer to talk about central bank financing of government spending. This can be direct or indirect. Direct forms include:

- Ex ante financing of government expenditure;
- Ex post monetization of deficits; and
- Purchases of bonds in primary auctions.

Indirect forms include:

- Purchases of bonds on secondary markets;
- Direct purchases of bonds from government-sponsored agencies and public development banks; and
- Yield curve control.

Since March 2020, all Western central banks have indirectly financed their governments, simply because of the scale of QE and other exceptional programs. I include the European Central Bank (ECB) in this. Despite its much vaunted treaty independence and the prohibition of monetary financing under Article 123 of the

Lisbon Treaty, the extent of the ECB's intervention in sovereign debt markets has enabled eurozone governments, including even Greece, to spend far more than their fiscal space would otherwise have permitted.

Some Western central banks have come close to direct financing of government expenditure. The Bank of England, for example, stood ready to use the Ways and Means overdraft to finance the exceptional government expenditures in the early days of the pandemic. Admittedly, this was to prevent sudden very large debt issuance hitting gilt markets at a time when they were already severely disrupted by pandemic fears. But it nonetheless amounted to a commitment to finance the U.K. government directly if necessary—even if only overnight. The Bank of England also said it was considering intervening in primary auctions, though it has not done so.

During the pandemic, governments and central banks have conducted a massive experiment. They have thrown off all limiting constraints and thrown money around on an unprecedented scale. One way or another, they have done everything that I recommended in my book.

But then the crisis they were dealing with was an unprecedented one. There has never in history been a coordinated shutdown of large parts of the global economy. Governments that were deliberately engineering the worst recession in 300 years because of a public health emergency had to keep people alive and businesses afloat through that recession—otherwise what would be the point of the shutdown? And central banks had to keep banks and markets functioning, and prevent a public health crisis becoming a sovereign debt crisis. It was an extraordinary time. It needed an extraordinary policy response.

I think it is fair to say that these unprecedented infusions of money into the economy have worked. People have stayed alive during the recession, and although many businesses have failed, many more have survived that otherwise might not have done. And although unemployment is elevated, it is much lower than was predicted.

But the experiment is not over. There is still a question to be answered—and the answer will determine the future path of both fiscal and monetary policy. Will all this money cause runaway inflation?

The Spectre of Inflation

We're now emerging from the pandemic. Economies are starting to recover. And inflation is already elevated. Indeed it would be surprising if it were not. Much of the money distributed during the pandemic is sitting in people's bank accounts and on asset markets. As the economy reopens, people are spending it. But the supply side is damaged: supply chains are severely disrupted, and production of essential goods is below its prepandemic level. So as demand is recovering faster than supply, prices are inevitably rising. What we don't know is whether the supply side can ramp up production sufficiently to mop up excess demand without central bank action. And if central banks now tighten policy to control near-term inflation, we may never know—which would be a pity. I'd like to remind central banks that it is medium-term inflation they should aim to control, not near-term inflation due to supply and demand disruptions in the aftermath of an unprecedented global recession.

Inflation is also elevated because of base effects, notably oil and gas prices, which fell sharply when demand crashed because of the shutdown and have now, because of supply constraints, rebounded to somewhat higher levels than before the pandemic. This is similar to what happened in 2010–2011, and the policy response should in my view be similar. The ECB's decision to raise interest rates in 2011 because of inflationary pressures arising from oil price rises contributed to the sovereign debt crisis of 2012, and sovereigns now have even higher debt levels than they had then. Premature interest rate rises could trigger another, and worse, sovereign debt crisis. It is important that we do not repeat the mistakes of the past.

However, we do need to be on our guard. At present, the indications are that inflation is mostly driven by supply-side factors and will therefore be insensitive to central bank actions and—hopefully—short lived. I think runaway inflation of the 1970s variety is unlikely. But it is not impossible that wage-price spirals could develop, particularly if supply-side damage proves intractable. I do, however, wish to scotch any notion that hyperinflation is a risk in Western economies. Exceptional though they are, the combined fiscal and monetary actions following the onset of Covid-19 are not so extreme as to trigger catastrophic loss of confidence in sovereign currencies, provided we establish a clear exit route from them.

While we are on the subject of mistakes of the past, I do not wish to see any repetition of the misuse of QE that we saw in the period between the great financial crisis and the pandemic. There will inevitably be some fiscal consolidation in the coming years. Indeed, in the United Kingdom, it has already started. But QE should not be used to offset fiscal consolidation. It is ineffective anyway if fiscal consolidation is targeted at the bottom end of the income distribution. And it means that central banks cannot meaningfully plan their exit from what is, after all, supposed to be exceptional support.

Compromising Central Bank Independence

I believe that there is now an even greater danger—namely, that QE, central bank financing of government, and helicopter money become normalized. I emphasized in my book that they should be used in exceptional circumstances only. I do not support the modern monetary theory argument that central banks should finance government even in normal times. We need a plan to restore normal market financing of government. And we also need to push back against expectations that central banks will continue to backstop everything that governments do.

Central bank independence has been significantly compromised by the exceptional support central banks have provided to fiscal authorities during the pandemic. It may prove very difficult to remove the punchbowl, especially when there are siren voices saying that central banks can simply finance everything without cost.

There may be a case for central banks helping to finance specific initiatives to address the challenges of climate change, aging populations, and the changing nature of work. But interventions on the scale we have seen during the pandemic should be reserved for exceptional situations. Helicopter money and fiscal QE are powerful tools. They need to be used sparingly.

Conclusion

As a result of the pandemic, central banks and governments have conducted an enormous "proof of concept" for helicopter money and people's QE. So far, it has been a resounding success.

It has prevented an engineered shutdown from becoming a disastrous and long-lasting depression. But the most difficult part of all is still to come, and that is landing our helicopters without crashing them.

Reference

Coppola, F. (2019) *The Case for People's QE*. Medford, Mass.: Polity Press.

18

CENTRAL BANK ACTIVISM: GOOD INTENTIONS, BAD POLICY

Kevin Dowd

Central bankers are fond of telling us how their "courage to act" got us through the Global Financial Crisis (GFC) and how the subsequent reforms they pushed through afterward have fixed the financial system once and for all. Such claims should be taken with a grain of salt. Following the GFC (2007–2009), Federal Reserve policies have created the "everything bubble." They have led to excessive risk taking, leverage, and debt; increased financial fragility, inequality, and zombification; and have had devastating impacts on savers, pension funds, and capital allocation. The longer these policies are sustained, the more the damage compounds.

Nevertheless, the Fed can't raise interest rates to precrisis levels without triggering a market meltdown and a new financial crisis. The "Fed put" (i.e., supporting asset prices by keeping interest rates "lower for longer") has left the financial system addicted to continued support. Moreover, given existing levels of debt, a significant normalization of interest rates has the potential to send federal, state, and municipal finances into a tailspin. The Fed has thereby painted itself into a corner: it can't continue indefinitely with its post-GFC policies and it can't stop them either.

Policymakers are not suggesting any solutions to this policy dilemma. Instead, they suggest that the problems caused by central bank activism can be solved by even more activism. As William

---

Kevin Dowd is Professor of Finance and Economics at Durham University Business School. He is also an Adjunct Scholar at the Cato Institute.

Hague, former leader of the U.K. Conservative Party, wrote: "Central bankers have collectively lost the plot. They must raise interest rates or face their doom" (Hague 2017).

In this chapter, I consider some of the alternative policy proposals on offer: helicopter money, modern monetary theory (MMT), negative interest rate policy (NIRP), climate change, and central bank digital currencies (CBDCs). I conclude that, although well intentioned, central bank activism has unintended negative consequences. Hence, it is best to recognize the limits of monetary policy and to keep it aimed at objectives that are simple, transparent, and attainable.

Helicopter Money

Helicopter money refers to a policy under which the central bank "prints" base money—physically or electronically—and gives it away to private parties or to the government.[1] While helicopter money might appear to be free, it isn't; and this is so even if the cost of printing or issuing additional base money is considered to be zero (Dowd 2018). To an economist, a good (including money in this context) is "free" only if it can be obtained at a zero opportunity cost (i.e., if some people benefit from an increase in the quantity of the good and no one else suffers any loss). But helicopter money always has an opportunity cost; it is not a free lunch.

To see why, it is helpful to think of the central bank as part of the government sector, and then consider helicopter money in the context of the consolidated government balance sheet. A helicopter drop to the public is fiscally equivalent to a tax cut, because people can use the money to pay taxes. If people respond this way, the government is then issuing money via its central bank, but receiving that money back in taxes. The impact of the helicopter money is akin to the IRS issuing bearer tax vouchers, which can be used to pay taxes. If we ignore any monetary consequences (e.g., inflation) from the helicopter money drop, then what we have here is a *fiscal operation*, which likely produces some degree of redistribution among the population depending on how it is implemented.

---

[1]"Base money" refers to currency plus member bank reserves (deposits) held at the central bank.

Likewise, a helicopter drop to the one part of the government—the central bank—issuing and handing over base money to another part of the government—the Treasury—is merely an intergovernmental transfer. There is no free lunch: helicopter money creates the illusion, but not the reality, of free money.

However, the illusion is important because it creates political demands for supposedly free Fed handouts. These demands, if successful, threaten to undermine Fed independence. Indeed, if the Fed acquiesces to such pressures, it will create precedents and encourage even more such demands. After all, if helicopter money appears to be free, then the demand for it should be infinite—one can never have enough.

Given that a helicopter drop to the public is inherently a fiscal operation, albeit one with monetary policy ramifications, it is critical to maintain a clear delineation between fiscal and monetary policy. Mixing fiscal and monetary policy is wrong on principle. Government spending should be financed by taxation or borrowing, not by the Fed printing money; and spending decisions should be made by Congress, not the Fed.

As David Stockman, former director of the Office of Management and Budget, emphasized: helicopter money is "a central bank power grab like no other because it insinuates our unelected central bankers into the very heart of the fiscal process." The Framers of the U.S. Constitution

> delegated the powers of the purse—spending, taxing and borrowing—to the elected branch of government. . . . "[T]hey did so because the decision to spend, tax and borrow is the very essence of state power. There is no possibility of democracy . . . if these fundamental powers are removed from popular control [Stockman 2016].

Bernanke (2016) suggests a solution. He proposes that the Fed simply deposit helicopter money in the Treasury's Fed account. The Treasury could then spend that money in accordance with congressional spending mandates. However, even this version of helicopter money would still leave intact the incentive for Congress to prefer helicopter money to taxation, on the grounds that the former avoids the adverse political consequences of the latter. Such an incentive is undesirable from the perspective of encouraging rational government spending decisions, the political costs of which should be clear and upfront, and not hidden behind an impenetrable monetary veil. You cannot have rational government spending decisions in a system in which finance appears to be free and legislators are spending money like it grows on trees. Rational fiscal policy is impossible when legislators operate under the illusion of a fiscal free lunch.

Modern Monetary Theory

Advocates of MMT propose that the government should spend a lot and run large deficits financed by printing base money. They claim that the government cannot default because it can always finance expenditures by printing more base money. MMT goes hand in hand with insouciance about large deficits and high levels of government debt. We are told that fiscal deficits don't matter (Kelton 2020); that printing money should be the primary source of government finance; and that taxation should be used mainly to pursue "sado-economic" policies designed to hurt the disfavored and to combat inflation.[2]

The reality, however, is that fiscal deficits do matter. Leave aside for the moment the possibility of financing deficits by printing money. If the government issues debt, then that debt will impose a burden on future taxpayers who will be called upon to finance its repayment. If too much debt is issued, the burden on future taxpayers will grow to the point where the government will default. This conclusion is not substantially altered if the government can finance deficits by printing money (see Dowd 2020).

MMT is best understood in terms of a simple Keynesian model under which a rise in inflation is to be countered by increasing taxes to depress aggregate demand. The underlying problem with that model and MMT is neither has any theory of the price level, because neither assigns any role to the quantity theory of money.

In *The Deficit Myth*, Stephanie Kelton recalls a revealing discussion between James Tobin and President John F. Kennedy:

> Tobin recalls JFK asking, "Is there any limit to the deficit? I know of course about the political limits. . . . But is there any economic limit?" When Tobin confessed that "the only limit is really

[2]The classic reference on sado-economics is Hutchinson (2012).

inflation," the president replied, "That's right, isn't it? The deficit can be any size, the debt can be any size, provided they don't cause inflation. Everything else is just talk" [Kelton 2020: 241].

But "Everything else is just talk" begs the central issue—namely, inflation. An MMT monetary policy would likely produce a similar outcome to that which followed the monetary policies pursued from the late 1950s to the early 1980s, that is, rising inflation and eventual crisis. In both cases, the root problem is the same: the absence of a coherent theory of inflation. Now, as then, the solution to that problem is the same: some version of the quantity theory of money needs to be used to connect the money supply to the price level, and thence to the inflation rate.

A further problem is that MMT ignores the fact that what might work at the margin may not produce the intended results, if pursued at the scale proposed by its advocates. Consider two examples.

First, suppose the government deficit were small. Then, in principle, it might be possible for an MMT policy to be pursued with minimal adverse side effects. But the current government deficit is large (about $3 trillion) and if that were financed by printing money, then the supply of base money (currently about $6.4 trillion) would increase by nearly 50 percent. It is difficult to believe that printing money at such a rate would not have serious inflationary consequences. MMT thus fails a basic reality check.

Second, unless the rate of growth of nominal deficit spending is constrained—and MMT advocates do not propose to constrain that growth rate—then MMT would eventually lead to both hyperinflation and government default.

Negative Interest Rate Policy

Advocates of NIRP recommend it as a means to "break through" the zero lower bound (ZLB) interest-rate barrier to set negative rates to stimulate spending.[3]

---

[3]In his well-publicized speech, "How Low Can You Go?" Andy Haldane (2015), Chief Economist at the Bank of England, proposes NIRP to address the problem of the ZLB being a barrier against the "effectiveness of monetary policy." However, he unfortunately does not answer his own question. Rogoff (2016) proposes NIRP to promote stimulus. Related objectives of NIRP are to stimulate the economy by reducing financing costs and saving, and to encourage more lending.

Abolish Cash

However, if a central bank were to push interest rates below zero, then individuals and firms would have an incentive to shift from holding bank deposits to cash. To implement NIRP, while avoiding such an outcome, policymakers would need to abolish cash.

Abolishing cash, however, would have a number of adverse outcomes. First, it would deprive users of the benefits of cash (e.g., cash's convenience for small payments, its usefulness as a store of value, and its anonymity). Second, it would expropriate assets that should by default be deemed to have been legitimately acquired. Third, by eliminating a key competitor, it would enable digital payments providers to increase their charges. Fourth, it would cause problems for vulnerable groups (e.g., the elderly) who would struggle to adapt to a cashless world. Fifth, it would make everyone dependent on digital technology that might fail when needed. For example, a payments provider might refuse to authorize a payment or the entire system might fail if the grid were to go down.[4] Finally, it would end financial privacy, because your payments provider (and possibly your spouse) would be able to see all your transactions (Dowd 2021).

Negative Interest Rate Policy

The key feature of NIRP is a negative central bank deposit rate that pushes down other bank deposit rates and bond coupons. NIRP was first implemented in 2009 when the Swedish Riksbank imposed a negative deposit rate for commercial bank holdings (i.e., reserves) with the Riksbank[5]—the first negative interest rate since

---

[4]To give an example, in September 2017, Puerto Rico was devastated by Hurricane Maria. The storm knocked out the electricity supply, bank ATMs and credit card verification stopped working, and people were unable to buy food and other necessities with their credit and welfare cards. Store security guards admitted only customers who could pay in cash, and the Federal Reserve had to fly in "a jet loaded with an undisclosed amount of cash" to meet payrolls and help avert disaster as peoples' cash holdings ran out (Levin 2017). "In a cashless world, you'd better pray the power never goes out," observed Ryan McMaken (2017).

[5]The Riksbank, however, did not make its main policy rate—the repo rate—negative until 2015.

at least Hammurabi.[6] Denmark, the eurozone, Japan, and Switzerland subsequently implemented their own versions of NIRP. The amount of negative yielding bonds rose to a peak of over $16 trillion in 2019 before falling back (Milne and Arnold 2020), by which time negative yielding bonds had risen to 30 percent of the market (Durden 2019). These NIRP experiments, however, were modest; rates only went as low as minus 75 basis points. Central banks didn't dare go further.[7]

We might reasonably expect NIRP to push down interest rates in general, but we should not expect it to make all interest rates negative. That is because the driving factors that lead to positive market interest rates—time preference, productivity of capital, and compensation for default risk—will not go away just because policymakers implement NIRP. Consider the following reductio argument.

Let's assume what we want to disprove, namely, that NIRP leads issuers to stop issuing positive coupon bonds. There is no reason to suppose that the demand for such bonds would disappear, because investors would continue to demand them for the same reasons they demand them now. So if I want to invest in a bond that pays a positive coupon and no one will issue one to me, I can financially engineer one from a portfolio of bonds that pay negative coupons—that is, I can create my own synthetic positive coupon bonds to invest in.[8]

---

[6]There are good reasons why interest rates had been positive over the previous 4,000 years or so. Positive interest rates reflect positive time preference, the expectation that the future productivity of capital will be positive, and compensation for default risk. Alasdair Macleod (2015) is to the point here: "NIRP is a preposterous concept. It contravenes the laws of time preference, commanding by diktat that cash is worth less than credit." If negative interest rates seem unnatural, that is because they are.

[7]Pushed too far, we would have NIRP on steroids that would cause major disruption to the financial system and lead to a downward spiral of falling prices, falling monetary aggregates and falling spending, resulting in nominally fixed debt burdens increasing in real terms, and increasing credit risk premia. Such a spiral would likely lead to the unraveling of the financial system and a depression–inducing debt–deflation "doom loop" of the sort that Irving Fisher set out in the 1930s (see Fisher 1933).

[8]To illustrate the financial engineering involved, suppose we have a floating rate note (FRN) with a maturity of two years, an annual coupon of −$3, and a face value of $100. Call this FRN0. We then decompose FRN0 into two further FRNs: FRN1 with the same maturity, an annual coupon of −$4 and a face value of $50; and FRN2 with a coupon of $1. FRN0 and the portfolio FRN1 + FRN2 have the same cash flows, so we can write FRN0 = FRN1 + FRN2. Subtracting FRN1 from both sides and rearranging, we then obtain FRN2 = FRN0 − FRN1, that is, we have financially engineered a positive coupon FRN as the difference between two negative coupon FRNs with different coupons.

So too can anyone else. The fact that those bonds are synthetic rather physically existent financial instruments does not matter. Similarly, if an issuer wished to issue such bonds, there is no reason why they shouldn't. They can even do so without taking on risk by issuing such bonds and simultaneously hedging their exposure with synthetics. The market for such bonds would then return along with other related markets.

For example, we can imagine financial institutions providing positive interest savings vehicles that serve the same role as traditional interest-bearing bank savings accounts. In short, NIRP would not lead to the disappearance of positive interest rates. Rather, it would produce a state of affairs in which positive rates (presumably, both nominal and inflation linked) and negative rates coexisted—and this would be the case regardless of how low the NIRP base rate might go.

Empirical evidence and the opinions of many observers point to the conclusion that NIRP has been a failure. Negative rates have failed to stimulate the economy; they are "a tax in sheep's clothing" (Waller 2016). NIRP led to greater rather than lower savings rates (Kantchev et al. 2016; Blackstone 2019; Durden 2019). It also led to reduced bank lending (Molyneux et al. 2020), reduced credit creation, and declines in banks' net interest margins and profitability (Molyneux et al. 2019).

NIRP had adverse impacts on savers, not just because it lowered their yields, often to below zero, but also because it reduced their investment opportunities (Stoller 2019) and pushed them to take on more risk in their search for positive yields. Likewise, negative yields made it more difficult for pension funds and insurance companies to meet their obligations, pressuring them to move up the maturity curve and take on more market or credit risk. However, since regulatory constraints hinder them from greater risk taking, they have difficulty avoiding negative yielding assets. Finally, NIRP was introduced because policymakers wanted to give their economies a short-term stimulus jolt, but central banks then experienced difficulties weaning their economies off the policy. "Overall, we are on a painkiller," one observer noted, "and it's very hard to get off it" (Blackstone 2019).

Yet, in 2019, the central bank that had pioneered negative interest rates, the Riksbank, ended it. The main reasons it gave were concerns about the long-term impacts if NIRP were to be continued—namely, that negative rates would weaken banks, discourage lending, encourage cash hoarding, and lead to further increases in already high levels of household debt (Milne and Arnold 2020).

Andersson and Jonung (2020), prominent Swedish economists, expressed other concerns about NIRP. In particular, its impact on the housing market, its ineffectiveness in helping to achieve inflation targets, and its impact on weakening the exchange rate. They gave a blunt assessment of the policy: "It is evident that the policy's effect on the inflation rate was modest, and that it contributed to increased financial vulnerabilities. The lesson from the experiment is clear: Do not do it again."

Climate Change

Then there is the issue of central banks getting into the climate change business. I would suggest they shouldn't. First, they don't have the legislative mandates to do so and have no right to appoint themselves to take on ambitious climate change or other fashionable social, environmental, or political causes without such mandates.

Second, they lack the scientific expertise to address multidecade or longer climate risks involved. To the extent they can claim any modeling expertise, it is on short-horizon financial modeling, on which their record is, to say the least, less than stellar. For example, consider their modeling failures on the Basel capital requirements. Any models central bankers might use to set such regulatory requirements are almost infinitely gameable and therefore useless.

Third, there is an insurmountable pretense of knowledge problem. To quote one leading climate change expert:

> The crucial, unsettled scientific question for policy is, "How will the climate change over the next century under both natural and human influences?" Answers to that question at the global and regional levels, as well as to equally complex questions of how ecosystems and human activities will be affected, should inform our choices about energy and infrastructure.

> But—here's the catch—those questions are the hardest ones to answer. They challenge, in a fundamental way, what science can tell us about future climates [Koonin 2014].

If the answers to those questions are not known, then no one, not even central bankers, can possibly know what should be done about them.

Fourth, even if they knew what they would like to do, central bankers lack policy instruments for the long horizons involved, and any instruments they do have such as "green" disclosure requirements are wide open to abuse—firms are already experts at "greenwashing."

Central bank climate policy is another lucrative make-work project for regulators and consultants. As Norbert Michel et al. (2021: 3) note:

> It is likely . . . that such [policies] will result in an army of well-paid consultants, lawyers, and accountants who will provide compliance advice to public companies subject to these rules, or to corporations seeking capital from the government on favorable terms, and that those living off this compliance and credit eco-system will become effective lobbyists for [the] maintenance of the system.

John Cochrane, a senior fellow at the Hoover Institution, has been a leading critic of having central banks move "headlong into climate change policy." In his view, it would "destroy central banks' independence, their ability to fulfil their main missions to control inflation and stem financial crises, and people's faith in their impartiality and technical competence. And it won't help the climate." His view is based on a fundamental principle governing the responsibility of a central bank in a free society.

> A central bank in a democracy is not an all-purpose do-good agency, with authority to subsidize what it decides to be worthy, defund what it dislikes, and to force banks and companies to do the same. A central bank, whose leaders do not regularly face voters, lives by an iron contract: freedom and independence so long as it stays within its limited and mandated powers [Cochrane 2020].

Once the precedent is created that the central bank should embark on one currently fashionable cause, and never mind that it has to violate its mandate to do so, then it opens up the floodgates to sponsor future fashionable causes. Such blatant politicking might be popular at Davos cocktail parties but it undermines whatever popular trust central banks might still enjoy.

Central Bank Digital Currencies

At one level, central bank digital currencies (CBDCs) are harmless but pointless. However, I would like to consider them in their most potent form whereby the central bank sets up a digital currency, compels everyone to use it, and abolishes substitutes like cash and bank demand deposits.

The first point to note is that such a system would entail seriously adverse effects on the banking system. These include the dangers of a major contraction in bank lending and having bureaucrats replacing bankers in allocating bank credit. These problems were nicely articulated by George Selgin in his recent open letter to President Biden's initial nominee for the post of Comptroller of the Currency, Professor Saule Omarova, regarding her version of a Fed CBDC scheme:

> According to your own description of it, your plan would ideally see public Fed Accounts "fully replace—rather than uneasily coexist with—private bank deposits." Consequently it would "likely cause a massive contraction in bank lending" to businesses and individuals. Most if not all of the lending now done by banks would instead be done by the Fed, either directly or through Fed purchases of securities issued by a National Investment Authority. Some of the Fed's lending would consist of "New Discount Window" (NDW) loans to "qualifying lending institutions" (QLIs). But in order to "maximize the allocative impact" of this arrangement, the Fed would be free, not only to determine which banks qualify for loans and what collateral they must post, but to explicitly prefer banks that fund particular firms or activities, while refusing funding to others. In short, despite allowing some banks to continue to make loans, the plan would have bureaucrats take the place of the thousands of bankers who now decide where bank credit goes [Selgin 2021].

Plans such as these also raise alarm bells because of their similarities to the Reconstruction Finance Corporation of the 1930s, which, besides being incompetent and monumentally wasteful, "was an unabashed, quintessential purveyor of cronyism" (Earle 2020).

CBDCs as Tools of Economic Policy

CBDCs have no end of (alas, undesirable) policy uses. They could be used as vehicles to implement helicopter money or NIRP.

They could give the central bank increased power to set the dominant interest rate in the economy and to apply differential interest rates. They could enable radically innovative monetary policies. If the central bank wanted to boost spending, it could announce that it will cancel or tax money holdings to encourage people to spend more. If it decided that it wanted to discourage money "hoarding," it could impose expiry dates to make people spend. If it wanted to reduce spending, it could increase the interest rate on money holdings to encourage people to save more, and so forth.

Demand management then becomes demand control. CBDCs could be used to complement MMT. If the central bank adopted MMT and then printed too much money, it could cancel some of that money once inflation became unacceptably high. CBDCs offer a new tool for central bank climate change and industrial policies. The central bank could apply differential treatment whereby preferred clients or sectors get better rates, whereas unapproved clients or sectors get penal rates or are denied credit altogether. CBDCs give the central bank increased power to punish and reward. They could also be used to compel people to buy government-approved products, or to set prices and quantities of everything bought and sold, and transform the central bank into the economy's central planner.

"Dark Side" Uses of CBDCs

CBDCs can also be used to implement sado-economic policies. CBDCs would entail total control over all spending by whoever controls the central bank and could be used to block unapproved expenditures or cancel anyone's money holdings. Cancellation can be partial or full, and done in an instant. As Peter Earle (2021) observes:

> Although it tempts speculation of a particularly Orwellian tenor, one may imagine . . . the tying of anything from mandatory insurance coverage to getting vaccinated to compulsory voting to be enforceable under the threat of individually-targeted monetary penalties. . . . [A] currently innocuous programmable digital currency may, over time, morph into nothing less than weaponizable money.

CBDCs could be used to impose any political agenda; go after political enemies; and punish those who express incorrect views, spread misinformation, and are deemed "oppressors" or "privileged" because of their race or sex. Punishments could vary from mild (e.g., fines or temporary blocks on permissible purchases) to permanent cancellation, rendering victims unable to make any transactions ever, thereby exiling them from the monetary economy.

CBDCs also make for a powerful future lockdown tool. They could be programmed to ensure that people could only spend within a certain distance from their home and could only spend at approved times on approved items and do everything else they are told. Last but not least, CBDCs could be used to implement Chinese-style social credit policies. CBDCs are the ultimate accessory in digital totalitarianism.

Conclusion

While those who propose a more activist central bank, broadly conceived, may have good intentions, their policies would have significant unintended negative consequences for economic and financial stability, as well as personal freedom.

In the past, central banks had straightforward mandates—in essence, to deliver monetary and financial stability. Those tasks are not difficult to perform, yet policymakers couldn't even do them properly. It is naive to believe that the problems caused by central banks' failures to deliver on their easy-to-achieve past mandates will be solved by vastly expanding their mandates and hoping for better results the next time around. It is therefore stretching credulity to believe that any of the extreme policies currently being bandied about, and discussed in this chapter, would end well.

The root problem is that central bank expansion—whether of its balance sheet or its mandate—is logically the worst response because it kicks the can down the road and makes the long-term outcome so much worse. But it is politically the easiest response, because it allows policymakers to avoid taking personal responsibility for necessary but politically unpopular decisions, such as normalizing interest rates.

Advocates of hyperactive central banking have forgotten why old-fashioned central banking was deliberately limited in its scope. On that subject, former Bank of England (BOE) governor Mervyn King put it well:

> Our ambition at the Bank of England is to be boring. . . . Our aim is to maintain economic stability. A reputation for being boring is an advantage—credibility of the policy framework helps to dampen the movement of the [economic] see-saw [King 2000: 1].

The "see-saw" King was alluding to was turbulence of the 1990s—the Barings debacle, Black September, and all that—which gave the BOE a (well-deserved) rough ride but pale in comparison to the "excitement" of the last 15 years.

Fast forward to the present day and King is now warning about central banks meddling in politics and overextending itself:

> The global financial crisis and its aftermath greatly expanded the role of central banks. . . . Amid widespread frustration with the inability of elected policy makers to address the critical issues of the day, influential voices—including politicians, economic luminaries and the general populace—increasingly called on central banks to step in. Central banks became "the only game in town." Central bankers responded willingly, moving into the political arena [King and Katz 2021].

By stepping into the political arena, central banks voluntarily surrender their own independence. By taking on tasks they are unsuited to carry out, central banks are sure to fail in their essential tasks. If we are to have central banks, their mandates need to be kept to the absolute minimum—on the presumption that the less ambitious they are, the less damage they will do. As far as central banking is concerned, keep it simple and above all, boring.

References

Andersson, F. N. G., and Jonung, L. (2020) "Don't Do It Again! The Swedish Experience with Negative Central Bank Interest Rates in 2015–2019." *VoxEU* (May 8).

Bernanke, B. S. (2016) "What Tools Does the Fed Have Left? Part 3: Helicopter Money." *Ben Bernanke's Blog* (April 11). Brookings Institution.

Blackstone, B. (2019) "Negative Rates, Designed as a Short-Term Jolt, Have Become an Addiction." *Wall Street Journal* (May 20).

Cochrane, J. H. (2020) "Central Banks and Climate Change: A Case of Mission Creep." *Hoover Institution blog* (November 15).

Dowd, K. (2018) "Against Helicopter Money." *Cato Journal* 38 (1): 147–69.

_____ (2020) "Review" of S. Kelton, *The Deficit Myth: Modern Monetary Theory and the Birth of the People's Economy.*" *Cato Journal* 38 (1): 147–68.

_____ (2021) "The War on Cash Will Have Catastrophic Consequences." *Daily Telegraph* (August 14).

Durden, T. (2019) "12 Reasons Why Negative Rates Will Devastate the World." *Zero Hedge* (August 17).

Earle, P. C. (2020) "No, We Don't Need a New Reconstruction Finance Corporation." *AIER blog* (March 27).

_____ (2021) "Make No Mistake: Programmable Digital Currencies Are Weaponizable Money." *AIER blog* (April 24).

Fisher, I. (1933) "The Debt-Deflation Theory of Great Depressions." *Econometrica* 1 (3): 337–57.

Hague, W. (2017) "Central Bankers Have Collectively Lost the Plot. They Must Raise Interest Rates or Face Their Doom." *The Telegraph* (October 17).

Haldane, A. G. (2015) "How Low Can You Go?" Speech at Portadown Chamber of Commerce (September 18). Available at www.bankofengland.co.uk/speech/2015/how-low-can-you-can-go.

Hutchinson, M. (2012) "Sado-Economics." *The Bear's Lair* (December 24).

Kantchev, G.; Whittall, C.; and Inada, M. (2016) "Are Negative Rates Backfiring? Here's Some Early Evidence." *Wall Street Journal* (August 8).

Kelton, S. (2020) *The Deficit Myth: Modern Monetary Theory and the Birth of the People's Economy.* New York: Public Affairs. Kindle edition.

King, M. (2000) "Balancing the Economic See-Saw." Speech (14 April). Available at www.bankofengland.co.uk/-/media/boe /files/speech/2000/balancing-the-economic-see-saw.

King, M., and Katz, D. (2021) "Central Banks are Risking their Independence." *Bloomberg* (August 23).

Koonin, S. E. (2014) "Climate Science Is Not Settled." *Wall Street Journal* (September 19).

Levin, J. (2017) "New York Fed President Sent Puerto Rico a Jet Filled with Cash." *Bloomberg* (October 9).

Macleod, A. (2015) "From ZIRP to NIRP." *GoldMoney* (September 24).

McMaken, R. (2017) "In a Cashless World, You'd Better Pray the Power Never Goes Out." *Mises Wire* (October 10).

Michel, N. J.; Burton, D. R.; and Loris, N. D. (2021) "Using Financial Regulation to Fight Climate Change: A Losing Battle." *Heritage Foundation Backgrounder* No. 3634 (June 24).

Milne, R., and Arnold, M. (2020) "Why Sweden Ditched Its Negative Rate Experiment." *Financial Times* (February 20).

Molyneux, P.; Reghezza, A.; Thornton, J.; and Xie, R. (2020) "Did Negative Interest Rates Improve Bank Lending?" *Journal of Financial Services Research* 57: 51–68.

Molyneux, P.; Reghezza, A.; and Xie, R. (2019) "Bank Margins and Profits in a World of Negative Rates." *Journal of Banking and Finance* 107: 1–11.

Rogoff, K. (2016) *The Curse of Cash*. Princeton, N.J.: Princeton University Press.

Selgin, G. (2021) "In Defense of Bank Deposits: An Open Letter to Professor Omarova." *Alt-M* (October 12)

Stockman, D. (2016) "Helicopter Money: The Biggest Fed Power Grab Yet." *David Stockman's ContraCorner* (July 14).

Stoller, M. (2019) "How Monopolies Broke the Federal Reserve." *BIG* (August 13).

Waller, C. J. (2016) "Negative Interest Rates: A Tax in Sheep's Clothing." *Federal Reserve Bank of St. Louis blog* (May 2).

INDEX

Note: Information in figures and tables is indicated by f and t; n designates a numbered note.

ABOUT THE EDITOR

James A. Dorn is Vice President for Monetary Studies, Senior Fellow, and Director of Cato's Annual Monetary Conference. He has written widely on Federal Reserve policy and monetary reform, and is an expert on China's economic development. He has edited more than ten books, including *The Search for Stable Money* (with Anna J. Schwartz); *The Future of Money in the Information Age*; *Monetary Alternatives: Rethinking Government Fiat Money*; *Monetary Policy in an Uncertain World*; and *China in the New Millennium*. His articles have appeared in the *Wall Street Journal*, *Financial Times*, *South China Morning Post*, and scholarly journals. He has been a columnist for *Caixin* and *Forbes.com*. From 1982 to 2022, Dorn served as Editor of the *Cato Journal*. He was a member of the White House Commission on Presidential Scholars (1984–1990), and a visiting scholar at the Central European University and Fudan University in Shanghai. He holds a PhD in Economics from the University of Virginia.

About the Cato Institute and Center for Monetary and Financial Alternatives

Founded in 1977, the Cato Institute is a public policy research foundation dedicated to broadening the parameters of policy debate to allow consideration of more options that are consistent with the principles of limited government, individual liberty, and peace.

The Institute is named for *Cato's Letters*, libertarian pamphlets that were widely read in the American colonies in the early 18th century and played a major role in laying the philosophical foundation for the American Revolution.

The Cato Institute undertakes an extensive publications program on the complete spectrum of policy issues. Books, monographs, and shorter studies are commissioned to examine the federal budget, Social Security, regulation, military spending, international trade, and myriad other issues. Major policy conferences are held throughout the year.

The Cato Institute's Center for Monetary and Financial Alternatives was founded in 2014 to assess the shortcomings of existing monetary and financial regulatory arrangements, and to discover and promote more stable and efficient alternatives.

In order to maintain its independence, the Cato Institute accepts no government funding. Contributions are received from foundations, corporations, and individuals, and other revenue is generated from the sale of publications. The Institute is a nonprofit, tax-exempt, educational foundation under Section 501(c)3 of the Internal Revenue Code.

Cato Institute
1000 Massachusetts Avenue, N.W.
Washington, D.C. 20001
www.cato.org